THE FRIEND

The British Secret Intelligence Service has been
the unseen, undercover arm of the nation's overseas policy. Although there has often been speculation about its involvment in particular incidents,
no authoritative account has ever been attempted
of its post-war history.

Now, for the first time, its story is told in
convincing detail, the triumphs and the disasters:
the defection of Grigori Tokaev, the first senior
GRU officer to escape from East Berlin; the
ruthless sabotage campaign authorized by the
Foreign Secretary to stem the flow of Jewish
refugees from Europe to Palestine; the brilliant
coup masterminded in Tehran to save the West's
oil supply; the secret deals and the collapse of a
spy-ring which led to the ill-fated Suez invasion;
and the remarkable exfiltration from Moscow of
Oleg Gordievsky, SIS's star agent for more than
a decade.

These events, woven into the background of
treachery provided by Kim Philby and George
Blake, and the bizarre purges conducted to rid
the organization of other suspect moles, combine
to make a compelling story which will fascinate
amateur historians and professional intelligence
officers alike.

About the author

Nigel West is a military historian specialising in security matters and is the European editor of *Intelligence Quarterly*. He has also written several controversial histories of Britain's intelligence organisations, including A MATTER OF TRUST: MI5 1945–72, MI6: BRITISH SECRET INTELLIGENCE SERVICE OPERATIONS 1909–45, GCHQ: THE SECRET WIRELESS WAR 1900–86 and MOLEHUNT: THE FULL STORY OF THE SOVIET SPY IN MI5.

The Sunday Times has commented on his books:

'His information is often so precise that many people believe he is simply the unofficial historian of the secret services. West's sources are undoubtedly excellent. His books are peppered with deliberate clues to potential front-page stories.'

The Friends

Britain's Post-War Secret
Intelligence Operations

Nigel West

CORONET BOOKS
Hodder and Stoughton

For Nikki

Copyright © 1988 by Westintel Research Ltd.

First published in Great Britain in 1988 by George Weidenfeld & Nicolson Limited

Coronet edition 1990

British Library C.I.P.

West, Nigel
   The friends: Britain's post-war secret intelligence operations
   1. British intelligence services: MI6. History
   Rn: Rupert Allason I. Title
   327.1'2'0941

ISBN 0-340-51120-6

Printed and bound in Great Britain for Hodder and Stoughton Paperbacks, a division of Hodder and Stoughton Ltd, Mill Road, Dunton Green, Sevenoaks, Kent TN13 2YA (Editorial Office: 47 Bedford Square, London WC1B 3DP) by Cox & Wyman, Ltd, Cardiff Road, Reading.

'MI6, a department known in the Foreign Office, politely, but not very sincerely, as the Friends'

The Hon. Monty Woodhouse
SIS Head of Station Tehran 1951–5,
in *Something Ventured*

CONTENTS

ILLUSTRATIONS

The Olympic Stadium Building in West Berlin where the local SIS station operated under cover of the British Control Commission for Germany (*author's collection*).

All that remains today of the American radar station in Rudow, West Berlin, where SIS sank the shaft for Operation PRINCE's tunnel (*author's collection*).

Colonel Grigori Tokaev, SIS's first imporatant post-war defector (*Weidenfeld Archives*).

Colonel Harold Perkins (*author's collection*).

The bodies of Clifford Martin and Mervyn Paice, the two SIME NCOs murdered by the Irgun during the ruthless undercover conflict in Palestine (*Topham Picture Library*).

Sir Stewart Menzies, Chief of SIS from 1939 to 1952 (*Weidenfeld Archives*).

Kim Philby pictured in 1955 after he had been publicly cleared by the Government of any involvement with the defections of Burgess and Maclean (*The Keystone Collection*).

Monty Woodhouse, SIS's Head of Station in Tehran until 1955 (*courtesy of Monty Woodhouse*).

Sir John Sinclair, the SIS Chief who took early retirement following the death of Buster Crabb (*author's collection*).

Buster Crabb, an accomplished diver whose participation in an authorized SIS operation led to his mysterious death under a Soviet cruiser in Portsmouth Harbour in April 1956 (*The Keystone Collection*).

The entrance to 5/6 Pushkin Street, Moscow, where Oleg

Penkovsky used a radiator in the hallway as a dead-letter drop (*author's collection*).

The lamppost on Kutuzovsky Prospekt used by Penkovsky to signal his Western case officers (*author's collection*).

The entrance to the Peking Restaurant where Penkovsky kept a rendezvous with Greville Wynne and first spotted a KGB surveillance team (*author's collection*).

Greville Wynne and Oleg Penkovsky at their trial in Moscow (*The Keystone Collection*).

Greville Wyne on arrival at Northolt airstrip after being swopped for Konon Molody, April 1964 (*BBC Hulton Picture Library*).

George Blake, formerly SIS's Head of Station in Seoul and KGB spy (*The Keystone Collection*).

Maurice Oldfield, the counter-intelligence expert and former SIS Chief (*The Keystone Collection*).

The old KGB headquarters in Moscow (*author's collection*).

Oleg Gordievsky, once the KGB's *Rezident* in London who spied for SIS for twelve years (*Associated Press*).

The British Embassy in Moscow where Oleg Gordievsky was smuggled out of Russia (*author's collection*).

ACKNOWLEDGEMENTS

My thanks are due to the independent research under-taken by John Miller and Charlie Brown. I am also grateful to the staff of the Foreign Office Library, the Public Records Office, and Admiral W. A. Higgins of the Ministry of Defence's D Notice Committee for his guidance.

ABBREVIATIONS

AIOC	Anglo-Iranian Oil Company
ANA	Arab News Agency
ASIS	Australian Secret Intelligence Service
BCCG	British Control Commission for Germany
BfV	West German International Security Service
BSC	British Security Co-ordination
CIA	Central Intelligence Agency
CICB	Combined Intelligence Co-ordination Bureau
CID	Criminal Investigation Department
CIFE	Combined Intelligence Far East
CPGB	Communist Party of Great Britain
CRPO	Combined Research and Planning Office
CSS	Chief of M16
DSO	Defence Security Oficer
EOKA	National Organization of Cypriot Combatants
FBI	Federal Bureau of Investigation
GCHQ	Government Communications Headquarters
GRU	Soviet Military Intelligence
IRD	Information Research Department
ISLD	Inter-Services Liaison Department
JIB	Joint Intelligence Bureau
JIC	Joint Intelligence Committee
KGB	Soviet Intelligence Service
MCP	Malayan Communist Party
MI5	British Security Service
MI6	British Secret Intelligence Service
NID	Naval Intelligence Division
NKVD	Soviet Intelligence Service
OPC	Office of Policy Co-ordination
SCIU	Special Counter-Intelligence Unit

SDECE	French Overseas Secret Intelligence Service
SHAEF	Supreme Headquarters Allied Expeditionary Force
SIFE	Security Intelligence Far East
SIME	Security Intelligence Middle East
SIS	Secret Intelligence Service
SLO	Security Liaison Officer
SOE	Special Operations Executive
UB	Polish Intelligence Bureau

ORGANIZATIONAL CHARTS

Post-War Chiefs of the Secret Intelligence Service

Sir Stewart Menzies	1939 – 52
Sir John Sinclair	1952 – 6
Sir Dick White	1956 – 68
Sir John Rennie	1968 – 73
Sir Maurice Oldfield	1973 – 8
Sir Dickie Franks	1978 – 81
Sir Colin Figures	1981 – 5
Sir Christopher Curwen	1985 – 9
Colin McColl	1989 –

British Intelligence Liaison in Washington

MI6

Peter Dwyer	1945 – 9
Kim Philby	1949 – 51
Machlachlan Silverwood-Cope	1951 – 2
John Bruce Lockhart	1951 – 3
Leslie Mitchell	1953 – 6
Machlachlan Silverwood-Cope	1956 – 8
John Briance	1958 – 60
Maurice Oldfield	1960 – 64
Christopher Phillpotts	1964 – 6
Stephen de Mowbray	1966 – 8
Christopher Curwen	1968 – 71

MI5

Dick Thistlethwaite	1945 – 9
Geoffrey Paterson	1949 – 54
Harry Stone	1954 – 64

Michael McCaul	1964 – 9
Barry Russell Jones	1969 – 72
Cecil Shipp	1972 – 5

Chairmen of the Joint Intelligence Committee

Victor Cavendish-Bentinck	1939 – 45
Harold Caccia	1945 – 8
William Hayter	1948 – 9
Patrick Reilly	1950 – 53
Patrick Dean	1953 – 60
Hugh Stephenson	1960 – 63
Bernard Burrows	1963 – 6
Denis Greenhill	1966 – 8
Edward Peck	1968 – 70
Stewart Crawford	1970 – 73
Geoffrey Arthur	1973 – 5
Antony Duff	1975 – 9
Antony Acland	1979 – 82
Patrick Wright	1982 – 4

Foreign Office Advisers to the CSS

George Clutton	1952 – 5
Michael Williams	1955 – 6
Geoffrey McDermott	1956 – 8
Robin Hooper	1958 – 60
Peter Wilkinson	1960 – 63
Geoffrey Arthur	1963 – 6
Christopher Ewart-Biggs	1966 – 70
Kenneth Ritchie	1970 – 73

INTRODUCTION

The British Secret Intelligence Service (SIS) has been in continuous existence, under various guises, since its inception on 1 October 1909. Originally it was designated the Foreign Section of the Secret Service Bureau, but during the First World War it adopted the military intelligence cover of MI1(c). Therafter it became known as MI6, and that title has stuck, albeit unofficially, to the present day. To insiders it has always been known as 'the firm' or, by the less respectful, 'the racket'. In more recent years initiated outsiders, mostly Foreign Office regulars and business contacts, have referred to the organization simply as 'the Friends'. This popular euphemism has extended to SIS's advice, which is often described as having come 'from friendly circles'.

Today, as before the Second World War, it is officially denied that SIS has a peacetime existence. Of course, this subterfuge fools no one, but it does enable government ministers to avoid awkward Parliamentary Questions and allow British Foreign Service officers to disavow the organization which, by its intrinsic nature, is distinctly undiplomatic and is not infrequently the cause of an embarrassing rumpus. In short, although the ruse of SIS's lack of acknowledgement appears a trifle anachronistic, while the initials of its American and Soviet counterparts, the CIA and the KGB, are universally recognized, it does serve a practical purpose.

Because SIS has no official peacetime existence it follows that there are, therefore, no documents or records to be placed in the Public Records Office, as is required by law of most government departments. And since there are no files, none can be declassified after the elapse of the appropriate period of time. Indeed, almost the only SIS documents ever known to have slipped past the ever-vigilant 'weeders', who scrutinize everything before it is shipped to the Public Records Office at Kew, is a batch of pre-war administrative files relating to the Passport Control Office.[1] This now defunct department operated for several decades as SIS's main cover, thus allowing intelligence officers to be posted abroad as Passport Control Officers. Clearly the deception, although well known to Britain's enemies, was sufficiently effective to distract at least one of the ubiquitous 'weeders'.

SIS's lack of an official entity or form is supported by a blanket ban on public disclosures from its employees and a permanent embargo on the release of personal memoirs. In contrast, no less than eight former members have produced accounts of their work in the Security Service. Sir John Masterman, Sir Percy Sillitoe, Derek Tangye, Lord Rothschild, Stephen Watts and, most recently, Peter Wright have all had their autobiographies published.[2] Sir Gerald Glover even had his printed privately,[3] while the late Jack Morton's recollections on a career that continued until 1971 is still in manuscript form. The Cabinet Office has also officially allowed another MI5 officer, Anthony Simkins, who was Deputy Director-General between 1965 and 1971, to have his collaboration in the preparation of the final volume of *British Intelligence in the Second World War*[4] acknowledged. He was also commissioned, with Professor Sir Harry Hinsley, to compile *Security and Counter-Intelligence*,[5] a wartime history of the Security Service.

SIS, on the other hand, is rather more strict in its approach to this sensitive issue, and the amount of printed material available from those with first-hand experience of SIS's operations is sufficiently limited to be listed here in full.

The first person to make the attempt was (Sir) Compton Mackenzie, who tried to give a highly detailed account of his experiences of his tour of duty for MI1(c) in the

Eastern Mediterranean during the First World War. All copies of *Greek Memories*[6] were seized on publication day and the author was convicted of breaching the Official Secrets Act. He was fined £100 with £100 costs, no mean figure in 1932, and all the books were ordered to be destroyed. Only a few valuable first editions survive, including one in the British Library which still cannot be read without MI5's permission!

Two years later another MI1(c) veteran, Captain Henry Landau, avoided a similar posecution by releasing *All's Fair*, the first of his three volumes of memoirs, in New York. They were never brought out in England and, as the author was a South African living in America, there was little the British authorities could do to prevent him.

During the post-war era only a handful of reminiscences have got through the net. The first to break ranks was Leslie Nicholson, who had long since retired from SIS and, in 1966, persuaded a New York publisher to issue *British Agent*. As a precaution Nicholson concealed his identity under the pseudonym John Whitwell. Having already emigrated to America, like Landau, the author kept out of the jurisdiction of the British courts and thus escaped being prosecuted or injuncted. When an edition was published the following year in London, the Government, presented with a *fait accompli*, took no action. It had also received advance warning that Kim Philby, having defected to Moscow four years earlier, had held an auction for the rights to *My Silent War*. Once again, no attempt was made to prevent publication in England.

With these precedents having been established, there was only official disapproval for Fred Winterbotham, a wartime SIS officer who wrote *The Ultra Secret* in 1974, and Professor R. V. Jones, SIS's wartime scientific adviser who produced *Most Secret War* in 1978. Similar defiance was demonstrated by Philip Johns, another emigrant to the United States who in 1979 wrote *Within Two Cloaks*, his recollections as SIS's Head of Station in wartime Lisbon.

Passing reference to their wartime service in SIS has

been made by literary figures like Somerset Maugham, Graham Greene, Malcolm Muggeridge, A. J. Ayer and Hugh Trevor Roper, but none have risked going into matters in any depth. Other books by retired SIS officers with a peacetime contribution behind them, such as Nigel Clive, John Bruce Lockhart and David Cornwell (rather better known by his *nom de plume* John le Carré), have discreetly omitted mention of anything other than their cover roles as regular diplomats from their autobiographical details.

When Charles Ransom joined the team of Professor Hinsley's academics preparing the official history of British intelligence for the Cabinet Office, his twenty-year career in SIS was referred to simply as having been 'in the Foreign Service, 1946–66'; in fact, he had joined the Friends in 1946 and had served abroad only once, heading the Rome Station from 1958 to 1961.

The unique exception is Monty Woodhouse, who succeeded in writing *Something Ventured* without official interference. This fascinating book describes his activities as SIS's Head of Station in Tehran and his efforts to have Dr Mussadeq removed from power, after which he left the Friends and was elected the Conservative Member of Parliament for Oxford.

More recently, two others, Anthony Cavendish, who was based in Germany after the war, and Desmond Bristow, latterly SIS's Head of Station in Madrid, have received stern warnings to discourage them from putting pen to paper. Daunting legal obstacles were placed in the path of the former's *Inside Intelligence*, so the author chose to have his book printed and distributed privately. Bristow has yet to complete his project.

The Friends are determined to prevent those seeking to capitalize on their secret careers and, when compared to the Security Service, have been quite effective in discouraging disclosures. Because of its structure of watertight compartments and the strict use of the 'need to know' rule, only a handful of senior SIS officers have ever been in a position to give anything like a comprehensive overview of its operations, even though the organization is itself, in number, a tiny fraction of the CIA, the KGB or even the French DGSE.

Even when individual agents run by SIS case officers have decided to reveal their handiwork, very little of substance about the Friends has been forthcoming. Only a few over-embroidered books have been published, the most recent being *Break-In* by Bill Graham,[7] the story of a contractor and part-time SIS agent who spent two years inside the Soviet trade delegation in London fitting double-glazed windows while simultaneously accumulating useful order-of-battle data about Soviet personnel. Freelancers like Graham, hired for one-off operations, can only give a small snapshot of the organization and are never allowed to gain enough information to paint a complete picture.

Where information can be traced directly to a particular insider, the Crown has the choice of wielding some awesome weapons: a criminal prosecution under the Official Secrets Act, which governments sometimes find politically uncomfortable, or the civil remedy of bringing a suit alleging breach of confidence. Unlike the Official Secrets alternative, the latter can be undertaken virtually anywhere and can be prohibitively costly to defend. Both merits were demonstrated recently in the Australian courts when the British Government tried to suppress the publication of Peter Wright's illicit memoirs, *Spycatcher*.

That particular controversy achieved two unexpected goals, one for either side. The Defence got a world-wide bestseller, but the Plaintiffs showed the lengths they were prepared to go, regardless of cost or unpopularity, to impose silence on the Crown's secret servants.

The introduction of a publications review board along the lines operated by the CIA and FBI seems an attractive alternative to the present system for all concerned (apart from the lawyers), be they taxpayers, historians, frustrated memoirists or even those directly concerned with maintaining the nation's security. However, not even the most optimistic members of the intelligence establishment anticipate such an event for some years. One consequence is that histories like this one are bound to be incomplete, quite apart from the excisions made voluntarily after requests from 'the relevant authorities'.

This account is not intended as a work of disclosure in the sense that the pages are filled with revelations of appalling wrong-doing, although some episodes, such as the ruthless sabotage campaign conducted by Harold Perkins from SIS's Rome Station against the Palestinian refugee ships in 1946, are hard to justify. Nor is it a whitewash. It is instead intended to be a factual account of Britain's efforts in the field of secret intelligence during the decades following the end of the war. No names of living agents are compromised and no secret sources in current use placed in jeopardy. But it is a nuts-and-bolts description of how the country's overseas, clandestine intelligence-gathering arm made the transformation from Empire to membership of the EEC.

The question most frequently posed nowadays in this context is whether, post-Empire, and with a vast signals intelligence capability employing many thousands, Britain really needs a Secret Intelligence Service. In the pages that follow it will become evident that successive governments of both persuasions have found SIS's arcane skills indispensable. Certainly, Ernest Bevin and Anthony Eden made heavy and persistent calls on the organization's resources. But is there still a requirement? The invasion of the Falklands in 1982 is surely eloquent testimony of a continuing necessity to acquire, collate and distribute, in a timely manner, secret information to the right quarters. As had previously been demonstrated at Pearl Harbor in 1941 (more than half a decade before the creation of the CIA), there had been plenty to indicate an impending attack if only there had been a properly responsive mechanism to interpret the signs. The short-comings of Whitehall's modern intelligence structure were subsequently investigated by Lord Franks, whose report[8] recommended significant improvements in the chain linking a covert source to the Chairman of the Joint Intelligence Committee (who, in turn, passes his staff's considered advice to his political masters), but did not suggest dramatic changes in SIS's role.

Lord Franks's criticisms centred on what was perceived as a poor performance by the JIC's Assessments Staff when dealing with 'an area of low priority' like the Falklands before the Argentine invasion. In that instance SIS's advice never filtered up beyond the Latin America Central Intelligence Group, the conduit for drawing the JIC's attention to particular issues at its regular meeting in the Cabinet Office every Wednesday morning. This was one of the 'defects in the Joint Intelligence machinery' that was subsequently corrected by breaking the tradition requiring the JIC Chairman to be appointed from the Foreign Office.

The Falklands intelligence lapse confirmed Peter Hennessy's truism that 'the shortcomings of the JIC and the secret agencies tend only to be exposed after the kind of failure they exist to prevent.'[9] What made the Franks Report so remarkable was not just the fact that it went 'considerably further than any disclosures at the end of the statutory thirty years in the amount of intelligence material displayed',[10] but that so much of it was released for public consumption. Previous post mortems on intelligence mistakes, like the complete absence of any secret intelligence during the Omani Campaign in the late 1960s, have never been published. Indeed, Sir Edward Bridges's enquiry into the Buster Crabb affair in 1956 has never even been admitted as actually having taken place!

The increased availability in recent years of previously classified documents, most notably in the United States, has done much to reveal the extent to which vital foreign policy decisions have been influenced by secret intelligence. Some have exposed the scale of covert operations mounted by administrations that only gave consent to them on the basis that the failures could be repudiated. Thus Clement Attlee's Government authorized a deadly counter-terrorist action in Palestine and perpetuated what added up to a virtual guerrilla war in the Ukraine. Similarly, Eden made astonishing demands on SIS in the run-up to Suez. As we shall see, SIS not only master-minded the Anglo-French adventure in the first place, but later conveyed the devastating news that the Soviets intended to intervene, thus turning a well stage-managed plot into a fiasco that wrecked the careers of both (Sir) Patrick Dean (then Chairman of the JIC) and Michael Williams (SIS's Foreign Office Adviser), to say nothing of Eden himself.

It is SIS's task to pursue policy objectives by unortho-dox means and to amass useful information from secret (and open) sources. The operation that goes wrong is an occupational hazard, although it is only accepted as such by politicians with reluctance. Usually both the triumphs and the disasters are kept under wraps. The infiltration of well-equipped partisan groups into the Soviet Union from the Baltic, and the joint Anglo-American sponsored attempt to undermine Enver Hoxha's regime in Albania, must be counted as failures. So should SIS's embarrassing endeavour to place a frogman under the *Ordzhonikidze* during Nikita Khrushchev's goodwill visit in 1956. All were to have profound effects on 'the firm'. Yet there were also the achievements – the skilful management of Soviet defectors like Colonel Penkovsky and Oleg Gordi-evksy; the brilliant 'technical coverage' of Soviet diplo-matic premises during the late 1960s; the elimination of Mussadeq and the manipulation of Greek policy towards Cyprus during the Emergency of 1955. Indeed, Britain's painful transition from a colonial power to a European leader with just nine possessions left scattered around the world might have been a lot more fraught without the rearguard intelligence battles won behind the scenes.

Finally, for those who may have reservations about the advisability of telling this story, the reader is reminded that another routine danger of collecting intelligence is every agency's inevitable susceptibility to hostile penetra-tion. All realistic case officers now recognize that dealing with *émigré* groups is, at best, a chancy affair. At one time they were considered excellent sources of infor-mation about their homeland and useful pools from which to recruit agents and foment subversion. Unfortunately, experience has shown that most Eastern Bloc *émigré* organizations have been hopelessly compromised, if not actually run directly from Moscow. Nor has SIS been immune to the phenomenon of the mole, the ideologically motivated convert to the opposition's cause. Both Philby and George Blake confessed to having betrayed every secret that ever passed over their desks, which means that what the KGB did not know about SIS during their periods of employment was probably not worth knowing. Nor did the damage stop when Blake was arrested in April 1961 or when Philby vanished from Beirut in January 1963. There is plenty of evidence to show that after their respective escapes, both men continued to nullify SIS's activities by exposing its overseas order of battle, the intelligence officers posted abroad as the organization's front-line. In essence, there is nothing in the pages that follow that is not already well known to the KGB and its many surrogates.

1

TRANSITION

'Deception has undeniably a part to play in diplomacy. In connection with gathering the intelligence on which to base a sound policy it is often essential, just as it is in war. But certain rules apply. It must be used selectively or it can become a bad habit.'

Geoffrey McDermott, *The Eden Legacy*[1]

At the end of the war in Europe, the British intelligence community consisted of numerous separate organizations exercising either a security or an intelligence function, or a combination of both. Some, like Colin Gubbins's Special Operations Executive (SOE), Sir Robert Bruce Lockhart's Political Warfare Executive (which co-ordinated psychological and propaganda operations) and Lord Selborne's Ministry of Economic Warfare, had no expectation of a peacetime existence. Their usefulness was judged to have come to an end, and they were to be dismantled and their personnel demobbed. SOE's task had been to foment resistance inside enemy-occupied territory and, at the conclusion of hostilities, had, in theory at least, worked itself out of a job. Its very success had made it redundant. There was, nevertheless, a core of units which were destined to survive: the Secret Intelligence Service, otherwise known as MI6, and the Government Communications Headquarters (GCHQ), which, at this point, was still under the departmental control of MI6's Chief, known by convention as the CSS, Chief of the Secret Service; the Security Service, more widely referred to by its cover military intelligence designation of MI5, under the leadership of its Director-General, Sir David Petrie; and the three service intelligence departments of the Air Ministry, the War Office and the Naval Intelligence Division (NID).

One of the difficulties faced by the CSS, Sir Stewart Menzies, upon the German surrender in 1945 was the new administration's interest in returning people to their civilian occupations. During the previous five years, special arcane skills had been acquired in such diverse areas as irregular operations and psychological warfare. Menzies was anxious to retain a capability to conduct the former, while the Foreign Office recognized a continuing need for the latter. Accordingly, key officers from SOE, such as Robin Brook and Dickie Franks, were persuaded to join SIS and continue their clandestine interests. It was not until 1947, after the Political Warfare Executive had been dismembered, that its value was realized belatedly; the Government, therefore, reconstituted it as the Information Research Department (IRD) of the Foreign Office.

Before embarking on a description of SIS's transition from peace to war, it might be as well to examine the scope of the three principal British intelligence machines which were themselves then under study, at Winston Churchill's request, by Sir Findlater Stewart, formerly the Chairman of the recently disbanded Home Defence Executive. Stewart's secret report, dated 27 November 1945, has never been published, but it was essentially a comprehensive survey of British intelligence with recommendations, based on evidence submitted by both Menzies and Petrie, for Britain's future intelligence requirements. By the time Stewart had completed his deliberations, Churchill had been replaced as Prime Minister by Clement Attlee; but the Cabinet Secretary was still Sir Edward Bridges, and it was to him that Stewart's report was delivered. In short, it favoured MI6's continued, covert life, with an added, limited capacity to undertake clandestine SOE-style operations. The time-honoured, parallel system, which had so neatly divided the nations's intelligence and security responsibilities since 1909 between MI5 within the Empire and SIS elsewhere in the world, was endorsed, although Stewart apparently suggested the construction of a combined headquarters in London so as to avoid wasteful duplication. At the time, SIS was still occupying its huge offices at 54 Broadway, in Victoria, and MI5 had transferred from St James's Street to the recently vacated Headquarters London District in Curzon Street. The idea of combining the two was later dropped, although a convenient location – the site of some old gasometers in Horseferry Road – was earmarked for the stillborn project.

Upon the advent of peace, or at least a cold war, SIS settled down to coping with two challenges: the threat to European independence posed by Josef Stalin and the Soviet Union, and the organization's own unwieldy structure.

The war with Germany over, SIS now anticipated a period of struggle to contain Soviet territorial and political ambitions. The collective brainpower of its intellectuals – A. J. Ayer, Hugh Seton-Watson, Robert Carew-Hunt and David Footman – predicted a potential threat of global conflict from the Comintern's ideological successor, the Cominform. In their work can be found the recognition of the unpalatable fact that, whatever the cost of the recent war, Moscow was just as committed as ever to world revolution. For example, in 1944 Footman, a distinguished novelist,[2] had published *Red Prelude*, a biography of Andrei Zhelyabov and the first of several scholarly books on Russian revolutionary history. Two years later, in *The Primrose Path*, he documented the life of Ferdinand Lassalle, founder of the German Labour Movement and a powerful influence on Marx and Engels. Footman was to comment that Marx

> had, he felt, discovered the scientific laws of historical development which made [world revolution] inevitable. The question was when it was

going to happen. But the final and happy state of affairs that was to follow on after the proletarian revolution was so desirable that it was obviously one's duty to hurry on the revolution by every possible means.[3]

Footman's critical analysis was in line with Seton-Watson, who left SIS in 1946 to return to academic life at Oxford. He later wrote *Neither War Nor Peace, The East European Revolution* and *The Pattern of Communist Revolution*, each a study of the malign influence of totalitarianism. Carew-Hunt subsequently wrote *Marxism Past and Present* and *The Theory and Practice of Communism*, a textbook on modern Marxist philosophy which promised that 'the entire fabric of society is to be turned upside down'.[4]

However, in the first uncertain months of peace, SIS's intelligence bureaucrats were mainly preoccupied by matters of internal politics. That 'the firm' would contract at the conclusion of hostilities was to be expected. Most SIS members were only too anxious to get back to civilian life, where many had jobs waiting. SIS's greatest wartime expansion had taken place within Section V, a self-contained counter-intelligence adjunct whose sole function was the assessment and exploitation of intercepted Axis wireless signals. Since 1940, more than 450 specialists had been drafted into Section V, the London base of which was housed in Ryder Street, but the collapse of the Nazi regime had terminated their mission. As the Sicherheitsdienst's radio stations went off the air, and once the much vaunted 'Werewolf' guerrilla movement was evidently not going to materialize, there was little reason for Section V to continue its operations. The head of Section V, Felix Cowgill, certainly saw the writing on the wall and took up a non-intelligence job with the military government in Munchen-Gladbach. The rest of the service prepared itself for a structural reorganization which would reflect the change in priorities brought about by peace.

SIS's Broadway headquarters was essentially split into

two halves: the SIS stations which were scattered around the globe and accommodated under diplomatic or military cover in missions overseas, and the ten 'consumer' headquarters sections. In brief, the individual stations gathered information which the London sections collated, analysed and then distributed to the right quarters. Each section had a special responsibility for liaising with SIS's clients, the external services and government departments in need of a supply of secret intelligence. Thus Section I handled political matters, II the military, III the Royal Navy, IV the Air Ministry, V counter-intelligence, VI economic, VII financial, IX Soviet and X the press. Section VIII dealt with SIS's complex communications and provided a link with GCHQ.

The hierarchy at Broadway was headed by the CSS, Sir Stewart Menzies, who had his own small department consisting of his Staff Officer (known as the CSO/CSS), Peter Koch de Gooreynd, who liaised with the Chiefs of Staff and the Joint Intelligence Committee, and his Foreign Office Adviser, Robert Cecil.

Menzies had three Deputy Directors, each nominated by their respective services: John Cordeaux for the navy, Air Commodore Lionel Payne for the Air Ministry and Major-General William Beddington for the army. In addition, he had both a Vice-Chief, Major-General John Sinclair, and a Deputy Chief, Air Commodore (Sir) James Easton. Cordeaux had reached the rank of lieutenant-colonel in the Royal Marines before his posting to naval intelligence in 1938, and had switched to SIS in 1942. 'Lousy' Payne, who had won the Air Force Cross in 1919, when he was twenty-five, was soon to leave SIS to become the air correspondent of the *Daily Telegraph*. Beddington, an Eton- and Oxford-educated veteran of the First World War who had seen action at Gallipoli, was to retire to his country home in Northamptonshire in 1947 and devote himself to hunting foxes. 'Sinbad' Sinclair, a cricket enthusiast who had started his career in the navy, had come into SIS early in 1945 after just a year as the Director of Military Intelligence

15

at the War Office; he was to be appointed Menzies's successor in 1952. Easton remained in SIS until 1958, when he was knighted and given a regular diplomatic post abroad.

During the summer of 1945, Menzies appointed six prominent SIS personalities, under the chairmanship of Maurice Jeffes, to review the organization and recommend changes which would make 'the firm' more responsive to the needs of peacetime intelligence-gathering.

Jeffes had been in SIS since 1919 and had served as Head of Station in both Paris and New York. The other committee members were Christopher Arnold-Forster, Captain Edward Hastings RN, David Footman, John Cordeaux and Kim Philby. Arnold-Forster, the SIS Chief Staff Officer, was shortly to take up his pre-war occupation of stockbroking in the City. Hastings, the CSS's personal representative at GCHQ, had spent much of the war at Bletchley Park masterminding the administration of the signals intelligence product codenamed ULTRA. This was to be his last significant contribution to SIS before his well-earned retirement to his Sussex estate in 1949. Footman, the long-serving head of Section I, was to stay on with SIS until 1953 when he moved to St Antony's College, Oxford. Cordeaux was briefly to succeed Arnold-Forster as CSO, before leaving SIS in 1946. He unsuccessfully contested the Bolsover constituency for the Conservatives in 1950 and 1951, but was eventually elected to Parliament in 1955 as the MP for Nottingham Central. Philby, the wartime recruit from SOE, had excelled in counter-intelligence work and, late the previous year, had been entrusted with the development of the new, anti-Soviet unit, Section IX. The Committee's secretary was Alurid Denne.

Together these seven officers thrashed out a new, streamlined, internal order of battle, with 'R' and 'P', requirements and production, sections superceding the old arrangements. The first would assess the demand for particular types of information in certain fields, leaving it to the production staff to acquire it. Section V, the counter-intelligence unit, was abolished along with Section IX, and R5 became exclusively Soviet-orientated, absorbing an area that had previously been Section IX's parish. This particular recommendation had been initiated by Philby, who, of course, had his own motives, as he later admitted in his autobiography. His sole interest had been in 'keeping, for the time being at any rate, the whole field of anti-Soviet and anti-communist work under my own direct supervision'.[5] R8 liaised with the codebreakers at GCHQ and R9 embraced all scientific intelligence.

The committee's lengthy report on reorganization suggested a simplified structure of five directorates: finance and administration, production, requirements, training and development, and war planning.

The CSS accepted much of the report and appointed Frank Slocum as his Director of Administration. Slocum had joined SIS from the Royal Naval Tactical School in 1937 and was to remain at Broadway until 1954, when he was posted abroad as Head of Station in Oslo. The new Director of Production (known simply by the abbreviation DP) was Kenneth Cohen, an old SIS hand who once claimed to have been the only Jew in the Royal Navy. He had joined SIS in 1935 and subsequently had headed the Vichy French country section. The Director of Training and Development was John Munn, formerly the commandant of SOE's training school at Beaulieu in Hampshire. His new department was established in Princes House, Princes Street, close to Oxford Circus, with additional facilities at Fort Monckton, Gosport.

Subordinate to the post of DP were three Controllers, who each looked after the stations in their individual geographical regions. Thus Simon Galienne, as Controller Western Area, handled France, Spain and North Africa. In conversation and internal correspondence he was simply referred to by the initials CWA. The Controller Northern Area was Harry Carr, who had spent fourteen

SIS's Post-War Reorganization

CSS

(Foreign Office Adviser)

Vice-Chief   Deputy Chief

Director of Administration
Director of Training and Development
Director of War Planning

Director of Production

– DP1: Controller Northern Area; P1: Soviet Union,
         Scandinavia
         Controller Western Area; P2: France, Spain,
         North Africa
         Controller Eastern Area; P3: Germany, Austria,
         Switzerland
– DP2: Controller Middle East; P4: Egypt, Iran, Iraq,
         Syria, etc.
– DP3: Controller Far East; P5: Latin America, Far
         East
– DP4: London-based operations

Director of Requirements

– R1: Political
– R2: Air
– R3: Naval
– R4: Military
– R5: Counter-intelligence
– R6: Economic
– R7: Financial
– R8: GCHQ
– R9: Scientific

years as Head of Station in Helsinki before being evacuated to Stockholm in 1941. The Controller Eastern Area
in charge of the key German, Swiss and Austrian stations

was Andrew King, fresh from having spent the war in Switzerland, latterly as Head of Station in Berne.

Between the Controllers and the stations was a second management tier of Production or 'P Officers'. Each P Officer supervised SIS's activities in two or three countries. Thus the P3, Peter Lunn, son of the veteran skier Arnold Lunn, supervised SIS operations in Austria and Germany, reporting to his immediate superior, the CEA.

This pyramid-like system was designed to channel information from agents in the field, through local stations, to Broadway. From there it was the task of the requirements section to circulate information to its numerous clients, including the Joint Intelligence Committee and a newly created body, the Joint Intelligence Bureau (JIB). Late in 1945 the JIC's wartime Chairman, Victor ('Bill') Cavendish-Bentinck,[6] was appointed Ambassador to Warsaw and Harold (now Lord) Caccia took over the reins. The JIB was headed by Major-General Kenneth Strong, himself a well-established intelligence officer who had served as Eisenhower's intelligence chief at the Supreme Headquarters Allied Expeditionary Force (SHAEF). The JIB was intended to be the country's first attempt to integrate the handling and analysis of all types of intelligence, and Strong gathered an impressive quantity of skilled analysts from the services to launch it. He later said that 'the formation of the Bureau represented the first attempt at the unified handling and objective analysis of intelligence needed by more than one government department and a first step towards the integration of intelligence'.[7] Although he admitted that 'none of my friends thought that the Bureau would last longer than six months', the organization was to remain in existence until 1963, when it was swallowed up by the Defence Intelligence Staff at the Ministry of Defence.

It was SIS's task to supply sufficient secret intelligence for the JIB staff to prepare their own assessments. Much of this material was to come from agents run by SIS's global network of stations. The stations themselves, consisting of a Head of Station, up to a dozen assistants and a small secretarial staff, provided coverage throughout the world. The tasks of a particular station could range from providing illicit support to a regime, carrying out reconnaissance missions in a neighbouring state, recruiting agents to penetrate a hostile target, or preparing local stay-behind resistance cells in anticipation of an invasion. Every station had a different set of priorities decided by the relevant Controller. In a typical station, such as Ankara, the Head of Station would be accredited at the relevant embassy, legation or consulate as a First or Second Secretary and would act as a link with the local authorities, from whom he might occasionally extract 'UA', the abbreviation for unofficial assistance. His role, of course, would be well known among the rest of the diplomatic mission and even the expatriate community, who were required to exercise discretion.

The thorny problem of suitable concealment for professional intelligence officers, which had so dogged SIS before the war when the Foreign Office's Passport Control Department had provided cover of the most transparent variety, had been largely overcome. Intelligence-gathering was still regarded with distaste by some Foreign Service stalwarts, but the war had generally transformed the hostility of all but the most stubborn. The fact that SIS's epithet of 'the firm' changed to the more affectionate 'the Friends' is an indication of the transformation in the regular Diplomatic Service's attitude. Yet, in spite of this broad acceptance, the old cover did perpetuate and seems to have had its advantages. The Passport Control Department survived within the Foreign Office until 1968, when it was finally merged with the regular Passport Office. Even more suprisingly, all three of the post-war Directors of Passport Control, Maurice Jeffes, John Teague and Leslie Mitchell, were really senior SIS officers. The Passport Control Department also provided Harold Caccia with a suitably misleading entry in the Diplomatic List, and several Heads of Station around the world still use 'Visa Officer' as their local cover.

In most Allied countries the identity of the Head of

Station was well known to the local intelligence authorities with whom he was expected to develop a good working relationship. Usually he was not just tolerated, but actively welcomed and given every opportunity to capitalize on wartime friendships and favours. He also provided a useful alternative channel for semi-official, non-diplomatic communications. In some countries, such as the United States, SIS and MI5 both maintained permanent representatives. During the war, a combined office called British Security Co-ordination (BSC) had been run from New York by Sir William Stephenson, encompassing SOE, the Political Warfare Executive, MI5 and SIS; but the terms of a secret 'no poaching' Anglo-American security pact required that the BSC be wound up as soon as the Japanese had surrendered. An interesting feature of the post-war era was British and American respect for the jealously guarded sovereignty of each other's territory; SIS agreed not to recruit US citizens in return for an American undertaking not to conduct covert operations within the Empire without prior consent.

The removal of Stephenson from New York, however, did not mean the end of a British intelligence presence in America. In fact, Peter Dwyer, formerly the SIS Head of Station in Panama, opened an SIS office at the British Embassy in Washington and ran it until 1949, when he retired to Ottawa. MI5's Security Liaison Officer (SLO) during the same period was Dick Thistlethwaite. They were then replaced by Philby and Geoffrey Paterson, respectively.

In Singapore, the situation was a little more complex, as MI5 had its own intelligence unit there, the Counter-Intelligence Co-ordination Bureau (CICB). Headed by Colonel Dickie Dixon, the CICB's function was to mop up enemy stay-behind organizations. It had only a short life because the Japanese had been very unsuccessful in building up networks of agents. At the end of 1945, Dixon returned to London, leaving his two deputies, John Harrison and Courtney Young. MI5's only Japanese-speaker, to build Security Intelligence Far East. SIFE extended to

Borneo, Kuala Lumpur, Colombo, Hong Kong, Rangoon and Australia, where SLOs maintained a link between the local police Special Branches and MI5's overseas branch in London, designated E Division.

SIS's parallel system, also based in Singapore, was headed by (Sir) Denys Page, the Oxford academic who was subsequently appointed Master of Jesus College, Cambridge. His *Who's Who* entry modestly recorded his brief role as '1945–6 Head of a Command Unit, Intelligence Division, HQ South-East Asia'. His office had outposts in Canberra, Rangoon, Kuala Lumpur, Hong Kong, Tokyo and Bangkok (and, latterly, Vientiane and Hanoi), and answered to SIS's Controller Far East, who, until 1950, was Dick Ellis, another old intelligence hand who had first joined MI6 as an assistant Passport Control Officer in Berlin in 1924. In 1940, he had been posted to New York as Stephenson's deputy in BSC. When Malcolm MacDonald, the Governor-General of Malaya, was appointed British Commissioner-General in South-East Asia in 1948, both MI5 and SIS's organizations reported to his local liaison committee, known as the Joint Intelligence Committee Far East, or JIC/FE.

The set-up in Singapore, with a joint intelligence apparatus answering to the local British Minister, was similar to the arrangements in the Middle East, where John Teague maintained a regional headquarters for SIS in Cairo masquerading as the Combined Research and Planning Office. This cover, usually known as CRPO (pronounced 'Creepo'), was a translucent successor to the Inter-Services Liaison Department (ISLD), which had long been compromised. CRPO operated within the British Middle East Office structure; had important stations in Beirut, Baghdad, Tehran, Amman, Basra, Port Said and Damascus; and worked closely with MI5's rather more overt outfit, Security Intelligence Middle East (SIME). Headed by Brigadier Douglas Roberts, a veteran SIS agent who had even worked under commercial cover as an 'illegal' in Russia, SIME distributed staff in British territories throughout the Middle East, working closely with the colonial authorities in Aden, Cyprus, Palestine and the Sudan. They were usually in the guise of Defence Security Officers (DSOs), but other, more convenient covers were employed when the occasion demanded. MI5's man in Iraq, Jack Morton, was seconded as Civil Assistant on the Staff of the Air Officer Commanding RAF Habbaniyah. SIME was only to have a relatively short existence, but it played a crucial role in the post-war development of British intelligence. Both Douglas Roberts and his deputy, Maurice Oldfield, were to transfer to 'the firm', bringing with them many of SIME's most talented case officers. Among them were Myles Ponsonby and Harold Shergold. Several other senior SIME officers, including Bill Magan, Alex Kellar, Philip Kirby Green and Bill Oughton, were to become directors of MI5.

Immediately after the war, the practice of duplicating representatives was more common, with MI5 officers attached to overseas embassies to sort out old counter-espionage cases or research aspects of the Soviet apparatus exposed by the Germans. Thus, when Charles de Salis and John Bruce Lockhart were manning the Paris Station during the immediate post-war period, there were also two Security Service officers on the staff: Jasper Harker, working from the Military Attaché's office, and (Sir) Peter Hope, seconded as a temporary First Secretary.

Unlike their counterparts in the NKVD, the Soviet intelligence and security apparatus, SIS staff behind the Iron Curtain made little attempt to avoid being identified for what they really were. George Berry, for example, who had taken over the Moscow Station in June 1943, remained there until 1951. Before the war he had served as British Passport Control Officer in Riga and Vienna, so he was thoroughly 'blown' long before he ever set foot in Russia. Similarly, Harold Gibson, another old stager with a long intelligence career who had been Head of Station in Prague for six years before the war, resumed his post in 1945. Concealment, of course, would have been somewhat futile, considering that up until January 1947, when Philby handed R5 over to Brigadier Roberts, responsibility for co-ordinating SIS's anti-Soviet operations was in the hands of a colleague who was to be revealed as a long-term NKVD 'mole'.

In reality, it was not the Eastern Bloc stations that undertook the management of anti-Soviet operations. The real 'front-line' stations in SIS's world-wide network were actually in the European zones of occupation. Many of the most dramatic post-war intelligence battles were fought in (and under) the Allied sectors of Germany and Austria.

2

THE BRITISH CONTROL
COMMISSION FOR GERMANY

'The democracies, who find no difficulty in defining
Intelligence objectives, methods, etc., in time of war, find
themselves in a dilemma in a grey period half-way between
war and peace. The satisfactory solving of this dilemma is a
major and pressing problem.'

John Bruce Lockhart, *Intelligence: A British View*[1]

Germany's post-war future had been the subject of three
inter-Allied conferences at Tehran, Yalta and Potsdam.
It had been agreed that the country was to be divided into
separate zones of occupation and, as soon as the enemy
had been subdued, that the various forces were to withdraw to their own prearranged sectors. The Russians were
to take the north-east, the British the north-west, leaving
the Americans in command of the southern end, plus the
port of Bremen on the North Sea. On 21 June 1945,
American troops withdrew from their combat positions
and the new zones formally came into being. As well as
agreeing to carve up what was left of the Reich, the Allies
had also decided to restore Austria's pre-war frontier, the
country being regarded, somewhat controversially, as
having been a victim of Nazi aggression rather than a
willing participant in Hitler's Third Reich.

This rather over-generous interpretation of Austria's
role before and after the *Anschluss* in 1938 did not prevent
the country from being divided into zones of occupation.

BERLIN

French Sector

Tegel

Soviet Sector

British Sector

Hohenschonhausen

Olympic Stadium

Sankt Antonius hospital
Karlshorst

Tempelhof

Gatow

Tuefelsberg

American Sector

Marienfelde

Rudow

Schönefeld

Wünsdorf

The Soviets took the eastern third of the country, comprising of Lower Austria, Burgenland and Upper Austria north of the Danube. This left the British with Styria, Carinthia and the East Tyrol, with a zone extending from the Italian frontier, and the Americans with an area of the Alps, taking in the province of Salzburg and Upper Austria south of the Danube, which conveniently neighboured the southern limit of their German territory. Arrangements for Berlin and Vienna, which both lay deep inside the Soviet zones, had also been thrashed out long before the German surrender and had first been raised in a Soviet proposal presented to the Moscow conference in October 1943. Berlin was to be divided into three zones, the British and Americans taking the western end of the city. Vienna was to be divided into four zones, with the fourth, the city centre, being under tripartite control. The

Soviets had ratified the plan for Berlin at a meeting held at Lancaster House in London in September 1944, and so, on 4 July 1945, they handed over control of the western sectors to British and American troops.

None of these considerations took account of French sensibilities, eloquently expressed by General de Gaulle, who demanded, and obtained, part of the British and American zones in Germany, the North Tyrol and Vorarlberg in Austria, and part of the western sectors of Berlin and Vienna. Accordingly, the city centre of Vienna came under quadripartite control, and jeeps carrying a representative from the military police of each of the four countries became a familiar sight.

Thus Germany and Austria were effectively partitioned, with a visible, imposed frontier stretching from the Baltic to the Adriatic, which was dubbed an 'iron curtain' by Winston Churchill in his historic speech delivered at Fulton, Missouri, on 5 March 1946. To a greater or lesser extent, Prague, Warsaw, Bucharest, Budapest, Belgrade and Sofia had fallen into Russian hands.

Certainly, the Allied occupation was an extraordinary undertaking, which was generally expected to last for about twenty years. Germany was to be governed by the Allied Control Council, drawn from the separate Allied Control Commissions, and Berlin, some 200 miles into the Soviet zone, was to be run by a joint body known as the Kommandatura. Given Berlin's strategic position in the heart of East Germany, and considerably closer to Poland than Hamburg, it was inevitable that the city would become known as the *agentensumpf* or 'spy swamp'. Every country established at least one intelligence headquarters there. SIS had offices in the British Control Commission for Germany (BCCG) at Lancaster House on the Fehrbelliner-Platz and requisitioned a building adjoining the Olympic Stadium, where SIS opened a station in 1946. Since the BCCG was eventually to employ a total of 22,520 staff, it was easy enough to provide further cover by attaching SIS personnel to the BCCG's

27

Intelligence Division (ID), a small unit run discreetly by Brigadier J. S. ('Tubby') Lethbridge.

For its part the NKVD, under the notorious Ivan Serov, took over the old Sankt Antonius hospital in Karlshorst, with the Soviet military intelligence service, the GRU, operating from an undamaged block in Wünsdorf. The fledgling American intelligence organization (which was not to be formally created as the Central Intelligence Agency until September 1947) was to occupy a building that had once been the Kaiser Wilhelm Institute for Physics, before moving to the ClayAllee.

In the year immediately following the German surrender, numerous British intelligence outposts were established. The main centre of SIS operations was located at Bad Salzuflen, with Harold Shergold in charge, with outstations in an abandoned SS barracks at Herford and in the British Consulate at Düsseldorf. However, SIS by no means enjoyed a monopoly on British intelligence functions in the occupied territories. In overall command was the Director of Civil Affairs and Military Government at 21st Army Group HQ, Major-General (later Field Marshal Sir) Gerald Templer. He had previously run SOE's disastrous German unit, X Section, which had attempted to infiltrate anti-Nazi agents back into the Third Reich with appalling losses, and had enjoyed considerable intelligence experience earlier in the war. His military intelligence staff commandeered an elegant gaming casino at Bad Oeynhausen, a small spa which, together with two neighbouring undamaged market towns, Lübeck and Bunde, had become the seat of the military government. There Templer and General Bill Williams, Field Marshal Montgomery's principal intelligence adviser, began to construct an impressive empire, which extended via the BCCG regional offices throughout the British zone. Further afield, in Austria, a former *Glasgow Herald* journalist, George Young, ran SIS's Vienna Station, and a sub-station to liaise with the British military headquarters was maintained by Cyril Rolo at Klagenfurt. Many other senior SIS personalities, including Daphne Park, James Fulton and John Bruce Lockhart, were to use the BCCG as cover during the following three years.

Quite apart from the above, dozens of sites throughout the occupied lands sprang up to house intelligence personnel, train special forces, provide wireless interception bases, debrief potentially useful sources and interrogate suspects. Most of these may be found on Map 2.

The real 'front line' of the intelligence war conducted in Germany was the BCCG. Very little has ever been written about the activities of its Intelligence Division and its influence on post-war Germany. Among its leading members were Niall Macdermot, later the Labour MP for Lewisham; Dick White, the counter-espionage expert on loan from MI5 who, a decade later, was to be appointed CSS; David Strangeways, a deception specialist from

SHAEF who eventually took up holy orders; D. A. G. Heakes, from Cambridge University, who edited the ID's fortnightly *Counter-Intelligence Bulletin*; John Simmonds, later the Librarian of All Souls, who headed the ID's sub-section responsible for the examination of captured enemy documents; Hugh Seton-Watson on loan from SIS; and Leo Long, from MI14, who attempted to run agents into the East. His efforts were largely nullified by his then undiscovered dual role as a Soviet spy.

The ID's task was chiefly liaison: to keep in close touch with MI5, SIS, the German Political Branch of the Foreign Office and the BCCG's regional offices, and to supply the newly set-up denazification tribunals with relevant information. It was a tall order and, given the difficult local working conditions, the BCCG's inadequate budget and the restrictive political limitations imposed by the Foreign Office, one that was impossible to achieve with any measure of success. It certainly left little opportunity for running anti-Soviet operations which, in any case, were doomed thanks to the activities of Leo Long and another well-placed Soviet spy in the BCCG's Press Department.[2] Another handicap was the presence of two left-wing MPs, Austen Albu and Konni Zilliacus, who had both been attached to the BCCG by the incoming Labour Government in London. Their role, with Ernest Bevin's apparent consent, was to ensure that when German political parties were eventually allowed to operate, only the Social Democrats would be in a position to take power. Zilliacus was a particularly sinister influence and was destined to be expelled from the Labour Party for his pro-Soviet views.

The purposes of SIS's operations in Austria and Germany during the immediate post-war period were diffuse. On the security front there was a determination to uncover and eliminate all the Nazi or Soviet networks which signals intelligence reliably indicated had been left behind. As far as the acquisition of information was concerned, this was limited to the insertion of individual short-term agents into the East to obtain details of the

Soviet order of battle and possibly some indication of any military build-up which might betray a surprise move. There was also the political task of ensuring stability in the western zones and the additional objective of acquiring as much technical intelligence as might be available. Leading this latter mission was Sir Charles Hambro, formerly head of SOE, who, with help from an SIS team led by Eric Welsh, sought out physicists and other scientists who were judged to be of use. Welsh used to boast of being the only regular SIS officer with a scientific degree; as a result, he had worked on Britain's secret attempts to frustrate the development of a Nazi atomic bomb. The German experts selected by Hambro and Welsh were either debriefed at a special centre at Gottingen or flown to RAF Tempsford, home of the wartime Moon Squadrons, where a large house in nearby Godmanchester, Farm Hall, provided secure accomodation with microphones in every room. A great number of atomic researchers, including a few lacking anti-Nazi credentials, willingly passed along this route before obtaining a security clearance and permanent employment on classified work in England and the United States.

Another parallel project, codenamed BACKFIRE, recruited German experts to collaborate with Sir Alwyn Crow, in charge of Britain's top-secret guided missile programme at the Rocket Propulsion Research Establishment at Westcott, near Aylesbury. Werner von Braun was one of those who were taken to England for questioning. 'I must admit that I thought the British might be unfriendly to me, but I found I was wrong the first day,' he recalled.[3] Nevertheless, he subsequently got a better offer from the Americans. Major Robert Staver, who ran the London end of the US scientific intelligence operation, acknowledged that 'the British pulled a sneaky on us. Partly by chicanery, and partly through clever staff work, they were able to gain possession of many of the most important German engineers whom they used on BACKFIRE.'[4]

Although this particular recruitment programme

required the co-operation of the German experts, there was a quite separate operation run by the Americans, with the help of some rather desperate Eastern European *émigrés*, to obtain technical expertise through coercion. In 1948 one such scheme, aimed at a senior Soviet technician named Colonel Grigori Tokaev, rebounded against them and provided SIS with its first important defector in the post-war era.

Tokaev had been a lecturer in jet engine technology and rocket propulsion at the Zhukovsky Air Force Academy in Moscow, and had enjoyed a long career at the elite Institute of Engineers and Geodesics. However, after the Nazi surrender, he had been transferred to Berlin with very precise orders to snatch German scientists who might assist Soviet missile research. Although a committed Communist, Tokaev had been a supporter of Trotsky and was what might be termed today a dissident. He was utterly opposed to his instructions and, when he learned that Professor Kurt Tank, Focke-Wulf's chief aircraft designer, was to be grabbed by the NKVD, he underwent a crisis of conscience. At the very moment he considered defecting to the Americans, he himself nearly became the victim of a kidnapping by *émigrés* working for them. He later recalled how he

> received further warnings to beware of being
> kidnapped. I was hunted by *émigré* organizations
> dating from the revolution; they asked me to put
> them in touch with underground movements in the
> USSR; they also tried to persuade me to desert to
> the West. I had met their kind when I first came to
> Germany, but now some of them were strongly
> backed by foreign money, and their arrogance had
> grown beyond belief. They showed me how closely I
> was shadowed from outside the Soviet zone as well
> as from inside it.[5]

Tokaev was alone in his car *en route* to Schwerin from Berlin when he was forced off the road by two *émigrés*. Luckily he was armed, and the two would-be kidnappers fled. Badly shaken, and convinced that the NKVD was planning to arrest him for his membership of a group of dissidents, he defected to the British with his wife and daughter. He was received in Berlin by the local SIS station and flown straight to London, where he was debriefed by the Special Liaison Centre headed by Commander Wilfred Dunderdale RNVR.

'Biffy' Dunderdale, in common with other senior SIS officers like Harold Gibson and Harry Carr, had been born in Russia and spoke the language rather better than he spoke English. Having joined SIS in Istanbul, Dunderdale had run the Paris Station for fourteen years until the outbreak of war and had unrivalled contacts within the White Russian *émigré* community in France. During the war he had liaised with the Free French, but afterwards he went back to his anti-Soviet calling and took over Section V's old offices in Ryder Street. It was there that he created a highly secret SIS sub-office, staffed mainly by elderly *émigrés*, and sought to process defectors. His first subject, the head of the Soviet Reparations Mission in Bremen, Colonel J. D. Tasoev, came over to the West early in May 1948, but, much to SIS's embarrassment, changed his mind almost as soon as he reached London. He was promptly returned to the Russians, after enduring a spell in Hammersmith police station during which a lengthy debate was held at Broadway about the relative merits of dumping the recalcitrant Soviet into the North Sea from a height of 20,000 feet. Menzies vetoed that particular solution and Tasoev was delivered safely to the Kommandatura in Berlin, sparking off a minor diplomatic incident and a few awkward questions in Parliament.

In contrast, Tokaev's defection proved entirely successful as he provided a wealth of detailed information about Soviet activities in Germany. He later collaborated with one of his debriefers to write two volumes of autobiography, *Betrayal of an Ideal and Comrade X*. Tokaev, who changed his name to Tokaty, went on to a distinguished academic career at the City University in London, was followed by others, but none were ever of his stature, so the Special Liaison Centre was eventually closed down.

The other Western intelligence agencies had their own particular priorities, with the Americans placing heavy reliance on the Gehlen organization, which had been granted an extended life in a special prisoner-of-war compound at Oberursel, near Frankfurt. There General Reinhard Gehlen, once the mastermind in charge of the Abwehr's wartime networks on the Russian front, willingly negotiated a pact with Brigadier-General Edwin Sibert, the senior US intelligence officer in Germany, and activated his long-term agents in the East to provide his new American masters with an apparatus that was to become the *Bundesnachrichtendiest*, a ready-made intelligence-gathering machine. SIS had considerable reservations about the deal struck between Sibert and Gehlen, but was powerless to raise formal objections. It was not so much the principle of collaborating with such a recent enemy, but the anxiety that the Americans might find themselves in a master/servant role reversal. After all, Gehlen had had vast experience, whereas the Americans were relative novices in the field of espionage, despite their huge resources. In fact, the pact was founded 'on a verbal agreement and a handshake'[6] and had been endorsed by Kenneth Strong, who was 'asked not to enquire too closely into the matter'.[7]

SIS had no such advantage, and it was not until late in 1949 that its chosen nominee, Otto John, was placed in charge of the BfV, the federal internal security unit which had previously been limited to the running of three refugee reception centres, where defectors and others with useful scientific, military or political information could be debriefed. In contrast to the Gehlen organization, which actively ran high-risk networks of agents into the East, SIS's approach was to concentrate its limited resources on the interrogation of escapees. The BfV was an ideal vehicle for such an operation, although John himself was an unpopular choice, especially with Gehlen, because he had switched sides in 1944 after the 20 July plot against Hitler had failed. He had managed to escape to Lisbon, where he surrendered to the local SIS station, and subsequently had been put to work on various 'black propaganda' projects by the Ministry of Economic Warfare. After the war, he had joined the prosecution staff at Nuremberg, which had not endeared him to his former friends, and had actually interrogated Field Marshal von Manstein. Gehlen thought him 'unsteady and rootless, he was not a professional in this field',[8] and also despised him as a security risk. John was to defect to the East in July 1954, but then returned five months later, claiming to have been the victim of a kidnapping. The schism between John and Gehlen did little to foster good relations between the local representatives of their respective paymasters, SIS and the CIA.

Perhaps the most controversial aspect of SIS's post-war operations in Germany were those run from the British zone into the Russian heartland. Each mission was authorized by the CSS and his Deputy, Jack Easton, and received the Foreign Secretary's blessing. The reason for these missions was Whitehall's growing anxiety about Soviet intentions in Europe. Stalin's swift take-over in the recently 'liberated' countries, where he had undertaken to sponsor free and fair elections, was an unmistakable manifestation of old-style Russian expansionism. Liberal administrations throughout Central Europe were replaced ruthlessly with Communist regimes, and, in the view of the pugnacious Bevin, such behaviour could only be deterred by fomenting subversion. There were no illusions about overthrowing Communism or toppling Moscow's nominees, but there was a belief that a strategy of encouraging home-grown resistance would lead to more caution in the Kremlin.

The route into Russia was not overland, but took advantage of the Royal Navy's convenient presence in Kiel. A sympathetic Kriegsmarine veteran, Hans-Helmut ('H-H') Klose, had been recruited in Hamburg by Harold Gibson to run a clandestine ferry service from the Danish island of Bornholm, through the Baltic to Estonia and

Latvia, using captured E-boats. The case officer in charge was a recruit from SIME, Anthony Cavendish, who worked closely with the Naval Intelligence Division's senior representative in Germany, Commander Anthony Courtney. The Admiralty concealed the operation as an alternate minesweeping and fishery protection exercise, but the reality was that SIS infiltrated a substantial number of heavily armed White Russian *émigrés* into the Soviet Union, where they tried to organize a partisan resistance movement along the lines of those that had proved so successful against the Nazis. Among the Naval Intelligence personnel seconded to the operation was (Sir) John Harvey-Jones, a Russian interpreter who subsequently became Chairman of ICI. Courtney recalls

> providing the SIS with direct naval assistance in the Baltic. This work involved a close liaison with the Lürssen brothers of Vegesack, where I was struck by the potential capabilities of stripped-down ex-Kriegsmarine 'E' boat hulls, powered by the incomparable twin Mercedes-Benz 518 diesel engines. With my assistants, the Staff Officers (Intelligence) at Hamburg and Kiel, I was frequently at Lübeck and Flensburg and other smaller harbours such as Eckenforde and Kappeln, from which we mounted our operations. Little did I know that the penetration of the Foreign Office and the SIS by the Russian Intelligence Service must have not only doomed our efforts from the start, but had involved me personally in sending many a brave man into the jaws of a Soviet trap.[9]

SIS continued to support the operation long after it became clear to others that most of the missions were going hopelessly wrong and costing the lives of expensively trained agents. The drawback of these politically embarrassing, deniable covert operations is invariably the necessity to depend upon the participation of individuals who are unlikely to spark off a crisis when caught. Inevitably this limited deployment in the field to *émigrés*, and restricted the really experienced operatives to routine training duties in safe areas where they were unlikely to cause embarrassment. This is exactly what happened with Easton's anti-Soviet operations, and it was not for some years that Broadway realized that almost all of the Russian *émigré* groups in Germany had been thoroughly penetrated and that its own organization was not exactly immune to the KGB. Even though several of the illicit wireless contacts established deep in the Ukraine were shown to be compromised, Harry Carr, Harold Gibson and other senior SIS staff in London pursued the policy of extending the Cold War right into the Soviet Union. Incredibly, guerrilla bands were still roaming free, sabotaging the occasional Soviet train, until at least 1954. As we shall see, the Soviets responded by tightening their grip on the satellite countries already in their control, and took active measures to recruit sources within both the *émigré* communities and the West's intelligence services.

3

PALESTINE 1945–8

'The primary cause of our failure in Palestine was the failure of our intelligence service.'

Lord Altrincham (formerly Sir Edward Grigg),
British Minister in the Middle East

SIS's bitterly unhappy experience in Palestine is a less than creditable chapter in Britain's post-war history. It was a frustrating and much misunderstood attempt to achieve the impossible by reconciling the conflicting aspirations of Arabs and Jews.

Nowhere were the results of the 1945 general election, called by Churchill in July, more eagerly awaited than in Palestine, where the British Government had exercised its mandate for more than twenty years. Jewish demands for a homeland had been vocal since the Balfour Declaration in 1917, when the Foreign Secretary, Arthur Balfour, had said that

> His Majesty's Government view with favour the establishment in Palestine of a national home for the Jewish people, and will use their best endeavours to facilitate the achievement of this object, it being clearly understood that nothing shall be done which may prejudice the civil and religious rights of existing non-Jewish communities in Palestine, or the rights and political status enjoyed by Jews in any other country.

Over the years, the first half of this policy statement had received rather more emphasis than the latter, much to the anxiety of the Arab states in the Middle East. In order to allay their fears, Chamberlain's Government had issued a White Paper in May 1939, which proposed strict limits on Jewish immigration for five years, and what amounted to an Arab veto on further Jewish settlement thereafter. This reversal was a highly controversial decision, especially in the light of the systematic Nazi persecution of Jews in Germany, and had been denounced at the time by both Churchill and Attlee. It had also been the spark that had ignited Jewish extremism. Not surprisingly, in view of the commitments given by the leaders of both Britain's political parties, Zionists around the world anticipated a dramatic improvement in their fortunes immediately after the 1945 election. After all, both Attlee and Churchill had pledged themselves to oppose the policy based on the 1939 White Paper, so the result was presumed to be good news, whoever won. In the event, Attlee was swept to power and promptly decided to continue with the existing policy. This was seen by many in the Jewish communities of Palestine and Europe as nothing less than a betrayal, and served to inflame the Zionists.

The main representative body for Jewish opinion was the Jewish Agency for Palestine, headed by David Ben-Gurion, which also boasted a military wing, the Haganah. Technically the Haganah was illegal, but many of its members had been enrolled as armed special constables during the Arab revolts of 1936–9. By tradition the Haganah pursued a policy of *havlagah*, the Hebrew word for self-restraint, and as soon as war had been declared with Germany the Haganah had suspended its anti-British agitation for the duration. So too did the Irgun Zvai Leumi, a semi-independent underground organization, which had taken a more aggressive attitude to the question of a Jewish homeland in Palestine by carrying out armed attacks on Arab villages. Composed mainly of

Polish 'illegals', many of the Irgun's members had volunteered for service in the British army, while others fought in resistance movements in Europe.

One group of extremists, however, decided to continue their campaign against what they perceived as the British occupation of Palestine. Led by Avraham Stern, the self-styled 'Freedom Fighters of Israel' robbed banks, attacked military installations and murdered policemen. Stern was eventually tracked down on 13 February 1942 in an attic in Mizrachi Street, Tel Aviv, the home of another terrorist who had been wounded and captured two weeks earlier. During his arrest, Stern was shot dead by a British police officer but, undeterred, the Stern Gang continued its activities for a further six years achieving world-wide notoriety in November 1944 when the British High Commissioner in Egypt, Lord Moyne, was assassinated in a Cairo street by two young members of the gang.

By the end of the war, some 130,000 Palestinian Jews had served with the British forces, of whom 32,000 had joined the army, which, in September 1944, had formed a Jewish Brigade. In short, the Jewish opposition to Britain's continued role in Palestine was sophisticated, well-trained and brilliantly organized. Many, like Moshe Dayan of the Haganah's intelligence unit, the Sherut Yediot or Shai, had been taught by either SIS or SOE. Dayan had run a chain of twenty stay-behind clandestine wireless stations based around Jerusalem for SIS since August 1941, and no less than thirty-two others had been parachuted into Nazi-occupied territory by SOE. Dayan's direct superior in the Shai was Isser Harel, a future head of Mossad (Israel's intelligence service) who had himself been trained by the Palestine Police. He had been discharged for insubordination.

Once hostilities in Europe ended, the Irgun renewed its activities under the leadership of a Polish immigrant, Menachem Begin. He selected his principal opponent, the Palestine Police's Criminal Investigation Department

(CID), as his main target and wasted no time in master-minding a series of attacks on various police stations, including the CID's headquarters in Jaffa. In May 1945, the Anglo-Iraqi pipeline was bombed, and there were numerous other acts of sabotage perpetrated by the Irgun with the intention of making British rule untenable.

The British, however, had anticipated an escalation in Jewish violence and, in a pre-emptive strike in October 1944, had airlifted 251 detainees from the Latrun intern-ment camp to Kenya. This decisive move had left the Irgun with only an estimated thirty–forty activists in the field, but this was a sufficient number for the launch of a series of raids designed to build up a stockpile of arms. The campaign culminated on 6 March 1946 in an auda-cious operation in which Irgun members masqueraded as British personnel and penetrated the huge military com-pound at Sarafand. As well as being garrisoned by the crack 6th Airborne Division, the base also housed Brit-ain's largest overseas signals interception facility. Without even being challenged, the raiders simply drove up to the camp's armoury and loaded rifles, Bren guns and ammu-nition into a stolen truck while the quartermaster's staff were held at gunpoint. In spite of the presence of the paratroopers in the camp, the raiders escaped and all but two eluded arrest. When the Irgun realized that two of its members, Michael Ashbel and Joseph Simchon, had been caught, Begin responded by ordering the kidnapping of five British officers from the Yarkon Hotel in Tel Aviv to hold as hostages. A sixth, Major H. B. Chadwick, attached to SIME's office in Jerusalem, was also bundled into a car, but managed to negotiate his own release. The other five were freed when the death sentence on Ashbel and Simchon was lifted.

The Sarafand incident was an eloquent demonstration that the Palestine Police were quite unable to cope with the combined, growing strength of the Haganah, the Irgun and the Stern Gang, so the Colonial Office requested SIS assistance. Stewart Menzies was asked to help achieve two important objectives: the formation of a counter-terrorist intelligence group to operate within Palestine, and the recruitment of a clandestine team to reduce the flow of illegal immigrants from Europe. The plan had the support of the new Foreign Secretary, Bevin, who approved the creation of a small unit headed by General (Sir) Bernard Fergusson (later Lord Ballantrae). Until his attachment to the Palestine Police as Assistant Inspector-General, Fergusson had been Director of Combined Operations. Now he was given *carte blanche* to identify and eliminate the fanatics who had been widely condemned, especially by the Jewish Agency whose leadership generally regarded terrorism as a tactic to be counter-productive. As Fergusson minuted at the time:

> There is in the army a small number of officers, who
> have both technical and psychological knowledge of
> terrorism, having themselves been engaged in
> similar operations on what may be termed the
> terrorist side in countries occupied by the enemy in
> the late war.[1]

The problem of illegal immigration was rather more complex than the challenge of terrorism in Palestine. A substantial proportion of the survivors of the Nazi Holocaust were determined to settle in Palestine, yet British policy, as set out in the 1939 White Paper and enforced by Attlee's administration, was to reduce the number of entry certificates granted. In 1944, 14,600 certificates had been issued; by the end of the following year, the figure had been brought down to 13,100.

Spurred by outbreaks of officially sponsored anti-Semitic violence in Poland, the Jews of Central and Eastern Europe were moving westwards and joining the many thousands of 'displaced persons' sheltering in makeshift refugee camps. The three main routes used and supported by the Haganah were through Germany to Berlin and then Hamburg in the British zone; through the French zone in Germany and onwards down to Marseilles; and, the most popular path, via Vienna and then Villach in the

British sector. From there the Haganah ran two underground railroads, known as *brycha*, down the Adriatic coast of Italy, or to ports like Sizak in Yugoslavia. Having got thus far, the refugees were ferried to beaches in Palestine in an assortment of patched-up, war-surplus tramp steamers. Between August 1945 and May 1946 some 73,000 'illegals' were believed to have been carried to their homeland in around sixty-four unseaworthy ships. The Royal Navy attempted to enforce a blockade and intercept vessels thought to be carrying 'illegals', but its intelligence was inadequate and the highly publicized incidents involving the arrest of refugee ships in the Mediterranean and the internment of their human cargoes in Cyprus and Mauritius had a poor reception in the United States. This latter consideration was to become increasingly important as the Jewish community in America rallied to the Zionist cause. On a couple of occasions the Haganah preferred to blow up its own ships rather than face British detention, providing more embarrassing headlines in New York.

The exodus was entirely against the British Government's stated policy and, as Arab opposition grew, threatened to destabilize the region. Understandably, the Arab states in the Middle East viewed the influx of Jews into Palestine with alarm. As the Arabs controlled the oilfields, it was in Britain's long-term, strategic interests to be allied with its traditional friends and maintain a balance to ensure regional peace. Therefore numerous compromise solutions, such as the partition of Palestine, were under debate, but from the Jewish viewpoint no further discussion was necessary. A homeland had been promised to the Jews in the Balfour Declaration and, after the Nazi deathcamp experience, any hardship could be endured in their escape from Europe and in the fulfilment of that promise. The Haganah aimed to ensure the safety of the refugees *en route*, and the Irgun vowed that it would bring the mandate to a swift end.

In January 1946, Sir Noel Charles, Britain's Ambassador in Rome, reported to London that 'we are doing our utmost to check the clandestine influx of refugees from Austria',[2] but he did not go into details. In fact, in response to a directive from Menzies, information from the SIS stations in Paris, Vienna, Milan and Trieste were being collated in Rome, which was SIS's largest European station, by Colonel Harold Perkins, who had devised a scheme to disrupt the traffic of weapons and refugees: limpet mines were to be attached to the refugee ships so as to prevent them from reaching Palestine. The man chosen to undertake this sensitive task was Frederick Vanden Heuvel, a Count of the Holy Roman Empire and a director of Eno's Fruit Salts, who until recently had been the long-serving SIS Head of Station in Berne. Vanden Heuvel had been replaced in Switzerland by Nicholas Elliott in 1945 and, upon his return to Broadway, had been assigned the Rome Station, where Kenneth Benton was already in command, with secret instructions to launch an anti-Haganah operation. Vanden Heuvel chose two other SIS officers to accompany him: Perkins and Wing-Commander Derek Verschoyle.

Perkins had graduated from Prague University with a degree in engineering and had gone on to qualify as a master mariner. By the time war broke out, he had learned some Polish and had become the owner-manager of a small textile mill in Bielsko, Silesia. He had an awesome reputation for toughness, and one of his SIS colleagues, Bickham Sweet-Escott, recalled that 'Perks' was 'the only man I have ever actually seen bend a poker in his hands'.[3] He worked in the Polish section of SOE throughout the war and eventually headed it, along with the Czech and Hungarian sections. When the Germans evacuated Prague, Perkins had appointed himself the acting British Chargé d'Affaires, a post he kept for some weeks until the pre-war SIS Head of Station, Harold Gibson, had flown out to relieve him.

Although perhaps not quite as colourful as Perkins, Verschoyle was an Irishman, edcuated at Trinity, Dublin, who had been the literary editor of the *Spectator* before he had joined the RAF in 1940. Thereafter, he had served in Bomber Command and the Mediterranean Allied Forces before transferring to SIS. His cover in Rome was First Secretary. His deputy, responsible for liaising with the Italian authorities, had formerly served in SIS's Dutch country section.

Vanden Heuvel's plan was to infiltrate agents into the Haganah's network using the SIS representatives in Locarno and Milan, Lance de Garston and Edward de Haan. One early success was the discovery of an arms dump of over forty tons of weapons in the Magenta displaced-persons camp west of Milan. However, their main objective was to find out which Adriatic harbour had been selected for the 'illegals' next embarkation point. Once identified, Perkin's task was to procure the necessary equipment and then plant the explosives on the side of the vessel well below the waterline.

Exactly how many ships were sabotaged is unknown but the Haganah was quite aware of SIS's campaign. One particular vessel, the *Pan Crescent*, was attacked while in its berth at Venice on the day of its scheduled departure. Two hundred Italian workmen who had been preparing the ship for sea escaped the blast but the hull was ripped open and water had poured into its empty hold. According to David and Jon Kimche who documented the *brycha* in *The Secret Roads*, the Haganah held a post mortem into the Pan Crescent incident:

'At first it was attributed to an Arab terrorist group, but later investigation followed a trail which led the Mossad leaders to the conviction that it had been a 'British Made' explosion; the organization to counter illegal immigration was resorting to more direct preventive measures.'

A Greek ship broker had been recruited by SIS to report the ships bought by the Haganah, and Perkins had devised a scheme to attach a limpet mine timed to allow Verschoyle's saboteurs, who posed as cigarette smugglers, to escape into international waters. The plan was eventually abandoned when the Haganah retaliated.

Meanwhile, in Palestine, the level of violence had escalated. On 13 July 1945, a police constable was killed when a British army truck carrying detonators was ambushed. On 25 July, the Lydda-Kantara railway link was cut when a bridge was blown up. In the spring of 1946, two terrorists were killed in an attack on the police headquarters at Ramat Gan, and the Irgun launched its raid on Sarafand.

This was the atmosphere in which Fergusson operated, but he experienced great difficulty in obtaining help from the community or in recruiting agents. As Begin later remarked:

> British Intelligence did its best to introduce informers into our ranks and to acquire agents from among our members. In all the years of the revolt there were only three cases of treachery and the enemy Intelligence never once succeeded in introducing their own agents into the underground without their being discovered almost immediately. They never succeeded – and this is most important – in getting agents into positions high up in the direction of the struggle.[4]

Certainly, the one useful source inside the Stern Gang, Israel Prizker, was shot for 'helping British Intelligence'.

The British response to the Sarafand raid was Operation BROADSIDE, executed on 29 June 1946, in which all the Jewish Agency offices in Palestine were occupied and 3,000 people were taken into custody and questioned at a special purpose-built camp at Rafiah, near the Egyptian border. The exercise yielded the first solid information about the composition of the Irgun and the Stern Gang, and led the Haganah to issue a formal statement withdrawing its support from armed conflict. Menachem Begin was identified as the Irgun's leader and Yaacov Meridor as his deputy. A list of 1,500 Irgun supporters was compiled with the Haganah's help, and a further wave of arrests followed.

Begin, who had a £10,000 price on his head, was never caught by the authorities, but moved constantly from one safe-house to another in the Tel Aviv area, disguised as a bearded rabbi. He has subsequently described this period of his life in *The Revolt*, in which he admitted that, even though the Haganah had publicly dissociated itself from the Irgun, up to September 1946 they had maintained a close liaison and had held joint conferences to approve plans every fortnight.

The Irgun reacted to BROADSIDE by striking at the heart of the British administration. Seven milk churns packed with high explosives were placed under the south wing of the King David Hotel in Jerusalem, which accommodated the army's General Headquarters. Ninety-one were killed with 110 injured, including fifteen Jewish civilians, when the six-storey structure collapsed in the explosion.

The King David Hotel bomb, which had been detonated before a proper warning could be given or the south wing evacuated, created outrage in Britain, among many of the Zionists and certainly among the security forces, which urged a crackdown and an end to further immigration. However, for political reasons, neither followed. Bevin was then attempting with President Truman to find a compromise solution, involving autonomous but separate Arab and Jewish provinces in Palestine. Despite endless meetings the negotiations came to little, apparently because of Zionist pressure on Truman's domestic supporters. Their plan was to demand partition and then create a Jewish state.

The British response was to allow Perkins and his team in Italy a free hand in choking off the supply of arms and volunteers bound for Palestine, but the combined forces of the Irgun and the Haganah had anticpated the escalation. The first counter-attack took place on 9 September 1946, when the senior SIS officer in Tel Aviv, Major Desmond Doran, was assassinated by a grenade while sitting on the balcony of his house with his Romanian-born wife, Sanda, who was badly injured. Two other SIS officers escaped unhurt. Before the war Doran had served in Berlin and had been Head of Station in Bucharest before transferring to ISLD in Cairo. His death is thought to be the only 'active service' casualty SIS has suffered in the post-war era. On the same day, a Palestine Police CID sergeant with twelve years' experience was shot in the back outside the popular Windsor Hotel. He had recently masterminded the arrest, interrogation and deportation of Begin's principal lieutenant, an activist named Yitzhak Ysernitzky. The third incident occurred early in the morning of 31 October, when two suitcase bombs were placed against the front door of the British Embassy in Rome; the explosion rendered the building uninhabitable. The Italian police later arrested Israel Epstein, who was imprisoned for the offence.

Now the security situation in Palestine deteriorated badly. A young member of the Irgun, Israel Kimche, was arrested for carrying weapons and sentenced to eighteen lashes. The punishment was carried out on 27 December 1946 in Jerusalem's Central Prison, and prompted the kidnapping of a British major and three NCOs. Each was flogged and then released.

Conditions in Palestine were such that the Government ordered Operation POLLY to be implemented – the withdrawal of non-essential personnel – and the security forces were increased to reach their peak of 100,000. On 25 January 1947, another terrorist, Dov Gruner, who had been wounded and caught during the Irgun's raid on Ramat Gan, was sentenced to death. Like many other members of the Irgun, Gruner had spent three years in the British army during the war. None of the Jewish terrorists captured to date had been executed, but Gruner's case was markedly different. An Arab policeman had been shot in the raid and an automatic had been found in Gruner's hand. Forensic tests showed that it had been fired recently. The Irgun responded to the verdict by kidnapping a retired officer, Major H. A. Collins, in Jerusalem and a judge, Mr Justice Windham, the following day in Tel Aviv. They were later released, unharmed, when the curfew had been lifted, along with the threat of martial law.

The sentence on Dov Gruner, together with three other

Irgun activists, was carried out in Acre Prison on 17 April 1947. Six days later, another two convicted fanatics were due to hang in Jerusalem Prison, but shortly before the sentence was carried out both men blew themselves to pieces with a grenade that had been smuggled into the death cell by a rabbi.

The Irgun's most spectacular raid took place the following month, on 4 May, while the United Nations attempted to find a solution to the Palestine problem. On that day the Irgun attacked Acre Prison and blew a hole in the perimeter wall, allowing 251 prisoners to break out, including twenty-nine Irgun detainees. The attack had been planned by Dov Cohen, a veteran of Dunkirk and the Jewish Brigade, who was killed while giving covering fire to the escapers. Close by was the body of Michael Ashbel, one of those arrested after the Sarafand raid. Several Irgun terrorists were arrested in the aftermath and, later, three were sentenced to death. The British Commander-in-Chief, General McMillan, warned his troops only to leave the military compounds armed and in groups of four, but this was clearly an impossible restriction for members of SIME. Thus, on 12 June, two SIME sergeants, Clifford Martin and Mervyn Paice, were kidnapped late at night in Natanya and held as hostages for the lives of the three Irgun men. When they were executed, Martin and Paice were hanged and their bodies left, booby-trapped with a landmine, in a grove of eucalyptus trees near Natanya.

These events prompted a bloody, anti-Semitic reaction from soldiers and police alike, and resulted in several violent demonstrations in England. They also brought an end to General Fergusson's experiments with 'counter-gangs'. His method had been to deploy two teams of ten men each, headed by Alistair MacGregor and Roy Farran. MacGregor was an experienced intelligence operative who had been nominated for the job by his former employers, SIS, while Farran had fought a highly irregular war with Italian partisans and the 2nd Special Air Service Regiment and had seen action in the desert at El Alamein,

France, Norway, Albania, Syria and Crete, where he had briefly been a prisoner of war, before escaping and enduring nine days in an open boat. As a genuine war hero and living legend, Farran had been recruited by Fergusson while instructing cadets at Sandhurst. He was, of course, an enthusiastic exponent of counter-terrorist tactics, but in October 1947 he was charged with the torture and murder of an Irgun suspect named Alexander Rubowitz. Farran had been arrested soon after Rubowitz's disappearance, but had escaped from custody. He was eventually found in Damascus, where Fergusson visited him and persuaded him to return to Palestine to face a court martial. At the trial Farran's alleged confession was ruled inadmissible, and Fergusson declined to give evidence for the prosecution in order to avoid incriminating himself. With only very circumstantial evidence to link Farran to the crime, he was acquitted; but a price was put on his head by the Irgun. A year after these events, his younger brother Rex was killed when he opened a parcel-bomb simply addressed to 'R. Farran'.

The dissolution of Fergusson's secret unit ended Britain's clandestine involvement in Palestine. During 1947 a United Nations Commission, headed by a Swedish Supreme Court judge, Emil Sandstrom, toured Palestine in the hope of achieving a settlement. His Commission's recommendation, partition, was proposed on 31 August and was then debated at the United Nations. The Haganah proved itself to be extremely successful in political manoeuvring during this critical period, actively exploiting Jewish sympathy around the world. Leading the Israeli delegation to the United Nations was Major Aubrey Eban, a former Cambridge don and Chief Instructor at the British Army's Middle East Arab Centre in Jerusalem until he resigned his commission in 1946.

The Haganah used all its guile and experience to ensure that the United Nations vote established an independent Israel. It was discovered, for example, that the limousine company supplying the British delegation to the United Nations with transport was Jewish owned. As a result, every journey made by the delegates from their office in New York to the UN General Assembly's special session at Lake Success on Long Island was bugged, giving the Jewish Agency useful information about British intentions. Indeed, Jewish businessmen were also allocated rooms in hotels directly under or adjoining those of the debate's main participants. It was a skilfully conducted surveillance operation that eventually helped to ensure that, on 29 November, the final vote, of thirty-three to thirteen, was in favour of partition. Britain was among the ten abstentions. This was followed swiftly by Bevin's announcement of Britain's intention to withdraw from Palestine on 14 May 1948.

SIS's Palestine episode was in complete contrast to everything previously experienced. Unlike in Germany, where the local population broadly welcomed the Western occupiers, there was little relief from the hostility of civilians. Nor were the British forces perceived to be the victors. In fact, quite the reverse, with people on all sides acknowledging the futility of Britain's extended presence. Indeed, initially at least, there was a good deal of sympathy within the police and intelligence community for the Jewish cause.

Nor were SIS combating a structured organization, in the sense that the opposition did not have obvious lines of communication which could be tapped or disrupted. The potent but hidden weapon of GCHQ'S cryptanalytical skills were of little use, save for revealing the very close, covert relationship between the Irgun and the Haganah. This was discovered by routine monitoring of the Jewish Agency's traffic on the cable link between Tel Aviv and New York. Unfortunately, there were enough members of the Haganah with cryptographic knowledge to urge caution when sending coded messages to the United States. In any event these signals, although intercepted and read, showed only the political initiatives undertaken by the Agency and betrayed nothing of a tactical nature which could be of use to the authorities in the field.

The Haganah and the Irgun wisely made little use of the wireless for operational purposes and were resourceful opponents, unlike the Stern Gang who caused widespread resentment, even within the host community. Since they had been largely trained by the British, they knew exactly what to expect and thus were able to plan accordingly. They also had remarkable success in planting agents inside the Palestine Police. The veteran CID inspector in charge of anti-Communist surveillance, Yehuda Arazi, turned out to be a Shai mole, supplying the Haganah with the identities of the few police informers within the organization.

The Jewish Agency virtually controlled the propaganda battle from the outset and was extremely effective in manipulating public opinion overseas, particularly in the United States where President Truman proved a compliant supporter of Zionist aspirations.

From the start Britain was in a no-win situation. The principle of partition had long been resisted because of determined Arab opposition. Any British-sponsored solution dividing the territory would have led to conflict straightaway as actually happened immediately after the withdrawal. The underlying fear was that such a compromise would only alienate Palestine's Arab neighbours and maybe force them to look to the Soviets for support. There was also anxiety about Muslim opinion in India, where British relations with the Islamic population were highly volatile.

In strategic terms Israel was regarded as being of minimal long-term significance. The expensive military bases were redundant, a duplication of facilities already in use in Egypt and Cyprus. Even the listening-post at Sarafand was judged to be expendable because of the attractive alternative sites in Cyprus. The British Government recognized these realities, but was also keenly aware of its responsibilities under the mandate to achieve the impossible: the peaceful cohabitation of two warring communities.

The security and intelligence picture in Palestine was

always depressing. The British forces were entirely isolated and, after Operation POLLY, effectively imprisoned
themselves in fortified garrisons. The hanging of convicted
terrrorists failed to appease public opinion at home, which
could not understand why so many servicemen were being
killed and injured without any adequate response. Yet
the same hangings, particularly of Dov Gruner, who had
part of his highly articulate family resident in America,
were a propaganda disaster in the United States. The
Haganah was rich, influential, secretive and sufficiently
well organized to resist all the measures that the authorities might normally have relied upon. Nor could SIS
depend on Arab sources to provide accurate intelligence
information. The real humiliation of SIS's experience in
Palestine was that it was forced to abandon the country,
lock, stock and barrel. There was no unofficial liaison
between the Mossad and SIS, and both Nigel Clive and
his deputy were 'blown' almost as soon as they opened
their office in Jerusalem and had to be evacuated. In their
stead, David Balfour, who had taught at Athens University until the German invasion and had spent part of the
war as an agent disguised as Father Dimitri, a Greek
Orthodox monk, was appointed Head of Station, under
Oriental Secretary cover, at the Embassy in Tel Aviv.
There he remained, under constant and hostile Israel
surveillance, until his transfer to Smyrna in 1951.

Perhaps the last word on this episode should be left to
Menachem Begin, who observed:

> The British Secret Service is an institution enveloped
> in legend. Who has not heard of its achievements?
> The legend has been passed on from generation to
> generation, and from country to country, and from
> continent to continent – until some have come to
> believe that the British Intelligence is omniscient
> and infallible. Those who are interested in the
> dissemination of such stories know that in spying, as
> in war, the legend of success is in itself a success
> factor. The strength of British Intelligence however

does not lie only in the legend. This Service was, and may still prove to be, a tremendous factor in international relations. It has at its disposal the accumulated experience of centuries.

But during the revolt in Eretz Israel neither great experience nor the vast resources of the British Intelligence Service were of much help. The Hebrew underground smote the Intelligence hip and thigh. We proved that the Secret Service was neither omniscient nor infallible.[5]

4

MALAYA 1948–57

'The Emergency will be won by our intelligence system.'

General Sir Gerald Templer[1]

No sooner had the withdrawal from Palestine been completed than an entirely new Emergency was declared on the other side of the world to challenge the British intelligence bureaucrats. The start of the Communist-inspired insurrection in Malaya began on 15 June 1948 with the murder of three European rubber planters, but the roots of the matter went back much further.

The Japanese had invaded Malaya in 1942 and had remained in control for the next three years, thus eliminating any ideas about 'white supremacy' that the colonial authorities might have given to the local population. When the surrender took place in 1945, there were only a handful of Force 136 liaison officers on the scene from SOE, who were powerless to prevent the Chinese-dominated Malay Communist Party (MCP) from taking control of many of the rural areas. This unsatisfactory state of affairs was short-lived and British rule was slowly re-established.

The origin of the sudden rise in anti-British agitation in 1948 was a secret meeting of the Cominform held in London in January the same year, followed a month later by a much larger gathering in Calcutta, under cover of an international Asian youth congress. Both had been monitored by MI5 and the Security Service's local representative organization, Combined Intelligence Far East

(CIFE). The second meeting had been attended by British, Australian and Soviet delegates, as well as individuals from the Communist parties of various Far Eastern countries. The assembled group was given a message from Andrei A. Zhdanov, the Cominform's leading theoretician, that Burma, Malaya, French Indo-China and the Dutch East Indies were ripe for the 'armed struggle against Imperialism'.

This claim was not entirely relevant to Malaya, where Britain had already agreed to the principle of 'ultimate self-government' and had taken the first step by creating the Federation of Malaya. However, this did not stop the MCP from stepping up its campaign of demonstrations, labour unrest and violence against the more isolated rubber estates. Its plan, as confirmed by captured documents, was to drive the European planters off their land and to sabotage the tin mines, thus making a continued British presence uneconomic and impractical. Terrorist attacks would force the authorities to mobilize and concentrate their resources in certain limited areas. The MCP would, therefore, have an opportunity to create bases in the 'liberated' jungle from which guerrilla raids could be mounted. Finally, according to the MCP masterplan, the liberated areas would link up for a wholesale war against the Imperialists. That, at least, was the theory.

In reality, the MCP only had a few thousand active supporters, drawn mainly from veterans of the anti-Japanese resistance army that had been trained by SOE instructors and supplied with British matériel. Instead of being turned in at the time of the Japanese surrender, these weapons had been hidden in caches, ready to be used again. The inspiration behind these tactics was Chen Ping, the MCP's recently appointed General-Secretary . . . and holder of the Order of the British Empire. During the Japanese occupation he had organized Force 136 networks and the decoration had been awarded in recognition of his outstanding work. He had also attended the victory parade in London and had received Lord Mountbatten's personal thanks for his contribution to the

Japanese defeat. Aged twenty-seven, he had succeeded to power in the MCP largely due to the duplicity of his Vietnamese predecessor, Lai Teck, who had been a long-term double agent working for the Malay Special Branch. A series of breaches in security had compromised Lai Teck and he had been withdrawn from the field in March 1947, allowing Chen Ping to take control of the movement. His first initiative was to impose a militant, confrontationalist policy and embark on an armed struggle against the British designed to make them repeat their all-too-painful experience in Palestine.

The parallels with the situation in Palestine are evident, but in spite of being well trained and well equipped, the MCP did not enjoy the popular support of the Malayan natives who were easily intimidated by Chinese terrorism. However, the greatest similarity was to be found in the intelligence community, which included many men with experience in Palestine. Indeed, the High Commissioner, Sir Henry Gurney, had been the Chief Secretary in Palestine, and the Police Commissioner, Colonel Nicol Gray, a former Royal Marine commando, had been Inspector-General of the Palestine Police until the end of the mandate.

The Malayan Federation's police force also boasted a Special Branch, headed by Ian Wylie, and a semi-independent Security Service run by Colonel John Dalley. Both organizations were handicapped by a lack of records, which had been completely destroyed during the Japanese occupation, and a morale-sapping internal rivalry that stemmed from the British surrender in 1942. The police officers who had obeyed orders and remained at their posts had endured appalling conditions in Changi Gaol; these old hands, who had experienced being 'in the bag', bitterly resented their colleagues who had slipped away before the collapse to fight what they perceived to have been a glamorous war with SOE's Force 136 in the jungle. It was widely known that one particular group of diehards in the Malay civil service had actually condemned the escapees to death and had refused to speak to them after the war.

Gray, Dalley and Wylie liaised with MI5 and SIS through two separate chains of command: the Security Liaison Officer in Kuala Lumpur, and Courtney Young's successor at CIFE in Singapore, Jack Morton. Representing SIS was Dick Ellis, on attachment to Malcolm Mac-Donald's staff at the office of the UK Commissioner-General for South-East Asia.

When Morton had been sent out to run CIFE in 1948, he was quite unprepared for the chaotic intelligence arrangements that prevailed. Half of the Malayan personnel refused to co-operate with the other half, and they all resented the influx of Gray's hundred or so 'Palestinians'. Partly as a consequence of all this hostility, the army had taken it upon itself to conduct its own anti-terrorist operations, guided by the Director of Military Intelligence, Colonel Paul Gleadell. A series of unfortunate incidents had followed, including several where army patrols had been ambushed in error by the paramilitary police jungle units, and *vice versa*.

The security situation continued to deteriorate throughout the following year, so Morton requested the appointment of an Intelligence Adviser to execute the administrative reforms he believed essential to beat the MCP. His nominee was Sir William Jenkin, formerly the Deputy Director of the Indian Central Intelligence Bureau. Jenkin had a wealth of experience dealing with Indian nationalist subversion and was believed to be of sufficient stature to cope with the bitter internecine jealousies which were crippling the anti-insurgency programme. Yet even Jenkin found the strife too difficult to cope with and demanded the creation of an entirely new post, Director of Intelligence, to supervise the functions of the Special Branch, the Security Service and CIFE. Although there were optimistic expectations of this new hierarchy, it was not to last long. Jenkin eventually quarrelled with Gray over a demarcation dispute involving the Special Branch and suddenly resigned, returning to London without bothering to say the customary farewells to his staff.

The complicated disputes which soured the atmosphere within the intelligence community in Malaya spilled over into MI5 and SIS, and eventually affected every area of security. Certainly for years afterwards, the 'Malayan mafia' was a powerful group within the Security Service. Few have written about this unhappy episode in Britain's post-war experience, but Sir Robert Thompson, the Director of Operations appointed in 1950, has lectured on counter-insurgency policy and the following passage in particular sums up the position in Malaya at the time:

> Ideally there should be one single organization responsible for all security intelligence within the country. If there is more than one, it is almost impossible to define the respective responsibilities of each organization or to devise any means of co-ordinating their activities. All sorts of things will start to go wrong. For example, agents, especially the less reliable, will get themselves on to the payroll of several organizations and feed them the same unreliable information. Such information seemingly confirmed from different sources will be accepted as authentic. The different organizations will withhold information from one another in order to exploit it and obtain the credit for themselves. A promising line of intelligence promoted by one organization may well be cut inadvertently, or even intentionally, by another organization. Mutual suspicion and jealousies will arise, quite likely with the result that the separate organizations merely end up spying on each other. The intelligence, on which government plans should be based, will be both patchy and unreliable. The best organization to be responsible for all internal security intelligence is the special branch of a police force rather than a completely separate organization. It is a great advantage if intelligence officers have police powers and are able to call when necessary on the other branches of the police for support and assistance for developing their intelligence network.[2]

An attempt was made to persuade Dick White, then MI5's Director of B Division, the counter-espionage branch, to take on Jenkin's vacant post, but he declined the offer. Instead, Morton succeeded to it and acquired Maurice Oldfield, formerly the head of SIS's R5, who joined CIFE's joint service section. Together Morton and Oldfield proved a formidable team, reorganizing the Special Branch and creating a training centre at the Federal Police headquarters in the Bluff Road complex outside Kuala Lumpur. Under Morton's direction, the arrangements for the internment of suspects was expanded, with over 6,000 taken into custody, and some 700 Malay Chinese were deported to China.

The disunity within the Malay intelligence community only served to encourage the MCP, which enjoyed a multiplicity of sources, including the High Commissioner's butler and several agents planted within the Special Branch. On 6 October 1951, following a leak of information, disaster struck. Sir Henry Gurney's official Rolls-Royce was ambushed on the road to his regular weekend retreat at Fraser's Hill, a hill-station some forty miles to the north of Kuala Lumpur. Gurney was shot dead as he walked away from his wrecked, bullet-riddled car, and all his police escorts were wounded. Gurney's assassination plunged Malaya into further uncertainty. The European estate managers, who had feared the worst the previous year when Britain had given formal recognition to the Communists in China, lost what little confidence they had left. Simultaneously, the adminstration was thrown into disarray – which was not helped by the absence of the Chief Secretary who happened to be abroad on leave – and the Government in London was distracted by the general election then in progress. Morale was at an all-time low. The police had no information about the perpetrators of the crime and most evaded capture, with only two of the insurgents being killed in brief fire-fights.

Gurney's murder proved to be a turning-point for the security situation. Once the general election was over, the new Colonial Secretary, Oliver Lyttelton, conducted a tour of inspection and was appalled by what he found. It was, he recalled, far worse than he had imagined possible and he remarked that he had 'never seen such a tangle as that presented by the Government of Malaya . . . . The police itself was divided by a great schism between the Commissioner of Police and the Head of the Special Branch. Intelligence was scanty and unco-ordinated between the civil and military authorities.'[3] Lyttelton made a second, clandestine visit to Kuala Lumpur to prepare a damning report on the situation, and then returned to London to invite General Sir Gerald Templer to take the two jobs of British High Commissioner and Director of Operations. The proposal met with fierce opposition from Malcolm MacDonald and the Foreign Office, on the grounds that the appointment should not have been a military one, but they were won round. After that the situation changed swiftly.

In January 1952, Nicol Gray resigned and went to work for the Jockey Club in Newmarket. His replacement was Colonel (Sir) Arthur Young, a career police officer who had just completed the reorganization of the colonial police in the Gold Coast. The next month Templer swept into office and, together with Young, restored morale. Although there may have been some initial apprehension about Young's appointment, for his previous experience had been strictly limited to routine police work, he soon demonstrated his high regard for the Special Branch. Templer, too, was popular. As well as having taken on responsibility for security matters in Germany immediately after the war, he had served in most branches of intelligence: he had been the intelligence liaison officer with the British Expeditionary Force in France on the outbreak of war and, more recently, had been Director of Military Intelligence between 1946 and 1948.

Templer recognized that the predominantly Chinese insurgents would only be beaten through a combination of excellent intelligence and what he termed a campaign to win 'the hearts and minds of the people'. Accordingly, he threw himself into the execution of a controversial scheme that had become known as the Briggs Plan, after its architect, Sir Harold Briggs, his predecessor as Director of Operations. This called for a ruthless resettlement programme involving the relocation of up to half a million squatters, who eked out an agricultural existence in the rural areas and were easy prey for the MCP and its undercover intelligence unit, the Min Yuen. Briggs Plan required all the squatter hamlets to be destroyed and the inhabitants brought into 600 'new villages', their perimeters surrounded by wire fences and controlled by a police post. Before going out to work in the morning, each villager could be frisked by troops to ensure that they had no concealed food or weapons. The objective was to prevent the guerrilla bands from obtaining either money or food from the peasants, thus forcing the insurgents to rely on their own limited resources in the jungle. There they could be pursued by the 20,000 troops, 40,000 Home Guard and 60,000 police that had been deployed against them. Although initially unpopular, the concept of the 'new villages' soon caught on because, for the first time in their lives, the squatters were granted ownership of the land they occupied and cultivated. They also enjoyed running water, electricity, schools, medical care and even a degree of democracy through locally elected councils. Thanks to the land grants, they had a stake in the country – and, therefore, something to lose.

In fact, the Min Yuen probably never had more than 15,000 members, and the number of terrorists at any one time did not exceed 5,000. Nevertheless, they proved to be extremely versatile, well-armed opponents, slipping out of the jungle to launch surprise raids before disappearing back into its cover. In response, Templer's tactics involved the distribution of identity cards, curfews and collective fines. He would concentrate his men on small areas, clearing them of terrorists and destroying the food caches, so that they could later be declared 'white' and freed of the Emergency restrictions.

Just the issuing of identity cards was an immense undertaking. A common system of registering Chinese names was required, and the one adopted was the so-called Chinese Commercial Code, which transposed numerals to the components of particular Chinese characters of the script containing one word or name. Chinese scholars were recruited to transform the ideographs, which even the illiterate Chinese could use for their own names, into the appropriate CCC numbers. The fact that it takes a knowledge of 7,000 characters to be able to read a newspaper gives an idea of the scale of the task before the Security Service. None the less, the system was introduced and it worked extremely well, becoming a vital way of identifying suspects. Another related development was the construction of a secret military holding centre, where prisoners could be screened and defectors processed.

Very gradually the situation began to get better and, during 1952, some 1,097 insurgents were killed, a dramatic improvement on the performance of the previous two years. Many, but not all, of these contacts resulted from the change in methods adopted by both the army and the intelligence personnel. Instead of guarding fixed points and waiting, defensively, to be attacked, the military stepped up its ground patrols, dropping small teams of bandit hunters into the rain forest by Royal Navy helicopters. There they would wait in ambush for the insurgents, before clearing a space so that they could be air-lifted out to another location. Some teams spent weeks at a time in the jungle, being resupplied by air. To increase the harassment, incendiary bombs were dropped on all the crops in terrorist-dominated areas, thus forcing the rebels to keep on the move.

The idea was to exert a relentless pressure which could be exploited by the intelligence staff, who collaborated with a specialist psychological warfare unit to produce millions of morale-sapping leaflets and safe-conduct passes. Defectors were promised good treatment, the best food and a variety of rewards for any senior MCP cadres they identified. For those who were illiterate, 'voice aircraft' flew regular missions broadcasting persuasive messages from defectors calling on their comrades to surrender. The scheme was so successful that some deserters surrendered carrying bags of decapitated heads so that they could claim the bounties on their comrades.

Each defector added another piece to the intelligence jigsaw of the MCP, and gradually the Security Service could produce a list of all the active Communist terrorists, or CTs as they became known, in Malaya. It was a highly effective undertaking, aided by several innovative schemes. On one occasion, for example, specially prepared 'surplus' radios were allowed to find their way on to the Chinese black market, in the knowledge that they would be snapped up quickly by the Min Yuen. Indeed they were, but the insurgents were unaware that each wireless set also acted as a beacon, transmitting a homing signal which could be traced, thus betraying its location.

As the intelligence effort expanded, so more experienced staff were drafted in. Arthur Martin, one of MI5's molehunters, was sent out to Singapore to relieve the SLO, Keith Way, and ended up running the Kuala Lumpur Special Branch, with Guy Madoc heading the Security Service. Martin was joined by Alec MacDonald, a future Director of MI5's counter-espionage branch.

By May 1953, the tide had turned in favour of the security forces, who were becoming adept at exploiting the Special Branch's information. As a result, the number of successful contacts and fire-fights multiplied. In one particular ambush Ah Kuk, Chen Ping's military commander for most of Southern Malaya, was killed, an event that boosted morale amongst the security forces but had the opposite effect on the MCP. The number of MCP defections increased to such a rate that a new unit, the Special Operations Volunteer Force was created, made up exclusively of 'turned' guerrillas. In addition, eleven former members of Chen Ping's central executive committee switched sides. Although some had been tempted by the high rewards on offer, others recognized the futility of fighting on when the British had already announced that 'Malaya should in due course become a self-governing nation'. Indeed, when Templer's first 'white' area was declared in September 1953, it reportedly attracted quite a number of disaffected MCP members who had tired of the struggle and simply wished to live in peace, free of the Emergency regulations and safe in the knowledge that a representative political structure was in the process of being constructed.

In June 1954, his task almost completed, Templer returned to London as the new Chief of the Imperial General Staff (CIGS) and was succeeded by his deputy, Sir Donald MacGillivray. He was responsible for negotiating away the last chance the guerrillas had: a safe haven in Thailand. After a series of secret negotiations conducted by the SIS Station in Bangkok, a joint Thai–Malay intelligence centre was set up at Songkhla, just over the Thai frontier, where information on the insurgents could be exchanged. This important development, combined with an agreement allowing Commonwealth forces to chase insurgents up to twenty miles into Thai territory, sealed the fate of the Communists. They were unable to escape the security forces, and the Royal Navy patrols off the coast ensured that they could not be resupplied from the sea. In short, they were trapped.

In July 1955, a general election was held as a first step towards a new constitution, and the MCP was left even more isolated. Tunku Abdel Rahman was elected Prime Minister and the British Cabinet confirmed that he would lead his country into independence. One of his first decisions was to issue an amnesty for all MCP members not guilty of any criminal acts. This announcement seems to have prompted the elusive Chen Ping to come to the conference table, for he made contact with the Special Branch and a preliminary meeting was held with Ian Wylie to agree a suitable venue for the main talks. The site chosen was a tin mine at Baling. On hand to escort Chen Ping out of the jungle, on 28 December 1955, was his old Force 136 commander, John Davis, by then a senior officer in the Malay Police. The historic meeting lasted two days, with Chen Ping demanding that the MCP be allowed to participate in the new political processes of Malaya. But the Prime Minister, always a firm anti-Communist, insisted on unconditional surrender. No agreement was reached, so Davis took the guerrilla leader back to the fringe of the jungle, where the struggle was continued by a diminishing number of Chen Ping's supporters.

Although Malaya was granted independence on 31 August 1957, the Emergency was not formally ended until 1960. Its toll was 3,149 Communists killed, 915 captured, 752 surrendered and around 1,643 wounded. The security forces suffered 1,438 killed (including 353 British personnel) and 2,299 wounded. Chen Ping is still believed to be at large, probably smarting over one betrayal above all: in April 1957, his chief lieutenant, Hor Lung, took a reward of £55,000 and the promise of a new life to sell out his comrades.

As has been seen, the Malayan episode largely involved MI5 personnel, with SIS having a peripheral involvement from Singapore and, of course, from the neighbouring stations at Bangkok and Rangoon. Nevertheless, the Emergency became the principal preoccupation of the JIC's Far East sub-committee, on which SIS sat, in the persons of Dick Ellis, Maurice Oldfield and his successor at the end of the active period, James Fulton. In addition, SIS also attended the British Defence Co-ordination Committee (Far East) and was, therefore, directly involved in the events in Malaya. It could be argued that the Bangkok Station's brilliant achievement in the creation of a joint Thai – Malay intelligence centre at Songkhla was one of the breakthroughs which enabled the campaign to end in success.

In intelligence terms Malaya's real contribution was to prove that, given adequate resources and the proper command structure, the security authorities could gain the upper hand in a conflict against home-grown insurgents who might otherwise be expected to be at an advantage against 'foreign occupiers'. There were, admittedly, special factors working in Britain's favour, such as the political initiative taken by the Cabinet to ensure the succession of a pro-British, moderate administration. Tunku Abdel Rahman was not the ideal choice of the local advisers, but he rose to the occasion and proved to be a leader who commanded considerable respect. Templer's determined promotion of the concept of a strictly Malayan political process effectively cut the ground from under the MCP, because the Communists could not pretend to be the only movement committed to ending colonial rule. Nor could the MCP be portrayed as the population's natural protector against British oppression. Many of the forces deployed in the Emergency were Commonwealth troops from Fiji, Australia and elsewhere, with the full backing of their respective governments. Templer made it clear that the country would only be ready for full independence when the terrorist atrocities had ended. Thus, the MCP itself unwittingly became an obstacle in the path of its own stated objective. By the end of the Emergency, when the country had been granted full independence, the MCP had become an irrelevance without any political power-base, alienated from both the Chinese community and the rural peasants.

The depth of knowledge achieved by the local Security Service and the Special Branch, with SIS's help, was truly astonishing. An enormous amount of information was accumulated about each individual terrorist and sympathizer, which was used to great effect in the military holding centre where suspects underwent interrogation. The 'menu' system of graded financial rewards linked to the stature of captured Communist terrorists was also a tremendous incentive for defectors to trade really valuable intelligence.

There is certainly a temptation to draw parallels between the situation in Palestine and the Malaya Emergency, considering that the opposition on both occasions were partly SOE-trained in the first place and that many of the British police personnel were deployed in both places. That, however, is the limit of the similarities. Although the Haganah was quite confident that the British would eventually pull out, it was uncertain about the terms. Withdrawal was never a real issue in Malaya, because the principle of independence for Malaya as a sovereign nation had been conceded at a very early stage. The chief difference between the two conflicts, and the key to the intelligence victory, was the willingness of the population to assist the security authorities. This never occurred in Palestine, where both Arabs and Jews were equally ready to shoot at British soldiers.

The Malayan campaign was a tremendous boost for MI5 and SIS, with both organizations claiming great credit after a somewhat sticky start. Many of the lessons learned were to be used to good effect again in Cyprus, where nationalist aspirations fuelled terrorism, albeit on a smaller scale, just as conditions in Malaya were returning to normal. But before examining the security and intelligence operation conducted there, we should return for a moment to SIS's London headquarters, which, during the period just covered, had found itself embroiled in a highly secret scandal that was to become known as the Philby affair.

5

KIM PHILBY AND VALUABLE

'The British security and intelligence services, the oldest and most experienced in the West, were gravely damaged by Blunt, Philby, Blake and others who worked for Soviet intelligence inside them for many years before being discovered.

Communist leaders appreciate the importance of good security work to their survival and to the constructive contribution that good intelligence can make to the success of their international strategy. Communist intelligence and security services are therefore free from the difficult, if not impossible, constraints imposed on the activities of their counterparts in democratic countries. They have an officially recognized and honoured place in Communist institutions. They have no problems to contend with from the press or public opinion in their own countries. They can afford to be more aggressive, especially in the recruitment of new agents.'

Anatoli Golitsyn *New Lies for Old*[1]

So much inaccurate information has been written about Kim Philby and, indeed, his supposed chances of becoming CSS, to say nothing of his alleged responsibility for the failure of numerous operations, that it is worth stating the facts again.

Harold Adrian Russell Philby was born in the Punjab on New Year's Day 1912, the only son of Harry St John Philby, a revenue assistant in the Indian civil service. His mother, Dora Johnston, was the tall, red-headed daughter of a Eurasian who worked in the Indian Public Works Department. Nicknamed Kim, after Rudyard Kipling's famous hero, young Philby was brought up in England by his paternal grandmother, the widow of a Ceylon tea planter. He was educated at a prep school in Eastbourne and then won a scholarship to his father's old public school, Westminster. Early in 1929, Philby won another prize, having come top of the three Westminster entrants for his father's old college, Trinity, Cambridge.

Philby went up to Trinity in October of the same year to read history, but three years later ended up with a good second-class degree in economics. Immediately after graduating he drove to Vienna on a motorcycle, where in February the following year he married Litzi Kohlmann, a Jewish Communist slightly older than himself.

Late in the spring of 1934, Philby brought his wife back to London, where they lived with his mother at the family home in Acol Road, Maida Vale. He supported himself as a freelance journalist, contributing articles to various literary magazines. His marraige to Litzi lasted just four years and, in 1937, she moved to Paris; Philby then travelled to Spain, where he began sending a series of unsolicited articles from Franco's Nationalist camp to *The Times*. Several were printed and, following one particularly impressive despatch from the Basque town of Guernica, soon after the Luftwaffe had devastated it, Philby was summoned to London and appointed *The Times*'s special correspondent.

Philby continued to cover the Spanish civil war until Franco's victory, remaining in Madrid until August 1939, when he returned to London. After three weeks' holiday, he was posted by *The Times* to the Arras headquarters of the British Expeditionary Force as a seasoned war correspondent, but was evacuated from Boulogne following the Nazi offensive in May. He made one further, brief return to France, to Cherbourg, before establishing himself in his mother's basement flat in Grove Court, Drayton Gardens, with his new girlfriend Aileen Furse.

Philby's first official contact with British intelligence was when he was interviewed for a job at the Government Code and Cipher School, SIS's pre-war cryptographic organization. He was turned down, but by the end of July 1940 he had secured a post with SOE as an instructor at its principal training centre, Brickendonbury Hall, near Hertford. From there he progressed to Lord Montagu's estate at Beaulieu, where he lectured potential saboteurs about the clandestine manufacture of propaganda and subversive material.

It was not until September 1941 that Philby was invited to join SIS's Section V, where he could put his knowledge of Spain to good use. Known as SIS's counter-espionage department, Section V was divided into geographical sub-sections; Philby's new post, V(d), headed by Dick Brooman-White, required the analysis of secret intelligence which originated from that most sensitive of sources, intercepted enemy signals. Based at Section V's war quarters in St Albans, Philby became a counter-intelligence specialist, concentrating on German decrypts. By sorting through the Abwehr's intercepted communications, he could spot the names of enemy spies and advise SIS's men in the field on how to anticipate and counter German moves in an area of Europe that had become a veritable cockpit of international intrigue and espionage. Philby excelled in the exploitation of this most secret source and proved adept in the construction of summaries, which concealed the true nature of their origin, for the distribution to SIS's four stations in Iberia: Lisbon, Madrid, Gibraltar and Tangier. He demonstrated all the qualities required of an intelligence bureaucrat, exactly the kind of individual the Service would need when peace eventually materialized.

In 1943, Section V moved to Ryder Street in London and Philby, who had taken charge of V(d), was given temporary responsibility for the whole of the Section while its new head, Colonel Felix Cowgill, visited America. Late in 1944, he was transferred across St James's Park to the seventh floor of Broadway Buildings to run a relatively new, anti-Soviet unit, Section IX, leaving his school-friend from Westminster, Tim Milne, in charge of Section V, which also happened to employ Philby's younger sister, Helena. Section IX had been formed in September 1944 under the aegis of an old MI5 hand, Jack Curry, with the former Head of Station in Shanghai, Harry Steptoe, as his principal assistant. Steptoe had been selected to make a tour of the Mediterranean stations to rebuild SIS's organization after the invasion of Italy, before becoming Head of Station in Tehran. Curry was anxious for retirement, leaving Philby in pole position to execute his take-over and 'sniff the breezes of office politics'. After SIS's reorganization, to which Philby made an influential contribution, Section IX was combined with Section V to form R5, of which he was named the head.

By the end of the war Philby and Aileen had had three children, Josephine, John and Dudley, and had bought a large comfortable house at 18 Carlyle Square, Chelsea. Having belatedly obtained a divorce from Litzi, Philby married Aileen in September 1946, just a few weeks before the birth of their fourth child, Miranda. Five months later, in February 1947, the entire family moved to Istanbul, where Philby had been posted as Head of Station, under First Secretary cover at the Consulate General, in succession to Cyril Machray. Before his departure Philby had attended a short training course, given by John Munn, and had then briefed his successor at R5, Douglas Roberts.

Philby's uneventful, standard, two-year tour of duty at Istanbul was followed by an even better appointment – Head of Station in Washington – to fill the vacancy caused by Peter Dwyer's decision to take up permanent residence in Canada. Philby handed over the Istanbul Station to an old wartime Section V colleague, Rodney Dennys, and returned to London to be briefed before moving into Dwyer's office in the British Embassy on Massachussets Avenue, where he remained until the defections of Burgess and Maclean in May 1951.

Up until this point Philby was, by SIS standards, a highly successful and polished operator. But contrary to speculation, there was never any chance of him succeeding Stewart Menzies as CSS. His private life was a complete mess, with two marriages, three children born out of wedlock and a well-known Communist past. Certainly, MI5 had a record of Philby's pre-war membership of the Communist Party of Great Britain (CPGB) and, in 1946, he had informed the Vice-Chief, Valentine Vivian, that Litzi had been a Communist activist. He could not have had any illusions about keeping his Party membership concealed, for Andrew King, one of his contemporaries at Cambridge and another rising star in SIS, had attended Party meetings with him at university.

In addition to all this, there was his unconventional father's record, which had included a five-month spell in prison under the wartime Regulation 18B. St John Philby had converted to Islam in 1930, and nine years later, after a lifetime in India and the Middle East, had fought the Epping by-election for the Labour Party and then the Hythe by-election for the far-Right British People's Party. He was also an Arabist of some note and a close friend of the Saudi royal family. It was his ignominious deportation from America, while on his way back to England from India in 1940, that had brought him to MI5's attention and had resulted in his detention.

St John Philby's fervently anti-British eccentricities, which continued until his death in Beirut in 1960, did not blight his son's progress as an able, bright, middle-ranking SIS officer. However, combined with Philby's hard drinking and Aileen's nervous collapses, the omens for promotion were not good. In any event, his career came to a swift full-stop in May 1951 when Burgess unexpectedly disappeared, apparently without trace.

Philby came under immediate suspicion when Burgess vanished for several reasons. It was perfectly clear, given the circumstances of Burgess's hasty departure on Friday 25 May, that he had received a tip-off from someone who had been privy to a long-standing Security Service enquiry into a leakage of information to Moscow from the wartime British Embassy in Washington. Over the four years that the investigation had been running, the field had been narrowed to just one suspect, Donald Maclean, who had been scheduled for a hostile interrogation the following Monday, 28 May. The confrontation never took place because Maclean had fled to France two days earlier, catching an overnight cross-Channel ferry to St Malo. Obviously he had been alerted to MI5's intention. Burgess's complicity strongly suggested that, as well as being an accomplice, he had also been the conduit for the timely warning. The only question remaining, which was on everyone's lips, concerned the identity of the 'third man'.

Philby had not known Maclean, but he had enjoyed a long friendship with Burgess stretching back to their university days together. More recently, Burgess had lodged with the Philbys in Washington, when they had both served in the same Embassy. When Philby's Communist past was added to the equation, the conclusion was irresistible. Philby was summoned back to Broadway by Menzies's Deputy Director of Intelligence, James Easton, to undergo a painful interview with Dick White at MI5's headquarters. This was followed up by a second session, which resulted in a detailed report being sent to Menzies stating that Philby had not been entirely candid; the Security Service recommended that his services should be dispensed with forthwith.

Menzies evidently found it difficult to hand out this kind of treatment to a colleague he knew and liked, so Philby's enforced resignation was mooted and accepted over two visits to the CSS's office. The financial settlement, in lieu of pension, involved an immediate severance payment of £2,000 and a further £2,000 paid in four half-yearly payments. Six months later, in November 1951, a formal enquiry into the Burgess and Maclean defections was conducted by MI5, and Philby was invited to give evidence to it. In reality, the so-called 'judicial enquiry' was little more than a concentrated effort by (Sir) Helenus Milmo, MI5's skilled wartime interrogator, to extract a confession before witnesses from the most probable candidate for the Soviet 'mole', or 'third man'. Milmo's inquisition failed, to the extent that Philby conceded nothing, but his poor performance satisfied all those present about the scale of his guilt. Philby endured a few more interviews with Jim Skardon, the ex-Scotland Yard detective who had persuaded Klaus Fuchs to admit to being a Russian spy, and then had one final meeting with Sir John Sinclair, Menzies's successor as CSS. Philby neatly avoided making any incriminating statements and, reluctantly, the Security Service was obliged to let him walk free.

Philby was now out in the cold. He moved to a small bungalow called Sunbox, at Heronsgate in Hertfordshire, and looked around for a new job. At one stage he flew to Spain, calling on the Head of Station in Madrid, Desmond Bristow, for a drink. Like all the European Heads of Station, Bristow had been ordered to keep clear of Philby, but he could not bring himself to abandon an old colleague. Instead, he entertained Philby and then sent a detailed report to Broadway.

While Philby wandered, apparently seeking employment as a journalist, his wife Aileen bought a large house, Leylands, in Crowborough, and went into a lonely decline. She needed constant psychiatric care, apparently quite convinced that her husband was trying to kill her. She eventually succumbed to influenza in December 1957, when Philby had finally got a job as a Fleet Street stringer in Beirut.

Philby's name is now a by-word for duplicity, yet for all the wisdom of hindsight, there were few clues to his true allegiances and certainly no evidence against him of the kind which could be brought before a court. He fitted neatly into the Bohemian, Left-orientated circle of intellectuals from which most of Britain's secret warriors were drawn; even his youthful flirtation with Communism was by no means unique and served to bolster his anti-Nazi credentials. However, although some details of his case became known outside SIS during the early 1950s, the organization closed ranks to prevent any further disclosures. Many of Philby's colleagues, who had not been indoctrinated into the substance of the evidence against him, believed he had been unjustly pilloried because of a few indiscreet friendships. Only a handful of senior SIS officers, who shared the truth with MI5's molehunters knew the weight of the case against him.

Although Philby is now recognized as an arch-traitor, very little is reliably known about the circumstances of his recruitment to the Soviet cause. He himself has given three versions of events: one in his self-serving autobiography; another in his extraordinary confession to a colleague in January 1963 (see Chapter 12); and a third in an interview recently with Phillip Knightley of the *Sunday Times*.

Philby has been described as being converted by his first wife, Litzi, in the turmoil of Vienna in 1934, and he himself told Nicholas Elliott, in his type-written confession, that he had been a willing volunteer then. However, in his memoirs, he says that he left Cambridge 'with a degree and the conviction that my life must be devoted to Communism'.[2] Anthony Blunt claimed that Philby had been recruited by Theodore Maly, a legendary NKVD 'illegal' who had operated in Britain during the late 1920s and '30s. This may well be the case, for in January 1988 Philby confirmed:

> On my very last day at Cambridge in the summer of
> 1933 I decided I would become a communist . . .
> [Maurice] Dobb [a Marxist economist] gave me an
> introduction to a communist group in Paris. . . .
> They in turn passed me on to an illegal underground
> communist movement in Vienna. My work in
> Austria must have caught the attention of the people
> who are now my colleagues because almost
> immediately on my return to Britain in the spring of
> 1934 I was approached by a man who asked me if I
> would like to join the Russian intelligence
> service. . . . I did not hesitate.[3]

However, when challenged to name his recruiter, Philby replied: 'For operational reasons I do not propose to name him, but he was not a Russian. . . .' The full truth of the matter is yet to be determined, but it is possible to quantify the damage sustained as a result of Philby's activities.

Although it is widely suspected that Philby reported everything he saw and did to his Soviet controllers, there is some reason to believe that he was sufficiently shrewd not to confide wholeheartedly in his NKVD case officer, however great his intellectual commitment to the Soviet cause. Blunt once recalled how clumsy exploitation of one of his tips had placed him in jeopardy. He had alerted his contact to the identity of an MI5 source inside the CPGB. This had been passed on instantly to the Party's General Secretary, Harry Pollitt, who had expelled the culprit without explanation, leaving the mole to deduce, correctly, that he had been betrayed. The Security Service had launched an internal investigation to find the leak, much to Blunt's discomfort, and he had narrowly avoided being compromised. Given Philby's considerable skill in the field, it is probable that he rationed his supply of information carefully, and may even have taken the prudent precaution of withholding certain items in order to ensure long-term protection from his Soviet masters.

It is possible that Philby did not get the opportunity to undergo a really lengthy, in-depth debriefing until some months after his expulsion from SIS. There may even have been a greater delay than that if Philby and the Soviets suspected he was under intensive surveillance and were reluctant to chance the necessary meeting. Nevertheless, whatever the date of Philby's eventual debriefing, he must have supplied enough damaging details of the personalities, structure and operations of the organization largely to nullify its existence. Unquestionably, his exposure in 1951 had a devastating effect on SIS. A few of the older hands, like Valentine Vivian, who had originally brought him into Section V, had just retired, but others, such as Kenneth Cohen and Cuthbert Bowlby, who had two and three years to go before retirement, felt bitter at the betrayal, almost as though their careers had been invalidated. Tim Milne was also caught up in the backwash and fell under suspicion.

Apart from the important SIS order-of battle information which, it must be assumed, Philby disclosed to the
Soviets, there must also have been a steady flow of
operational material. Up until his transfer to Section IX,
Philby had access to only a limited number of secrets in
which his contacts would have been interested. His daily
fare consisted of clues gleaned from German intercepted
signals, which were relevant to the Abwehr's activities in
the Iberian region – hardly the kind of sensitive data that
the NKVD would have regarded as vital. However, he
also gained access to SIS's source books, which revealed
details of SIS sources inside the Soviet Union, exactly the
type of information that the Russians would have been
extremely interested in. Philby recalled how he had
obtained these top-secret files from SIS's registry:

> These held the particulars and records of SIS agents
> operating abroad. It was natural for me to want
> information on the agents operating in the Iberian
> Peninsula, and my perusal of the source books for
> Spain and Portugal whetted my appetite for more. I
> worked steadily through them, thus enlarging my
> knowledge of SIS activity as a whole. When I came
> to the source book for the Soviet Union, I found
> that it consisted of two volumes. Having worked
> through them to my satisfaction I returned them to
> registry in the normal way.[4]

This sounds like a grotesque breach of security, especially
as Philby had no possible 'need to know' about SIS
activities outside his own geographical region. However,
the damage was not quite as bad as it might appear, as
SIS had virtually no sources inside Russia to boast of.
Apart from all the White Russian *émigrés* who were of
dubious value, there had only been one really good agent
run personally by Harold Gibson.

Gibson, like his brother Archie who was also an SIS
officer, was rather more Russian than English. He had
been born in Russia before the revolution and Russian
was his first language. He had attended Tonbridge School

and fought in the First World War, before joining SIS and being posted to Istanbul in 1919. Two years later, he transferred to Bucharest and, in 1930, was appointed Head of Station in Riga. Then in 1933, he met an old school-friend who happened to be private secretary to the Foreign Trade Commissar (and a long-surviving senior member of Stalin's Politburo), Anastas Mikoyan. Gibson moved to Prague to run his agent, but contact was broken late in 1940 after Gibson had been evacuated to London. When discreet enquires were made in Moscow, it was discovered that Gibson's agent had been arrested and executed. It was not until 1964 that Blunt admitted that he had deduced the agent's identity from an SIS report and had passed the word on to his NKVD contact.

Thus, when Philby came to examine the source books in late 1941, there was little for him to discover. Indeed, he would have learned that even GCHQ had been instructed to ignore Soviet signals for the duration of hostilities.

It was only when Section V and Section IX had been combined to form R5, when Philby had taken on responsibility 'for the collection and interpretation of information concerning Soviet and Communist espionage and subversion in all parts of the world outside British territory', that he really became indispensable to the NKVD. While in his new post, Philby made several sorties abroad during the summer of 1945. He visited France, Germany, Italy and Greece, partly to reconnoitre the facilities that might be available for extending SOE's covert war against the Soviet Bloc, and partly to indoctrinate SIS's field personnel into Menzies's plan for continuing irregular operations into the peace.

It had long been decreed by a JIC sub-committee chaired by Bill Cavendish-Bentinck that SOE as such would cease to exist after the Japanese surrender, but that much of its capacity to conduct clandestine operations would be integrated into a Special Operations branch of SIS under SOE's wartime leader, Colin Gubbins. In theory, the Special Operations branch was to build the foundations of a stay-behind network in Germany, Austria and Northern Italy. The contingency plan in the event of a Soviet invasion also allowed for a permanent skeleton staff that could be mobilized and brought up to full strength at very short notice. Initially, SIS's new branch was only intended to operate actively in the Middle East, chiefly Iraq and Persia, but Menzies had other ideas. With the first frost of the Cold War, preparations were made to foment subversion in the Soviet Union and its more vulnerable satellites. Even the Foreign Office, ever wary of SIS-inspired adventures, was later to give its broad approval to action that would 'liberate the countries within the Soviet orbit by any means short of war'.[5]

The targets for SIS's ambitious plan to limit Soviet hegemony in the Balkans centred on Yugoslavia, Bulgaria, Albania and Greece, each of which was in various stages of civil disorder. SOE's Balkans section, under the command of Brigadier C. M. Keble, had moved, along with part of its Middle East base, from Cairo to a small Italian fishing village, Torre a Mare, just outside Bari, in 1944. Its cover was Force 266, an offshoot of Force 133 which remained in Cairo until it was disbanded, along with the rest of SOE, at the end of June 1946. Since it was ex-SOE personnel who were going to be expected to spearhead SIS's anti-Communist campaign in the Balkans, Philby undertook a lengthy tour of inspection. His journey in the summer of 1945 took him to visit Charles de Salis and John Bruce Lockhart in Paris, Monty Woodhouse in Athens and SOE's outpost in Bari. There he was 'instrumental in getting a pet bugbear chosen for an airdrop in to Yugoslavia; but instead of breaking his neck he covered himself with glory'.[6]

If Philby intended to make his influence felt in the planning and execution of secret missions into the Balkans, he did not do so at this early stage of the peace. When one of Menzies's Deputy Directors, General Sinclair, offered him the post of Machray's successor in Istanbul, he undoubtedly had good reason to believe that he would still be able to take a hand in matters as 'Istanbul was then the main southern base for intelligence work directed against the Soviet Union and the socialist countries of the Balkans and Central Europe'.[7] Philby also had another motive for going to Turkey. He knew that his lack of overseas SIS experience would be a severe handicap in his future manoeuvrings. As he later confirmed, 'I could not reasonably resist a foreign posting without serious loss of standing in the service, and such loss of standing might well have prejudiced my access in the long run to the sort of intelligence I needed.'[8]

With these expectations Philby must have been a little disappointed when he was instructed, shortly before his departure for Istanbul at the end of January 1947, 'not to concentrate too much attention of the Balkans'. His 'first priority was the Soviet Union'[9] and, accordingly, he spent much of his two-year tour of duty engaged in a topographical survey for SIS's War Planning branch of Turkey's bleak frontier with Georgia and Soviet Armenia, leaving the management of individual agents to Roman Sulakov, the station's long-serving, White Russian assistant who had been recruiting and running spies in the region for at least two decades.

Philby has often been credited with masterminding the well-informed counter-insurgency measures taken by the Communist regime in Albania, but in reality he was not made privy to the details of SIS's intended assault until he had reached London, *en route* for his new post as Head of Station in Washington. Philby left Istanbul at the beginning of September 1949 and took up his new post in the middle of the following month, having arrived in New York aboard the SS *Caronia* on 8 October. During a series of numerous briefing sessions at Broadway, he was informed about SIS's officially authorized response to the Communist coup in Prague, the Soviet-inspired civil war in Greece and the ruthless blockade of the western sectors of Berlin. He was also told that SIS had finally been allowed to execute a plan that had already been more than two years in the making: the overthrow of Enver

Hoxha's hated regime in Albania, codenamed Operation VALUABLE.

The first stage in the operation was then just getting under way under the command of Harold Perkins, who had conducted the sabotage of the Haganah's illegal refugee ships three years earlier. Perkins had recruited a training officer, David Smiley, and acquired the use of a strategically located base camp named Fort Benjimma, not far from Mdina, Malta's ancient capital, where volunteers from the sizable Albanian *émigré* community could be put through their paces before being infiltrated back to their homeland.

At that time, in May 1949, Smiley was with his regiment, the Royal Horse Guards, in Germany. He was a professional soldier who had joined SOE in Cairo in 1943 and had been into Albania twice to fight with the partisans. The first time he walked overland from Greece; the second he was parachuted straight in. After the war, he had been posted to the SIS Station in Warsaw, but the Polish authorities had declared him *persona non grata* for spying. On his return to London, he had declined an offer from Bernard Fergusson to join his counter-terrorist unit of the Palestine Police and had joined Perkins instead. At the end of his secondment, he returned to regular soldiering as second-in-command of his regiment.

The SIS plan to destabilize Albania was no hit-or-miss affair, as it has sometimes been portrayed. It was a comprehensive project proposed by men who had actually spent months inside the country with the very groups who were seeking to overthrow the Communists. Apart from Smiley and Perkins, who were acknowledged experts in their trade, SIS selected career officers who knew all the risks from personal experience: The Hon. Alan Hare, for example, a veteran of two SOE parachute missions into Albania; John Hibberdine, who had spent months up in the north of the country organizing guerrilla bands before he had succumbed to paratyphoid; Anthony Northrop, who had been one of SOE's liaison officers with the headquarters of Hoxha's resistance movement; Professor

Robert Zaehner, an Oxford don and linguist who had spent much of the war working undercover for SIS, dressed as a local tribesman in Soviet-occupied territory in Northern Persia; and Peter Kemp, a survivor of the Spanish civil war and numerous raids on the French coast before being parachuted into Albania with an SOE mission. Even the tricky political negotiations, which had to be held with the exiled leaders opposed to Hoxha before any of the *émigrés* could be recruited, were conducted by another old Albanian hand, Julian Amery.

This was no madcap scheme, but one that involved much research into the backgrounds of the first batch of thirty raw recruits from the displaced-persons camps in Europe, and the acquisition of suitable transport and radio bases. The Head of Station in Athens, Pat Whinney, who had run SIS's flotilla of fishing boats in the Western Mediterranean during the war, was called upon to provide the transport. He arranged the purchase of a *felucca*, the *Stormie Seas*, and recruited two skilled seamen, John Leatham and Sam Barclay, as crew. Both had worked for the British Military Mission in Athens, running supplies into Piraeus during the civil war. Alan Hare manned a secret wireless station in the Villa Bimbelli, the Greek royal family's seaside retreat in Corfu, overlooking the Albanian coast.

The operation began in earnest in mid-July 1949 when the first Albanian volunteers arrived in Malta from Italy, having been flown in by the RAF on a flight organized by Cyril Rolo from the Rome Station. They had been living in the refugee camps dotted around Naples and all had impeccable political credentials. Some had already proved their opposition to the Communists by fighting with the resistance before trekking over the mountains to Greece. The Greeks, ever wary of their neighbours to the north with whom they were still officially at war, invariably expelled them to Italy, where they languished as stateless persons, providing SIS with an ideal pool from which to select guerrilla fighters.

Yet with all these preparations, the one commodity in

short supply was money. Attlee's Labour Government had demanded austerity to rebuild the war-shattered British economy, and SIS felt the pinch like everyone else. There was very little foreign exchange available and the main condition imposed on the Albanian exercise was the requirement of financial backing from the Americans. One of those charged with selling the idea to the US State Department was William Hayter, then Chairman of the JIC. He had flown to Washington with a high-powered Foreign Office delegation to sell the simple idea that the Soviets would only be persuaded to cease their encroachment on Europe if the West struck back at a suitably vulnerable ally, demonstrating the intrinsic weakness of the Soviet Bloc satellites. Once bitten in Albania, so the theory went, Moscow would hesitate before escalating the struggle in Greece.

Receiving the delegation at the State Department had been Frank Wisner, a former Wall Street lawyer from Mississippi, who had been appointed to the Office of Policy Co-ordination (OPC) in September 1948. In reality, the OPC was a covert operations branch separate from, but funded by, the fledgling CIA. Wisner was a determined Anglophile (he had had his son educated in England), who had headed the Office of Strategic Services' base in Istanbul before taking a detachment to Bucharest at the end of the war. As the Assistant Secretary of State for the Occupied Areas, before the creation of the CIA, Wisner had seen the first manifestations of the Cold War. It had left a lasting impression, so that when he was offered the chance to participate in the Albanian operation, he grabbed at it and assigned James McCargar to protect OPC's investment.

The first infiltration of Fort Benjimma-trained agents took place on the night of 3 October 1949, when nine well-equipped exiles were rowed ashore on the Karaburun peninsula, in the south of the country. It was not until 12 October that Hare received his first radio report, which was far from encouraging. One group of five men had gone to earth, hiding in a cave, because of intensive military activity in the area, and the others had either been killed or captured. Apparently, they had struck out on their own, heading north, but had been ambushed. Of the participants of this first operation, only four eventually made it safely to the Greek border.

Meanwhile, a second infiltration was under way, using the *Stormie Seas* again to land a team of eleven exiles, all armed to the teeth. They went ashore in the Gulf of Valona on 10 October and completed their mission without too many mishaps. They then slipped across the frontier into Greece, where they were temporarily imprisoned by Greek border guards. Rollo Young was despatched from the Athens Station to extricate them and escort them back to Malta for debriefing.

These preliminary, reconnaissance missions were intended to guage local feeling about the regime and to test reactions to the suggestion of a more ambitious scheme, involving many more men and much more money. The survivors from the first two operations gave a reasonably optimistic report of their encounters with the villagers they met, but they suspected that they had been betrayed. Claims of betrayal are often made by agents after such an experience, and case officers conducting debriefing sessions invariably dismiss them as excuses for poor tradecraft. This is what happened on this occasion. It was conceded, however, that the Albanian security forces had certainly been on the alert, but this was put down to an incident the day after the second landing when the *Stormie Seas* had actually been fired on by Albanian sentries.

There could be no question of reusing the *Stormie Seas*, as it was correctly assumed that it would have been compromised under interrogation by whoever had been captured from the first mission. Accordingly, the *felucca*'s crew were assigned to Istanbul, where they concentrated on running agents through the Black Sea to Bulgaria. Prepartions were also made for a third mission, overland from Greece.

Certain factions within the Greek authorities were

willing collaborators in the undertaking, because Pat Whinney had taken the precaution of bringing several of his most influential contacts, including the police chief and the head of the Greek intelligence service, into his confidence. Ever since Monty Woodhouse had reopened the SIS Station in Athens after the liberation, the British had been given complete freedom to operate from Greek territory, much of which anyway had been controlled by British peace-keeping troops. Indeed, several key members of the Government and the security apparatus had been recruited by SIS in Cairo during the war. However, discretion was essential because, even if Hoxha's regime was toppled, as intended, there was no guarantee that its replacement would be any the less hostile to the Greeks, who were, after all, the Albanians' traditional enemy.

The third mission, comprising of six exiles, began in July 1950, but the first attempt to get them over the border failed when a group of unfriendly Greek intelligence officers intervened. The six were detained, but Robert Zaehner managed to obtain their release and place them in a safe-house in Kifissia, on the outskirts of Athens, until the operation could be reinstated.

Owing to political problems the six were unable to start again for two months, during which Zaehner and Whinney's deputy, Frank Stallwood, tried to keep them under wraps. In order to ensure that there were no slips-ups the second time around, an additional organizer, Dayrell Oakley-Hill, was recruited to assist. Before the war he had served in King Zog's gendarmerie, which was largely staffed by British officers, so at least he was able to communicate with 'the pixies', as the Albania volunteers had come to be known, and make them behave, pending their departure. He also escorted them as close as he was allowed to the Albanian frontier before sending the group back into their homeland, where they stayed for two months.

After these first three operations, which were judged to be a limited success with quite acceptable losses, the training camp in Malta was scaled down and turned over to Anthony Newman, who was sent out from Broadway. David Smiley returned to his regiment in Germany. However, the Americans were determined to continue and set about drawing up a much grander plan.

Frank Wisner's concept of engaging and detaching the Soviet satellites was nothing if not ambitious. Everything was done to a grand scale. The Albanian volunteers were put into American uniform, given a fictitious military designation as a labour corps, 'Company 4000', and sent to an isolated compound at Wachterhof near Munich; in reality, they were trained as parachute saboteurs at Kaufbeuren and Bad Wiessee. The first mission of four *émigrés* was flown from Athens in an unmarked plane to their dropping-zone by Polish aircrew on 19 November 1950, but they were ambushed by the security forces soon after landing. Only two escaped, who gradually made their way north to Yugoslavia, recruiting and training small bands of monarchist partisans on the way. When they eventually reached the Yugoslav frontier, they gave themselves up. It would be years before Tito allowed them to leave.

In the nine months that followed, more agents were prepared for infiltration. The CIA made desperate attempts to contact the groups formed by their first two survivors, but in vain, so three new teams of four men each were sent in on 23 July 1951. This time none escaped. Ten were killed within hours of landing and the remaining two were captured, taken to Tirana and tortured before being made to participate in a show trial.

The court proceedings opened on 10 October with no less than ten defendants, including the two wounded survivors of the first US-sponsored mission, the two from the second and ten other agents who had been rounded up during the course of the year. All made abject confessions and were reported to be in extremely poor condition, but that did not prevent the well-publicized spectacle from lasting nearly a fortnight. At its conclusion just two were sentenced to death, but none ever emerged from prison. Furthermore, the Albanian secret police took their revenge on the families of those identified as having taken part in the missions by liquidating all their known relatives.

Incredibly, even while Radio Tirana was broadcasting the details of each day's revelations from the court, a third US mission was despatched. That, too, suffered losses immediately upon arrival with two of the company being killed by the security forces, who appeared to have surrounded the dropping-zone. The remaining three fled east to Yugoslavia, where they had to evade more patrols before eventually reaching Greece. A report describing their experience, plus the Radio Tirana transcripts of the trial, finally persuaded the CIA to call off the parachute missions.

David Smiley had returned to Germany 'very downcast and completely mystified as to what had gone wrong',[10] and Philby later recalled that 'the operation was quietly dropped without having made any noticeable dent on the regime in Tirana'.[11] However, there is no particular reason to believe that Philby played any sinister role in the Albanian fiasco. He has said that 'the operation, of course, was futile from the beginning',[12] but he has never claimed to have been instrumental in ensuring its failure. He was certainly aware of the initiation of the British programme shortly before the insertion of the first mission back in October 1949, but he had been aboard the SS *Caronia*, in the mid-Atlantic, when the operation actually took place. On that occasion two agents were captured, but on the second mission every man returned safely. That is hardly evidence of betrayal.

According to Smiley, Philby 'made several flying visits to Greece and Italy, and though he does not admit it in his book, he was quite certainly telling the Russians all the details of the operations I was running from Malta, and no doubt the Russians were passing everything on to Enver Hoxha.'[13] However, it could easily be argued that with two 'pixies' in custody, the Albanian secret police had little need of tips from Philby via the KGB. The two captives are known to have succumbed to torture, which would have compromised rather more directly useful information than Philby could ever have acquired on his 'flying visits'.

In retrospect, it has to be conceded that, despite the precautions taken during the Albanian operations, security was relatively lax. There could have been leakages of information from within the very divided Albanian *émigré* community in Italy, or from Malta or Athens. The political and religious differences of 'the pixies' were the sources of constant unrest. Some were monarchists, utterly committed to King Zog; others wanted to overthrow Hoxha so that he could be replaced with a democratic republic. Many of the factions were as opposed to each other as they were to the Communists. They were also typically Balkan when it came to the blood feuds which dominated particular families. Betrayal was a way of life, as might be expected in a country where Islam confronted Christianity and hostilities between different groups had been continuing for decades. In short, although a brave few were determined to end Hoxha's regime, there was never sufficient motivation among the exiles to get them to bury their differences and combine to fight a common enemy. Even King Zog, when first approached in Cairo to endorse the SIS/CIA-sponsored Free Albanian Committee, refused to co-operate on grounds that it contained anti-royalist elements. As if all this was not enough to make a complex situation even more complicated, Albanian agents were known to be operating in some strength in Italy and could easily have exerted a hold over many of the exiles who had left members of their family behind.

Therefore, although Philby may have been a convenient scapegoat, there were plenty of other explanations available for the venture's lack of success. Certainly, it would have stood a better chance if either Yugoslavia or Greece had given some measure of support to the operation, such as providing safe haven. In the event, 'the pixies' knew that even if they managed to evade Hoxha's secret police, they would receive a hostile reception if caught by either the Yugoslav or Greek authorities. While SIS and the

CIA could secure their release from Greek hands, a Yugoslav prison looked much the same as an Albanian one, and just as impossible to organize the extraction of a prisoner. Although not exactly doomed from the start, the SIS planners were guilty of exaggerating the amount of support 'the pixies' could expect from the local population after landing. This, of course, is understandable; their own experience had been limited to organizing guerrilla parties against the Nazi occupation. The task of persuading villagers to take up arms against Tirana had been rather underestimated.

Where Philby unquestionably inflicted heavy casualties, and wrecked a really promising opportunity to carry the Cold War right into the Ukraine, was on the joint Anglo-American attempt to build and support a partisan movement deep inside the Soviet Union.

The person chosen to conduct the campaign was Stepan Bandera, the extremist leader of the Organization of Ukrainian Nationalist Revolutionaries. Based in Munich, and taking money from both SIS and the CIA, Bandera supplied a steady stream of willing recruits for the CIA's training centres at Kaufbeuren, Bad Wiessee and Landsberg. Also located in Munich was the National Alliance of Russian Solidarists (NTS), which boasted its own independent espionage school at Bad Homberg. In Frankfurt, the British supported the General Russian National People's Movement, which accommodated the older generation of White Russians. All three movements were essentially fronts which produced agents for the CIA and SIS, but each was equally penetrated by the KGB.

Ukrainian exiles who were considered suitable for infiltration back into Russia were recommended by Bandera for SIS's intensive agent training course run by Peter Follis at a special school in Holland Park, London. They also attended the main facility at Fort Monckton, outside Gosport, before being transferred to Cyprus, where the RAF arranged for clandestine flights to be made across Soviet territory. The first insertions took place immediately following a joint SIS/CIA planning conference organized by the Controller Northern Europe, Harry Carr, and held in London in April 1951. Three six-man groups were parachuted into the Ukraine, but none were ever heard of again. Nor did the Americans have any better luck. They flew drops into the Ukraine from Greece, but few of the parties managed to transmit a short prearranged 'safe-arrival' message on their short-wave radios. Even the agents who were slipped across the Baltic on H.-H. Klose's E-boats from the joint SIS/British Naval Intelligence outpost on Bornholm fared badly. Of the handful who did acknowledge signals, most were believed to be operating under Soviet control. This appallingly high rate of failure is not entirely surprising, given Philby's recollection that, 'in order to avoid the dangers of overlapping and duplication, the British and Americans exchanged precise information about the timing and geographical co-ordinates of their operations. I do not know what happened to the parties concerned. But I can make an informed guess.'[14]

The Ukrainian disaster ruined Harry Carr, who had masterminded the entire operation and spent most of his career, which dated back to the North Russian expedition in 1919, fighting the Bolsheviks. He opted for a field post, as Head of Station in Copenhagen, in 1955 and eventually retired in 1961. Shortly before his final departure from Broadway, Moscow produced a booklet entitled *Caught in the Act* identifying twenty-three agents who had been captured and claiming that 'only an insignificant fraction of cases can be listed here'.

In spite of Philby's duplicity, the *émigré* recruitment programme was not entirely wasted, judging by the lengths the KGB went to in order to eliminate the exile leadership. The details are known because two professional assassins, Nikolai Khokhlov and Bogdan Stashinsky, defected. Khokhlov's target had been Georgi Sergeivich Okolovick, the NTS leader who had previously been the victim of an abortive kidnapping: but instead of carrying out his assignment, Khokhlov turned himself in to the CIA in Frankfurt in February 1954. He identified several other KGB agents and only narrowly escaped death himself when he was surreptitiously injected with thalium in September 1957 while attending a public conference.

Stashinsky defected in August 1961, two years after he had fired an exploding cyanide capsule into Bandera's face on the doorstep of his Munich apartment. By that time he had already stalked and killed another prominent Ukrainian *émigré*, Lev Rebet, outside his office. The defections prompted a shake-up inside the KGB, but the assassination policy continued.

The attempt to destabilize the forty-five million Ukrainians in the Soviet Union by reawakening their nationalist passion failed in large measure because of Philby's intervention. Whether it would have had more of a chance of success without him, or whether it was doomed anyway, like the Albanian fiasco, is an impossible question to answer.

Whatever else Philby achieved, he ruined his Chief, Stewart Menzies, who had led SIS since November 1939, and ensured that, to a greater or lesser extent, the careers of a good number of his colleagues had been invalidated.

It has been alleged that Menzies never accepted Philby's guilt and was obliged to accept his resignation in 1951 because of political pressure, following the defections of Burgess and Maclean, and leverage from MI5. Once again, this is a claim propagated by Philby. However Philby's close assocation with Burgess was, in Menzies's eyes, a sufficient indiscretion to preclude him from SIS. Nevertheless, the Chief must have been shattered by the possibility, whether he believed it or not, that Philby, star of the old Section V which had done so much to recover SIS's shattered pre-war image, could have been a wrong 'un. Whatever he thought, and he confided in no one, Menzies only waited a few months before submitting his resignation to the Foreign Secretary, Anthony Eden, at the end of June 1952 and recommending his Vice-Chief, John Sinclair, as his successor. The formalities over, Menzies took his recently acquired third wife, Audrey

Hay, down to his country house, Bridges Court, in the Wiltshire village of Luckington, to spend his retirement hunting with the Beaufort.

Menzies kept out of the limelight until late in 1962, when his name and wartime role was published for the first time by H. Montgomery Hyde in *The Quiet Canadian*.[15] The revelation caused a small sensation, with questions asked in the House of Commons (where Hyde had sat as the Unionist MP for North Belfast until 1959), but the furore soon died down. Menzies seemed not to take any notice, because virtually everyone in his narrow circle of polite society (his clubs were White's, Boodles and the Turf) had always known that he had 'run the Secret Service'. Even though he was informed when Philby finally confessed to having been a Soviet spy in January 1963, Menzies made no public comment, and his death in May 1968 prevented him from being hounded by Philby's vitriolic memoirs:

> He was not in any sense of the words a great intelligence officer. His intellectual equipment was unimpressive, and his knowledge of the world, and his views about it, were just what one would expect from a fairly cloistered son of the upper levels of the British establishment. In my own field, counterespionage, his attitudes were school-boyish – bars, beards and blondes.[16]

6

CYPRUS 1955–60

'If you were to take British information priorities after World War II, where quick accurate intelligence influenced decisions at government level, you would have to include Palestine, Malaya, Suez, Borneo, Kenya, Cyprus, Aden, Ulster and the Falklands. Much of the information in these "small wars" was supplied by two-legged spies.'

John Bruce Lockhart, *Intelligence: A British View*[1]

The Cyprus Emergency, which was formally declared in November 1956, had its origins in a secret meeting held between a young cleric named Michael Mouscos and Colonel George Grivas in Athens in July 1952.

In 1950, the charismatic, American-educated Mouscos had been enthroned as Archbishop Makarios III, leader of the Greek Orthodox Church in Cyprus. For several years, as the Bishop of Kition, he had been in the forefront of the popular campaign for *enosis*, political union with Greece. Grivas shared Makarios's Cypriot background, but had spent his career in the Greek army. After the army's defeat by the Nazis, he had organized a right-wing resistance movement known as 'X', which had ruthlessly prepared for the return of the monarchy at the end of the war by murdering members of the Greek Communist Party. At one stage of the civil war, Grivas had been extricated from almost certain death by British troops, but this incident had not affected his opposition to the British presence in Cyprus. He was totally committed to *enosis* and, in October 1952, had obtained a visa

94

from the British Embassy in Athens for a brief visit to Cyprus. His purpose was a thorough reconnaissance of the island in preparation for a series of guerrilla attacks on British installations.

Cyprus had been under British control since 1878, when Disraeli had acquired the island from the Turkish Ottoman Empire for Queen Victoria. During the First World War, Cyprus was offered to Greece in return for a declaration of war against the Kaiser, but King Constantine had backed the wrong horse. In 1925, Cyprus became a Crown colony, but Greek Cypriot support for *enosis* continued to grow.

It was Gamal Abdel Nasser's demand for the return of Britain's base in the Suez Canal zone (see Chapter 9) that transformed Cyprus's rather dubious strategic value. On 28 July 1954, the British Government announced the withdrawal of its troops from Egypt and the transfer of the British Middle East Headquarters to Episkopi. Henry Hopkinson MP, Oliver Lyttelton's junior minister in the Colonial Office, had responded to a Parliamentary Question by confirming that Britain would never change Cyprus's colonial status, thus dashing Greek hopes for *enosis*. When challenged about self-determination, Hopkinson had stated that Cyprus 'can never expect to be fully independent', and thereby lit a fire which would engulf the island.

The loss of the Canal zone and Anthony Eden's desperate gamble to recover it are dealt with later, but overnight Cyprus acquired a strategic importance that it had never enjoyed before, even though it boasted only a limited number of airfields and had no deep-water harbour. From the intelligence viewpoint, Cyprus had been designated the new home for SIS's regional base, then led by George Young, the former head of R6 (the economic requirements section) who had become Controller Middle East in 1951 in succession to John Teague. Young's busy empire originally took in the SIS stations at Beirut, Tel Aviv, Amman, Baghdad, Jeddah, Tehran, Basra, Damascus, Cairo and Port Said, and enjoyed good relations with

SIME's parallel organization of Defence Security Officers and Security Liaison Officers, then headed by Bill Oughton from RAF Fayid, outside Ismailia. Oughton had two representatives in Cyprus: Fitz Fletcher, the SLO at the High Commission in Nicosia, and Gerald Savage, the DSO at the Combined Middle East Headquarters at Episkopi. Under normal circumstances their tasks would have been routine. Instead, they found themselves in the midst of an emergency made all the more complicated by the Suez fiasco.

In anticipation of trouble, MI5's Director of E Branch (the overseas section), Bill Magan (himself a former head of SIME), had sent Phillip Ray to Nicosia to organize local intelligence. Ray began by creating a Special Branch within the CID and appointed George Meikle to run it. The Branch's first success, based on information supplied by a secret SIS source, occurred on 26 January 1955, when HMS *Comet* intercepted a caique, the *Ayios Georghios*, off the coast of Khlorakas and confiscated 10,000 sticks of dynamite. Thirteen Cypriots were arrested, including Sokratis Loizides, an Athens-based lawyer and *enosis* activist who had been deported from Cyprus and banned from re-entry four years earlier.

All thirteen prisoners were interrogated at Paphos Prison, but they claimed to be fishermen who had smuggled the dynamite for peaceful purposes. This story only lasted until naval divers brought up boxes of guns and ammunition that had been jettisoned shortly before the *Comet* had appeared. When Loizides was convicted of gun-running, he was sentenced to twelve years' imprisonment, which he served at Wormwood Scrubs and Maidstone.

Any complacency about having dealt *enosis* a crippling blow was quickly dispelled. On the night of 31 March, sixteen bombs went off across the island. The Cyprus Broadcasting Corporation's transmitters at Athalassa and Lakatamia outside Nicosia were attacked, as was the radio tower at Wolseley Barracks. The Episkopi power plant was sabotaged and explosives went off close to two

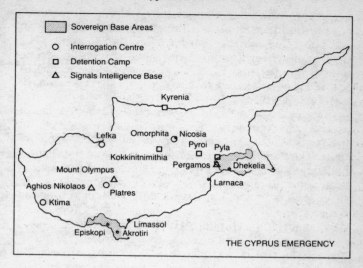

Sovereign Base Areas
○ Interrogation Centre
□ Detention Camp
△ Signals Intelligence Base

THE CYPRUS EMERGENCY

police stations in Limassol and the CID headquarters in Larnaca. Even the heavily guarded secret wireless interception base at Aghios Nikolaos, home of the No. 9 Signal Regiment, was rocked by a bomb. Another device was left near a hotel in Nicosia soon after the departure of the Governor, Sir Robert Armitage. Beside it was a number of leaflets from the self-styled *Ethniki Organosis Kyprion Agoniston* (National Organization of Cypriot Combatants) or EOKA. They were signed by 'Dighenis', the name of the Greek medieval hero. It did not take the Special Branch long to discover that Dighenis was the *nom de guerre* adopted by Grivas.

In June, EOKA struck again: a grenade was thrown at Sir John Sterndale Bennett, head of the recently arrived British Middle East Office. By this time Ray had returned to London and had been replaced as the Co-ordinator of Intelligence by an MI5 officer. The political atmosphere was deteriorating and members of the CID and the Special Branch were becoming the subject of calculated EOKA intimidation. Three Greek Special Branch officers were shot during the summer. One, Herodotus Poullis, was on routine surveillance duty at a Communist rally in Ledra Street, Nicosia's 'murder mile', on 28 August. His attacker, Michael Karaolis, was caught fleeing the scene and became the first EOKA assassin to be sentenced to death. He was hanged in Nicosia Central Prison on 10 May 1956.

The greatest disaster of the summer was the escape of sixteen EOKA leaders from a makeshift detention centre in Kyrenia Castle, of whom only seven were ever recaptured. The incident was a painful reminder of the island's inadequate security arrangements and served to give a tremendous, if unexpected, boost to EOKA morale.

On 25 September, the British Government responded to the escape by replacing Armitage with the CIGS, Field Marshal Sir John Harding. He took personal charge of security and, in a vain attempt to reduce leaks of information, shipped in 300 British police officers. He knew that the indigenous police force harboured many EOKA sympathizers, or victims of EOKA threats, and that even the Special Branch had been penetrated. George Lagoudontis was one of several Greek Cypriot officers who gave regular reports about the Branch's operations to EOKA contacts. In spite of Harding's efforts, the incidents continued.

Six soldiers were killed during October and November, compelling the Governor to declare a State of Emergency. This announcement on 25 November coincided with the detention of 100 EOKA suspects nominated by Meikle's Special Branch. Twelve thousand troops were placed on alert and Turkish Cypriots, from the minority section of the community which composed just eighteen per cent of the population, were brought into the police. New regulations were enforced which included a mandatory death penalty for the possession of fire-arms, life sentences for sabotage, collective fines on whole towns and a ban on strikes. By the end of the year, twelve British servicemen and twelve Cypriots had died in the violence.

Armed with the new emergency powers, the Special

Branch rounded up hundreds of EOKA suspects and questioned them at a series of purpose-built interrogation centres. At the height of the conflict, some 4,500 police and 28,000 troops were engaged in security duties, although EOKA probably never fielded more than two or three hundred terrorists. An information fund totalling £150,000 was set up to encourage informers and, gradually, evidence mounted of a direct link between Makarios and the elusive Grivas. Not all the informers were paid. One of the best 'hooded toads' who pointed out EOKA activists while concealing his own identity was a prisoner serving a life term for discharging a fire-arm. In return for his valuable help his sentence was cut to nine years in prison in England, but he was secretly released after just eighteen months.

Makarios, of course, denied having any links with EOKA and continued to negotiate for *enosis* with Harding; but when his palace was searched, the Special Branch found what it believed to be signs of a hastily evacuated arms cache. However, the best proof of Makarios's illicit support for Grivas came in February 1956, when a company of men from the 3rd Battalion, the Parachute Regiment, ambushed an EOKA group near the Kykko monastery. Codenamed PEPPERPOT, the lengthy operation was centred in the Troodos foothills, an area identified as an EOKA stronghold by an informer named Pascalis. During the five-week search, Grivas literally went underground and moved into a collection of rough hides hewn out of the mountainside, which offered perfect concealment. Although Grivas himself narrowly evaded the paratroops, he entrusted his diary to Pascalis, who promptly sold it to his Special Branch contact. This remarkable document had been kept by Grivas in case he should ever fall out with Makarios and gave a detailed account of how the two leaders had conspired together and planned EOKA's campaign of assassination and terror. It was an extraordinary lapse of security, apparently born out of mutual mistrust, and it provided damning evidence of the Archbishop's involvement with

EOKA. On 9 March, Makarios was due to fly to Athens for consultations with the new Prime Minister of Greece, Constantine Karamanlis, but when he reached the airport at Nicosia his party was guided to an RAF transport aircraft. Once aboard he was served with a deportation order and flown to Mombasa in Kenya, where he was transferred to a Royal Navy frigate for exile on Mahé, the largest of the remote Seychelles Islands in the Indian Ocean. The following day, Harding outlined the evidence that had been accumulated against Makarios. It consisted largely of information gleaned from the incriminating Grivas diaries, but the Director of Intelligence insisted that the exact source should not be compromised.

With Makarios quarantined, the security pendulum seemed to swing against EOKA. Grivas was constantly on the run throughout the summer of 1956 and, on 20 August, more of his diaries were recovered from a hiding-place in a field near Lyssi. This second batch of indiscreet documents proved even more incriminating than those sold by Pascalis. They showed Grivas's complicity in no less than twenty-five murders, all believed to be EOKA informers. Despite protests from the Special Branch (now headed by Bill Robinson, a former Indian police officer from the Punjab), Harding decided to publish the Grivas diaries in the hope of alienating him politically. The Special Branch was furious at having lost what it saw as a golden opportunity to trap Grivas. According to the most recent entry in his diary, Grivas intended to move into the home of someone who also happened to be a police informer. Not surprisingly, when the Governor disclosed the existence of the diaries, Grivas failed to turn up.

At first it seemed as though Harding had succeeded in his objective of isolating Grivas, who called a truce and moved his secret headquarters away from the mountains and into a tiny room excavated under a house in Limassol. Only a couple of his most faithful EOKA couriers were entrusted with its exact location, which happened to have been used as a British army billet. But at the very moment that Harding seemed to be gaining the initiative, Eden embarked on his disastrous invasion of the Suez Canal zone, obliging the forces engaged on security duties in Cyprus to withdraw. Just as the tide had changed against EOKA, so it suddenly reversed its course. Always an impressive strategist, Grivas launched a renewed campaign of violence and intimidation which, during November alone, involved some 416 separate incidents. Harding responded by ordering more detentions, bringing the total held to 693, but by the end of the year the statistics had escalated alarmingly: 115 Greeks and eighty-one Britons had been killed, compared to just twenty-four for the previous year.

Following Eden's resignation as Prime Minister in 1957, the Cabinet decided to release Makarios from detention and let him return to Athens to begin negotiations again. His first step was to order Grivas to cease operations, but this manoeuvre was interpreted in Ankara as the first step in a British sell-out to the Greeks. In fact, EOKA was in considerable difficulties, especially after Grivas's principal lieutenant, Gregoris Afxentiou, had been betrayed for £5,000 and killed by troops in a cave. The imposition of a truce was actually quite convenient for EOKA, but it alarmed the Turkish Government, which, fearing the worst, started to arm VOLKAN, the Turkish Cypriot counter-terrorist organization. The Turks had been perfectly willing to accept British rule, but the moment the new British administration, under Harold Macmillan, showed signs of wanting to go back on Hopkinson's commitment to the word 'never', Ankara had taken an increasingly aggressive position against future Greek domination of the island, which, geographically, was only forty miles away from Turkey's coast. Turkish anxieties were fuelled in December 1957 when Harding, who had been so tough on EOKA, had hanged nine convicted terrorists and had recruited so many Turkish Cypriots into the police, was replaced as Governor by Sir Hugh Foot, a colonial civil servant but also a member of a family with strong Leftist sympathies. Foot's stated intention of finding his own constitutional solution to the bitter

conflict between Cyprus's two communities only aggra-
vated the security situation, which deteriorated towards
civil war. For many, partition looked like the only acceptable answer to an intractable problem.

By 1958, the level of violence had reached a peak, with
130 Greek Cypriots killed in the daily confrontations with
the security forces and the Turks; thirty-nine Britons were
also killed, including an MI5 officer who was shot in the
back in Famagusta. EOKA's campaign was not only
aimed against the Turks and Special Branch informers.
Many of those murdered were left-wingers and trade
unionists whom Grivas wished to eliminate before the
anticipated power struggle took place following British
withdrawal. The British response was a reorganization of
the security apparatus, with (Sir) John Prendergast
brought in from Kenya, where he had masterminded the
suppression of the Mau-Mau rebellion, to take over a new
co-ordinating post of Chief of Intelligence. A tough
Irishman, Prendergast had been in the Palestine Police
and had also been seconded briefly to SIME in the Suez
Canal zone in 1952. Supporting Prendergast was Philip
Kirby Green (known as 'K-G'), one of Britain's most
remarkable secret warriors, who had joined the Royal
Navy and served in the 1st destroyer Flotilla in the
Graeco-Turkish War in 1922. Since then he had been an
officer in the Merchant Navy and had spent ten years in
the Metropolitan Police, before joining MI5 in 1942. For
the rest of the war, he was DSO in Gibraltar and had then
been posted to the Caribbean as MI5's SLO.

Prendergast and K-G were a formidable team and, with
Magan's support, they devised a joint MI5-SIS scheme
codemaned Operation SUNSHINE to trace Grivas to his
hiding-place and eliminate him. John Wyke and Peter
Wright made all the technical arrangements, which
included placing surreptitious taps on Makarios's private
telephone, while (Sir) Stephen Hastings was tranferred
from the Paris Station to be 'in at the kill'. Hastings, who
was to be elected the Conservative MP for Mid-Bedford-
shire in November 1960 immediately after leaving the

Friends, enjoyed a daunting reputation and had been decorated with the Military Cross while serving with the SAS in 1944. An old Etonian, he had joined SIS in 1948 and completed a two-year tour at the Helsinki Station before moving to Paris in 1953. He was an experienced case officer and ran an agent who had been recruited from inside Makarios's immediate entourage. SUNSHINE also involved a fall-back plan, which developed out of the evidence that was accumulated of the Archbishop's rather unusual homosexual proclivities. However, before SUN-SHINE could be executed, it was scrapped because, against all the odds, the politicians began to make progress.

Secret negotiations between the Greek and Turkish Foreign Ministers opened late in 1958 at the United Nations, following one of the many stalemated votes taken on the issue, and continued into February the following year at Zurich, where a political agreement was almost reached. However, just when the Greek and Turkish sides thought they had reached a settlement, Makarios intervened at the signing ceremony in London and withheld his consent. Both the Greek and Turkish delegations protested that Makarios had been a party to every stage of the agreed compromise, but he would not budge. Reluctantly Selwyn Lloyd, who was chairing the conference, agreed to extend it for an extra twenty-four hours so as to allow Makarios to reconsider his proposed 'modifications'. After a night in his suite at the Dorchester, Makarios returned to Lancaster House the following morning and told the Foreign Secretary that he had decided to relent. At last he was ready to confirm the terms previously agreed. Exactly what occurred to persuade Makarios to change his mind and co-operate has never been revealed, but it is known that he made no attempt to contact Grivas to get his advice. One possible explanation for the Archbishop's uncharacteristic reversal is the likely impact the disclosure of the material that had been gathered during SUNSHINE relating to his private life would have had in Cyprus. There he was revered by the greater part of the island's population as a political leader and churchman. Any revelation about his homosexuality would have been terribly damaging, as he was well aware.

Makarios's change of heart meant Cyprus would gain independence, with a guaranteed role for the Turkish minority in the political framework, but no *enosis*. Britain would retain sovereignty over two of the principal bases on the island and pay rent for the others. It was brinkmanship on an astonishing scale, but it did achieve a temporary end to the bloodshed. Grivas, who had been excluded from the deal, was given a safe conduct to Athens, where he was welcomed as a hero; his EOKA supporters were granted an amnesty.

At the polls in December 1959 Makarios was elected President and, in accordance with the new constitution, Dr Fazil Kutchuk, the Turkish Cypriot leader, was appointed Vice-President. In August 1960, Cyprus became an independent republic and Polycarpos Georgadjis, one of EOKA's most resourceful members and the organization's district leader in Nicosia, was appointed Minister of the Interior in charge of police and security. He knew something of his assignment for he had been among those who had escaped from Kyrenia Castle back in September 1955. He had been recaptured, but had escaped again, this time from a hospital in a raid during which four others had been killed. He was caught again for the third time early in 1957 in the home of a senior Greek policeman. He then escaped from detention hidden in a dustbin. Fortunately, Prendergast did not have to stay on the island to deal with his old adversary. He was posted to Hong Kong to head the Special Branch there. In his place MI5 sent an officer who had seen active service in Greece during the civil war to set up a liaison office in the new British High Commission.

The Cyprus Emergency hardly compared to the Malayan campaign in terms of casualties, with only 104 British servicemen, twelve police officers and twenty-six civilians killed in total. Paradoxically, EOKA murdered rather more of its own people (about 112 Greek Cypriots). The security forces shot just ninety-seven terrorists.

What made Cyprus so important was the island's strategic value in a post-Suez empire which had left Britain with world-wide responsibilities, but precious little resources to service them. With Palestine gone, Suez a smouldering memory, Persia overwhelmed by nationalism and the Baghdad Pact in tatters, Britain required solid bases from which to defend its interests. Cyprus was far from ideal, but there simply were no alternative sites in the region; the prospect of two large sovereign bases, plus additional facilities for gathering signals intelligence, must have seemed extremely attractive, even if it did take months of exasperating negotiations for the minister directly concerned, Julian Amery, to tie up all the details with Makarios.

The key to the Cyprus success, which it certainly was, lies in the brilliant work done behind the scenes in Athens by the Head of Station, Christopher Phillpotts, and his CIA colleague, Al Ulmer. Phillpotts used characteristic initiative to mount a series of highly productive operations of a nature that is still too secret to be disclosed, while Ulmer and his staff bought influence by adding senior members of the Greek administration to the payroll. Phillpotts, an extremely amiable figure with a gift for amateur operatics and a great knowledge of the theatre, had first come into contact with SIS while operating patrol boats in the Channel during the war. His complaints about the unusual craft slipping in and out of the Helford River at night had ended in his own recruitment in SIS's private navy. To impress those who, like himself, had once doubted SIS's usefulness, he invariably quoted the oft-told story of how Menzies's predecessor, Admiral Sir Hugh Sinclair, had once forced Baldwin to return to Parliament to correct a misleading statement he had given about German air-force strengths earlier the same day. Sinclair had threatened to resign unless the Prime Minister had acted, and the incident had convinced Phillpotts of SIS's value.

Together Ulmer and Phillpotts used quiet, undercover diplomacy to convey a straightforward message to the Greeks: if they pressed for *enosis*, it would mean war with Turkey and the possible breakdown of NATO. It was only when Constantine Karamanlis's advisers were convinced of Turkish determination and Turkish military superiority that a solution was reached. The element that enabled Britain adroitly to guide both sides to Lancaster House was Phillpotts's technical sources of information, which more than compensated for the loss of so many individual agents to the Americans who enjoyed bigger budgets. These same sources ensured that the Royal Navy maintained an effective blockade to prevent EOKA from receiving supplies by sea and enabled the security forces to keep Grivas pinned down. In 1957, Phillpotts was rewarded with a CMG and promoted to the Paris Station, where he remained for an unusually long tour lasting five years; his place in Athens was filled by Alan Hare, who was able to capitalize on his groundwork.

7

BUSTER CRABB OBE GM RNVR

'In the modern age there are many contrivances for
overlooking or overhearing the proceedings of others.
Peeping Toms and flapping ears have gadgets never thought
of before.'

Anthony Eden, *Full Circle*[1]

By any standards 1956 proved to be a catastrophic year
for SIS. The first disaster occurred on Saturday 21 April,
when Colonel Grimshaw, SIS's communications specialist, reported the collapse of Operation PRINCE to the
Head of Station in Berlin, Peter Lunn.

Operation PRINCE was a technical project involving a
tunnel dug from Rudow in the American sector of Berlin
to an underground cable conduit in the East, which
housed the main telephone landlines of the Soviet military
headquarters in Karlshorst. The exercise was a repetition
of Operation LORD, which had been conducted in
Vienna in 1950 by John Wyke, SIS's technical expert,
under the direction of Lunn, who had been the Head of
Station in Vienna before moving to Berlin. LORD had
been a great success, as had its commercial cover at the
shaft head, a textile shop selling original Harris tweed
imported from Scotland. The tunnel had been dug from
the basement of the shop, which was located in the suburb
of Schwechat, to a junction box beneath the busy road
outside. The tapped line gave access to all the communications that passed between the old Imperial Hotel, which

had been requisitioned by the Red Army for its head-quarters, and Moscow. On that occasion, Lunn had been forced to abandon the commercial cover because it had become embarrassingly popular and had attracted too much attention. Nevertheless, the project had continued from a large mansion nearby, where Wyke had been installed in the guise of a rich, retired, expatriate army officer.

PRINCE was a similar undertaking, but on a much larger scale, and was completed with American assistance. Grimshaw's partner had been Bill Harvey, the legendary hard-drinking, gun-toting former FBI Special Agent who was the CIA's Station Chief in Berlin. His collaboration had led to the operation being nicknamed 'Harvey's hole', but he had secured the use of an American radar station as a convenient location from which to sink the shaft.

PRINCE had produced a huge quantity of raw intelligence, in the form of telephone intercepts which required time-consuming transcription and analysis; this was also undertaken on a joint basis by SIS and the CIA. Exactly how the existence of the tunnel was discovered by the Soviets was not known in April 1956, but it later emerged that Grimshaw's deputy, who had been responsible for supervising the tunnel's logistic support, was George Blake, a long-term Soviet mole. It had been his job to gather the sophisticated recording equipment needed to tap the Russian lines and monitor their performance. He had also acted as secretary for the Berlin Station's liaison committee, which had managed the day-to-day running of the tunnel with the Americans.

The loss of PRINCE was a great blow to Broadway and provided the Soviets with an enviable opportunity to make propaganda. Certainly, they wasted no time in inviting journalists down the tunnel to inspect the undeniable evidence of foreign espionage. However, just as Broadway was absorbing the news from Berlin, there was another, even more serious, débâcle which was to have appalling consequences for everyone.

Once again, the origins of the incident, which was to

become known as the Crabb affair, went back some years to the development of Section R3, SIS's naval liaison unit. In the immediate post-war period, the section had lost control over Frank Slocum's private navy, which had instead been taken over by the Admiralty's Naval Intelligence Division. Its principal target was, of course, the Soviet Union, but because of hostile surveillance the Naval Attaché in Moscow had little chance of gathering any really useful information and was rarely allowed to visit a Soviet port. On the few occasions he did so, he was under tight escort. Accordingly, the naval section developed its contacts with members of the merchant navy and, in particular, with shipping companies that regularly had vessels visiting ports of interest. Frank Slocum had been the SIS regular in charge of these activities, but in 1954 he had been appointed to Oslo as Head of Station. His successor was Ted Davies, a former RNVR officer who had served with Pat Whinney and Christopher Phillpotts in Slocum's wartime private navy.

In the mid-1950s, the Soviet navy was relatively small and its movements could be plotted with ease, both by 'shadowing' at sea by submarines, surface vessels and aircraft, which was carried out by NATO navies and air forces, and by signals interception. There was, however, an additional need to monitor Soviet technical developments so as to remain one step ahead in the complex area of electronic counter-measures. Whenever an opportunity presented itself, efforts were made to take radar profiles of Soviet warships so that an up-to-date index of the fleet could be maintained. Attempts were also made to take acoustic recordings of every Soviet warship at sea, and it was not unknown for clandestine hull surveys to be carried out. Most of these undertakings involved virtually no risk. For the recordings to be made a submarine was simply placed under the intended path of a Russian ship. The radar profiles involved rather more preparatory work, with special equipment moved into a secure location close to where the target Russian ship was going to come into range.

Just such an operation had been completed in October 1955 when the Soviet cruiser *Sverdlov* had docked in Portsmouth Harbour. Radar equipment had been installed in a huge, secret, nuclear bunker hewn out of the chalk under Dover Castle, and its bulky antenna fixed on one of the galleries halfway up the cliffs. Scarcely visible from below, the galleries held generators and the bunker's air-conditioning plant, and provided an ideal vantage-point from which to capture the *Sverdlov*'s radar image. A submarine was positioned in the Channel exactly where the cruiser was expected to pass, and a covert hull inspection was arranged once the warship had docked at Portsmouth.

The diver selected to carry out the Admiralty's underwater mission to check the cruiser's hull for tell-tale 'blisters' used to house sonar equipment and to measure the pitch of the propellors was Commander Lionel Crabb, known to his friends as Buster. Crabb was an extraordinary, almost legendary, figure in the diving world who, paradoxically, was a poor swimmer. Now in his mid-forties, and constitutionally somewhat the worse for an excess of alcohol and cigarettes, he sported a monocle and swordstick and cut a somewhat eccentric, if broken-down, figure. During the war he had volunteered for bomb disposal work and had been posted to Gibraltar in 1942, where he had pioneered methods of clearing enemy limpet mines from merchant vessels. Italian midget submarines and frogmen had preyed on the Mediterranean convoys and many ships had been lost until an Underwater Working Party had been created to inspect every Allied and neutral ship. Using very rudimentary breathing gear, converted from the submarine escape kits issued to submariners, Crabb had become an accomplished diver and an expert in underwater bomb disposal and salvage work. He had also won the George Medal for removing an unexploded torpedo head from beside a troopship. The nature of his unusual job brought Crabb into contact with MI5 and SIS, which both maintained wartime offices on the Rock, and Slocum's navy, which operated a few *feluccas* in the region for landing agents into occupied France. It was through this personal contact, which was kept up after the war, that he was commissioned to do one-off tasks for SIS. Crabb was demobbed in 1948, but soon afterwards was employed by the Director of Boom Defence and Marine Salvage to assist on the development of underwater cameras. He was then seconded as a technical adviser to the Admiralty Research Establishment at Teddington. There, according to his biographer, Marshall Pugh, he 'began to dive, to photograph wrecks in harbours, to help salvage divers before they began; to film the behaviour of underwater weapons and equipment; to experiment with new cameras, new lights, new breathing equipment, new diving suits. Most of the work was secret and important.'[2] Equally secret was his parttime work for Slocum, which may have involved clandestine hull surveys in Soviet harbours operating from submarines.

Whatever Crabb's unofficial activities while based at Teddington, it is known that the last few months of his service until the end of his contract in March 1955 were spent at HMS *Vernon*, the Royal Navy's shore base in Portsmouth and the headquarters of the Admiralty's Underwater Counter-measures and Weapons Establishment. He had anticipated an attachment to the Iraqi navy as an adviser, but instead had taken a job with a friend, running a coffee-bar furniture business. He also kept up his freelance diving, going down to Portsmouth for the *Sverdlov* operation in October 1955, and again in April the following year.

This second operation was to examine the hull of the Soviet cruiser *Ordzhonikidze*, which docked in Portsmouth on 18 April with Nikita Khrushchev and Marshal Bulganin aboard. It was almost as though the *Sverdlov* had been a rehearsal, and virtually everyone concerned in the plan regarded it as a non-risk venture. Since the operation was in total breach of a directive prohibiting any clandestine operations while Khrushchev and Bulganin were in England, and the episode was to go so disastrously wrong, it is worth looking in detail at the role of all those involved.

The chief planner was Ted Davies, who worked out of the London Station, then headed by Nicholas Elliott. The Station was located in a large, nondescript office on the east side of the Vauxhall Bridge Road, not far from Victoria. It was unique because it conducted operations within the United Kingdom, almost as though it was located in a foreign country. In many ways it mirrored an overseas station, running agents and operations in the immediate territory as well as providing a base for activities in Europe, but it had a heavy bias towards technical facilities because of the coverage needed for all the diplomatic missions in the capital. Indeed, much of the rear of the building was taken up by a huge telephone intercept and transcription centre, which automatically recorded every call in and out of virtually every embassy in London. The authority for the entire programme was an annual warrant signed by the Foreign Secretary for each target country, whatever the number of telphone lines involved. In order to ease difficulties of jurisdiction with the Security Service, the Station boasted a permanent liaison officer, John Henry. Elliott had a long background in intelligence, having been recruited originally by MI5; he had worked briefly in its German double-agent section during the Phoney War before switching to Section V of SIS. He had spent most of the war as Section V's representative in Gibson's Istanbul Station before going to Berne in 1947. Four years later, he had returned to London as Chief of Production (CPR) before being assigned to the London Station. Elliott's immediate superior at Broadway was the Director of Production for Europe, or DP-1, a former parachute officer. Between the DP-1 and the higher echelons of the CSS, Sinclair, and his newly knighted Vice-Chief, Easton, was the Foreign Office Adviser, (Sir) Michael Williams.

Williams's anomalous post had been created in April 1942, when severe criticism of SIS's structure had led to a regular diplomat, (Sir) Patrick Reilly, being seconded to

Menzies with the title of Assistant Chief Staff Officer. In reality, Reilly was the direct link between the CSS and the Foreign Office, giving political guidance where necessary and ensuring that the Government's policy on sensitive issues was correctly interpreted. He had been succeeded by another diplomat, Robert Cecil, but at the end of the war the post had lapsed. It was only in 1950, when Reilly returned to the intelligence community as Chairman of the JIC, that he saw the dangers of Menzies's organization running potentially controversial operations without proper authority. He therefore recommended the reinstatement of a Foreign Office Adviser. The first post-war nominee in the job was (Sir) George Clutton, a former First Secretary in Belgrade and latterly Head of the Foreign Office's African Department. His appointment to SIS in 1952 followed a two-year stint in Tokyo as head of the UK's liaison mission to Japan. It was only discovered some years later that he was a homosexual and was suspected of having been the victim of a Soviet blackmail attempt. In 1955, he was appointed British Ambassador to Manila, and his place in Sinclair's hierarchy had been taken by Williams.

Williams had been educated at Rugby and Trinity, Cambridge, before joining the Foreign Office in 1935. He had served abroad at Madrid, Rome and Rio de Janeiro prior to his transfer to SIS in 1955. When the question of Davies's plan for the *Ordzhonikidze* had been raised early the next year, it had been referred by Elliott to Williams for his approval. But instead of consulting the Permanent Under-Secretary, or the Chairman of the JIC, he had simply given it his sanction. Apparently, he had done so because he had been 'faced with the Crabb scheme at the end of an exceptionally hard day, during which his father had died'.[3] His father, the Rev. Frederick Williams, had died suddenly at home on 7 April, the very day that Elliott's project had reached his desk. It was presumed by Elliott and the Director of Naval Intelligence, Rear-Admiral Sir John Inglis, that the operation had been given all the necessary clearances. In fact it had not, and the initiative was quite contrary to Eden's directive on the subject.

On the afternoon of Tuesday, 17 April 1956, Crabb and Davies checked into the Sallyport Hotel in Portsmouth High Street and spent the following two nights there. Davies, in fact, suffered a mild heart attack on the Wednesday, but decided to continue with the operation which was planned for early the next morning. On 19 April, Crabb dived from HMS *Vernon* and everything appeared to be normal. He returned briefly from one sortie under the *Smotriashchin*, one of the cruiser's two destroyer escorts, and, having added some extra lead weights to his belt, made a second dive from which he never returned.

Davies was in no condition to handle the emergency, but he did manage to alert the London Station to the fact that Crabb had disappeared. John Henry promptly drove over to Leconfield House and begged MI5's Director of Establishments (A Branch), Malcolm Cumming, to intervene. He ordered Henry and Hugh Winterborn, a member of A Branch, to go down to Portsmouth to remove any evidence of their connection with Crabb. The two officers went to the police headquarters in Portsmouth, where the head of the CID, Detective-Inspector Lamport, was persuaded to visit the Sallyport Hotel and warn the owner to keep quiet about his two guests. The relevant pages of the hotel register, bearing the signatures of Buster Crabb and 'Bernard Smith', who had given his address as 'attached Foreign Office', were removed and a receipt given.

If the London Station had hoped that the incident could be forgotten, the Soviets had no such intention. A complaint about illicit divers was lodged with the Admiralty by the Russians, but the Commander-in-Chief Portsmouth simply issued a routine denial. This was followed by a short announcement on 29 April that Crabb 'is presumed to be dead as a result of trials with certain underwater equipment'. A little later the same day, after several press enquiries, the Admiralty added that 'the location was in Stokes Bay',[4] some three miles away from the quay where the Soviet warships had been moored. However, it was the discovery that Lamport had torn out the pages of the hotel register that really fuelled speculation. Eventually the Soviets joined in, on 3 May, by leaking the content of an official diplomatic note, in which it was pointed out that the Admiralty's original denial about the existence of a diver had been contradicted by the latest admission that Crabb had disappeared while diving. The Russian protest brought further press speculation, including confirmation from one of Crabb's friends that he had been engaged to dive under the *Sverdlov* the previous October. Questions were raised in Parliament and, very reluctantly, the Prime Minister, who had only been told the story on 4 May, made a brief statement:

> It would not be in the public interest to disclose the circumstances in which Commander Crabb is presumed to have met his death. While it is the practice for Ministers to accept responsibility, I think it is necessary, in the special circumstances of this case, to make it clear that what was done was done without the authority or the knowledge of Her Majesty's Ministers. Appropriate disciplinary steps are being taken.[5]

Eden's attempt to stifle further comment on the affair failed, and a full debate was held in the House of Commons on 14 May. By that time Eden had asked the Cabinet Secretary, Sir Norman Brook, to investigate the matter and, after receiving a preliminary account from Sinclair, who had been on leave at the time, had commissioned a more searching enquiry from Brook's predecessor, Sir Edward Bridges. Opening the debate the Labour opposition leader, Hugh Gaitskell, remarked that 'presumably the Secret Service or a secret service and the Admiralty must have been mixed up in the plan from the start'.[6] Eden replied that 'I deplore this debate and I will say no more', but there were others willing to do so. Among them was Konni Zilliacus, who suggested that

Crabb 'had on this occasion been employed by the United States Secret Service with the complicity of their and his contacts in the British Secret Service'.[7] A number of Tory MPs with SIS experience contributed nothing to the debate. Philby's friend, Dick Brooman-White, who had won Rutherglen in 1951, and had actually spent a year in Turkey when Philby had been stationed in Istanbul, kept quiet. So did Henry Kerby, the wartime recruit into SIS who had seen service in Sweden in 1940 and had won the West Sussex seat in March 1954. One Member with intelligence experience who did comment was John Cordeaux, now sitting for Nottingham Central. He observed that 'it would be wrong for the House to lose faith in the Secret Service because of this case, but it was impossible to excuse it. It was approved as mistakenly and rashly as it was ineptly carried out', and he 'felt alarmed for the higher direction of whatever service might be concerned. Commander Crabb was of an age when he should hardly have been chosen for such a hazardous operation.'[8]

Eden was understandably furious about the taunts he had to endure in the Commons and about the blatant way in which SIS had ignored his specific instructions not to engage in any irregular activity while Khrushchev was in Britain. His retribution was in the form of the official (but secret) Bridges Report. Bridges interviewed all the principal participants and gave them all a surprisingly lenient hearing. Davies retired on health grounds soon afterwards, with generous compensation, and emigrated to the United States. Elliott escaped all criticism and received a posting as Head of Station in Vienna. However, Bridges's displeasure was reserved for higher mortals. In his report, submitted on 18 May 1956, he suggested to the Prime Minister that SIS was ready for some significant changes.

Eden's action was swift. He allowed Sir John Sinclair the early retirement he had previously requested and had the Foreign Office withdraw Michael Williams, who was transferred to Bonn with the rank of minister. Williams eventually rose to be Ambassador in Guatemala; his last post was Minister to the Holy See, before he received a belated knighthood in 1968 and retired two years later. The Buster Crabb affair had effectively wrecked his career and ruined Sinclair, who was rumoured, falsely, to have been sacked. Sinclair retired to East Ashling, near Chichester, and obtained directorships with two companies: the Universal Asbestos Manufacturing Company and Chinnor Industries Limited. By rights his successor ought to have been Jack Easton, his loyal Vice-Chief who had been in the Friends for thirteen years, but at the age of forty-eight he was considered too young for the post. Instead, Eden appointed Sir Dick White, the Director-General of the Security Service, as the new CSS, and imposed a permanent ban on all politically risky covert operations without a written ministerial sanction.

Much to SIS's eternal embarrassment, the *Ordzhonikidze* was later sold to Indonesia and discovered to be entirely deviod of any exotic equipment, either inside or outside the hull.

Crabb's body, or rather what remained of his torso, was not recovered until 10 June 1957, when a fisherman discovered it on a sandbank in the mouth of Chichester Harbour. Formal identification was impossible, but the Pirelli two-piece rubber diving suit was recognized as one owned by Crabb. An inquest was held, but there was insufficient evidence for the coroner to determine the cause of death. Crabb could either have got into difficulties while underwater on his second dive or, perhaps, had been murdered by Soviet frogmen who might have emerged from a hatch below the *Ordzhonikidze*'s waterline. The find reopened press speculation, and Chapman Pincher revealed in the *Daily Express* that 'Crabb was working for the United States Intelligence Service – not the British – when he disappeared last year'.[9] There were to be other, equally bizarre, theories about this *cause célèbre*. In 1960, a Czech *émigré* writing under the pseudonym J. Bernard Hutton suggested in his biography, *Frogman Spy*, that Crabb might have been kidnapped by the Soviets. This was a theme returned to eight years later, in *Commander Crabb is Alive*, which included photographs purporting to show Crabb in Soviet uniform talking to a group of Red Navy sailors. The stories have now entered the mythology of espionage, but none has any credence.

However, by the time the first of these claims had been made, White had taken control of SIS and had had to cope with another crisis, this time of Eden's own making.

8

OPERATION BOOT

'The British "station" is almost identical with that of the CIA, except, perhaps, that it is normally smaller, better covered, and better integrated into the embassy to which it is assigned. Also it is poorer, its budget normally being about a third of the budget of its American counterpart. For this reason it is in most parts of the world a primary duty of the British station chief to use his superior prestige and cunning to persuade his CIA colleague to join him in joint Anglo-American operations, for which he supplies the brains and the CIA colleague supplies the funds.'

Miles Copeland, *The Real Spy World*[1]

The Crabb affair was a bad experience from everyone's point of view. Eden referred to the incident as 'this sad event', but it was only one of several he would endure during the coming months. Ahead was the embarrassing public revelation that Philby's name had been linked in the 'third man' scandal to the defections of Burgess and Maclean, and the appalling Suez débâcle. But before describing Eden's attempt to overthrow Nasser, we should turn briefly to Iran, where the seeds of the major crisis in Egypt were to be found.

Iran had long been an area of strategic interest to Britain, not least because it supplied much of the West's oil through the Anglo-Iranian Oil Company (AIOC) refinery at Abadan, which was the biggest in the world. The British Government owned just over half of the company and, in accordance with a concession signed in

1933, virtually ran Iran's monopolized oil industry, providing most of the country's income from the AIOC's dividends and a royalty on sales. At the outbreak of war, the Reza Shah had declared his country neutral, but that status was ended in 1941 when the Allies invaded to secure a southerly supply route to the hard-pressed Soviet Union, The Shah was placed in detention in South Africa and his weak son, Mohammed, put on the throne leaving Iran under joint Anglo-Russian control. This state of affairs continued until 1946, when the Russians failed in their attempt to seize the country through their surrogates, the Tudeh Party, and reluctantly withdrew to their own border.

The Soviet withdrawal left Britain firmly in control, but in 1948 the Labour Chancellor of the Exchequer, Sir Stafford Cripps, announced that the depressed economic situation called for greater taxation and a limit on dividends of all companies. The implications for the AIOC were severe – a considerable drop in revenue from the dividends – and all pleas to regard the company as a special case were rejected by Cripps, who pointed out that the company represented Britain's largest overseas investment and, as such, was a key financial asset. No exception could be made to the Treasury's dividend rule; the Iranian economy would just have to cope. This attitude served to harden Iranian nationalist sentiments which had been exploited for some years by Dr Mohammed Mussadeq, a vociferous member of the Iranian parliament, the Majlis, and one of the few local politicians not to have been put on the British payroll.

Mussadeq used the Treasury's intransigence as another example of Iran's loss of sovereignty and began pressing for nationalization of the oil industry. These demands were skilfully resisted by the Prime Minister, General Razmara, but in March 1951 he was assassinated by a Muslim extremist. Two months later the Shah reluctantly appointed Mussadeq as his successor. Supported by huge street demonstrations, Mussadeq announced the nationalization of the AIOC; the company responded by ceasing its operations, thus bringing Iranian oil exports to a virtual standstill, apart from the small quantities destined for Israel and China.

The Labour administration in London found itself in some difficulties. It could hardly oppose the principle of nationalization, which it had applied ruthlessly in Britain, but nor could it simply wave good-bye to the country's largest overseas asset. To do so without taking firm action to enforce the sanctity of contracts would invite similar trouble elsewhere in the world where Britain had important interests. There was a strong desire to settle the matter with some old-fashioned gunboat diplomacy, but the Americans were convinced that any British military action in the south would provide the Soviets with an excuse to invade from the north. The SIS Head of Station in Tehran at the time, Monty Woodhouse, recalled that '[Foreign Minister Herbert] Morrison was willing to use force to recover the AIOC's rights and property, especially the great new refinery at Abadan. . . . One of my officers had suborned the Iranian Commander-in-Chief at Khorramshahr not to offer more than token resistance, so the operation would not have been difficult. But the Cabinet would not let Morrison proceed.'[2] Bowing to US pressure, the contingency plan codenamed Operation BUCCANEER was shelved.

The only alternative was a coup to remove Mussadeq from power, and this was 'first formulated by the Foreign Office itself rather than entrusted to its so-called Friends'.[3] But even if the original idea did not come from Broadway, the plan and its execution certainly did. Accordingly, the SIS Tehran Station in the British Embassy started drafting in suitable personnel. At that time, it consisted of 'three or four able young men in the Embassy [who] specialized in intelligence on Iran and the Communists. Another cultivated leading Iranians who were hostile to Mussadeq. Another conducted a useful liaison, approved by the Shah, with the chief of the security police, who was well informed about the Tudeh Party.'[4] They were John Briance, a former Palestine

Police officer who had been posted to Tehran in 1950; Norman Darbyshire from Cairo, who had done a tour of duty in Tehran at the end of the war and had been installed in 1950 as Vice-Consul at Reshed on the Caspian; Alexis Forter, an RAF officer of White Russian extraction, who was sent to open a sub-station in Basra; and Robert Zaehner, the hard-drinking Oxford don who had participated in the Albanian fiasco. The Head of Station, Woodhouse, was an SOE veteran who had won the DSO while fighting with Greek guerrillas (and was later to become the Tory MP for Oxford); he had been brought in to head SIS's War Planning Directorate in 1949.

Zaehner was to be one of the crucial players in the drama that followed, having spent four years under press attaché cover in Tehran from 1943 onwards. During that period he had recruited some important agents inside both the royalist camp and the opposition. Chief among them were the three wealthy Rashidian brothers, Seyfollah, Qodratollah and Assadollah, who exerted considerable influence and were believed by many to own numerous members of the Majlis, quite apart from their own very substantial holdings. All three were committed Anglophiles, having educated their children in England and having bought properties in London.

While Zaehner rallied political support for an acceptable deal with the AIOC, Woodhouse took care of the logistical back-up any mass uprising against Mussadeq would need, using RAF Habbaniyah in Iraq as a source of weapons to arm the royalist tribes. Caches of guns were secreted throughout the country to give Mussadeq's opponents confidence and to form the basis of a resistance movement to deter the Soviets from taking advantage of the situation. All went well until 17 October 1952, when Mussadeq suddenly broke off diplomatic relations with Britain and gave all the diplomatic staff just ten days to quit the country. This, of course, was an intelligence disaster, because the expulsion required the evacuation of all the SIS personnel operating under diplomatic cover and effectively left SIS's agents in the hands of the CIA station in Tehran. Quite apart from the obvious drawbacks to such an arrangement, the Rashidian brothers were as anti-American as they were pro-British. However, a link was provided in the form of a wireless contact with RAF Habbaniyah so that communications with the brothers could be relayed to the SIS station based in the British military headquarters in Cyprus, but clearly desperate measures were called for.

The first step was a conference in London at which Woodhouse, Zaehner and Sinclair's deputy, George Young, briefed the new Foreign Secretary, Anthony Eden, on the deteriorating situation. Woodhouse was optimistic about the chances of removing Mussadeq, but Zaehner 'gave Eden an extremely defeatist account of the capabilities of the brothers'.[5] No operations could be run without a base in Tehran and, in the absence of a diplomatic mission, that meant total reliance on the CIA. This presented further difficulties, because the US State Department had tried to keep a neutral stance over the oil dispute and was suspected of being more than a little sympathetic to Mussadeq, who was perceived as a bulwark against Communism and a not entirely unsatisfactory replacement for General Razmara. The Americans had always been uneasy about propping up British Imperialism and, anyway, considered Razmara to have been unusually corrupt, if not actually a fully paid-up SIS agent. The US State Department's viewpoint was also coloured by the inescapable strategic fact that a British boycott of oil products, or a Royal Navy blockade in the Persian Gulf, might easily force the Iranians to turn to their Soviet trading partners across the Caspian Sea.

With Eden's consent, Woodhouse flew to Washington with Darbyshire and the newly appointed SIS Foreign Office Adviser, George Clutton, to suggest a joint operation to get rid of Mussadeq once and for all. According to Woodhouse's own account, he 'decided to emphasize the Communist threat to Iran rather than the need to recover control of the oil industry'.[6] In America, the SIS delegation was received by the incoming Eisenhower administration's new Director of Central Intelligence, Allen Dulles, and his local man in Beirut, Kermit Roosevelt. Together they established the basis of Operation BOOT. All that remained to be finalized was a practical scheme. By February 1953 Young, Woodhouse and a new player, Dickie Franks, had been enrolled. (A former SOE saboteur, Franks was destined to become CSS in 1978, after an SIS career spanning thirty years.)

BOOT was finally formulated, as Woodhouse describes:

> Two separate components were dovetailed into the plan, because we had two distinct kinds of resources: an urban organization run by the brothers, and a number of tribal leaders in the south. We intended to activate both simultaneously. The urban organization included senior officers of the army and police, deputies and senators, mullahs, merchants, newspaper editors and elder statesmen, as well as mob-leaders. These forces, directed by the brothers, were to seize control of Tehran, preferably with the support of the Shah but if necessary without it, and to arrest Mussadeq and his ministers. At the same time the tribal leaders were to make a show of force in the direction of the major cities in the south. If there was any resistance by the Tudeh Party, the tribes would occupy Isfahan and Abadan.[7]

As Roosevelt later recalled, the British

> brushed aside my reservations and proposed that we have at least a thorough preliminary talk right then and there. I was dealing at this time only with Clutton, his principal lieutenant Monty Woodhouse and with his recently returned head of the Iranian office, Norman Darbyshire. They had already sketched out a plan of battle and, while they recognized that we might have political problems,

they could see no other reason for delay. We did take the time to go into their battle plan in some detail. In later talks the number of participants on both sides would be substantially increased. But at the beginning it was just the four of us.[8]

On their second visit to Washington in February 1953, the BOOT team from SIS was accompanied by the 'able, no-nonsense' Patrick Dean, then Chairman of the JIC. It was agreed that Mussadeq should be deposed by a military, pro-royalist coup, which would enable the Shah to name Mussadeq's successor. The only stumbling-block was the American nominee for the post, General Fazlollah Zahedi, who had been interned in Palestine during the war for his pronounced pro-Nazi sentiments. Dean declared the choice 'a bit of a shocker',[9] but it was accepted because in spite of his experience Zahedi was not known to be anti-British; the SIS idea that Roosevelt should be BOOT's field commander was also adopted. In reality, there was not much alternative, because SIS still lacked any facilities in Tehran.

The first hurdle to be overcome was to obtain the young Shah's consent to a *coup d'état*, so in mid-July Roosevelt travelled undercover to Tehran from Beirut and made contact with Ernest Perron, a well-placed British agent who was the Shah's Swiss-born private tutor and life-long friend. Roosevelt's initial overtures failed, as did an attempt to use the Shah's sister, Princess Ashraf, as an intermediary. Eventually Roosevelt was forced to make a direct approach by attending a secret rendezvous with the Shah at midnight on 1 August. Roosevelt presented himself as a personal representative from Eisenhower and Churchill, explaining that elaborate arrangements had been made to confirm his credentials: the President had agreed to insert a particular phrase into a speech he was due to deliver, and the Prime Minister had got the BBC to alter its usual World Service time signal on its Persian language broadcast; instead of baldly stating 'It is midnight', which was the usual routine, the announcer was to say 'It is now . . .', then pause briefly and add 'exactly midnight'. Eden had been seriously ill during the last vital weeks of planning and so Churchill had been indoctrinated into BOOT. As Woodhouse later observed, 'Churchill enjoyed dramatic operations and had no high regard for timid diplomatists. It was he who gave the authority for Operation BOOT to proceed.'[10]

The Shah was suitably impressed and, after much persuasion during several more secret meetings, agreed to do nothing to oppose the CIA's plan. Much of the credit for gaining access to the Shah and swinging opinion against Mussadeq was later taken by Roosevelt when, in the opinion of others involved, it should really have gone to (Sir) Shapoor Reporter, SIS's Bombay-born agent of influence in Iran who had served during the war in the Tehran Embassy as the public relations officer. Reporter was an SIS asset of long-standing, who had attached himself to the US Embassy in 1948 as 'political adviser'.[11] His advice to Roosevelt helped ensure BOOT's eventual success.

Operation BOOT centred on the recruitment of some 6,000 anti-Mussadeq Iranians, organized by a small, well-equipped group which itself was controlled by the Tehran CIA station and General Norman Schwartzkopf, the US police adviser attached to the Iranian army. Schwartzkopf allegedly recruited his armed insurgents (or mob, as others have accurately described them) with open suitcases of money. The total cost to the CIA has been put at around $20 million. The plan called for the Shah to issue an imperial decree, or *firman*, which would dismiss Mussadeq and establish General Zahedi in power with the legal support of the army. The *firman* was to be delivered by Colonel Nematollah Nassiry, the commander of the palace bodyguard, while the Shah and his queen flew up to their summer retreat on the Caspian to await events. If the coup was a success, the Shah would return in triumph to Tehran; if not, he would simply fly on to a safe haven and issue an ultimatum to his people requiring them to decide between himself and the increasingly irrational Mussadeq.

On 13 August, the rabble took to the streets in a series of violent and chaotic demonstrations, and Colonel Nassiry led a detachment of tanks to the Prime Minister's house. Unfortunately, the plot had been betrayed and Nassiry was met by a strong force of troops loyal to Mussadeq, headed by the Chief of Staff, General Raqi Riahi. Nassiry was promptly arrested, but as news spread of the attempted coup, so the demonstrators crowded back into the streets. Tehran's radio station denounced the intervention by 'foreign elements', and the Shah hastily departed for Baghdad before flying on to Rome, where a CIA-maintained hotel suite awaited him. Meanwhile, in Tehran General Zahedi went into hiding.

It was at this moment that the US State Department almost lost its nerve. The Under-Secretary of State, Walter Bedell Smith, was alerted to the failure of the coup and transmitted a 'get out quick' signal addressed to Roosevelt in Tehran. However, the CIA station lacked an independent method of contacting Washington and relied on SIS for all its external communications. Woodhouse, therefore, managed to intercept the message in Cyprus and declined to pass it on immediately. The critical delay in the onward transmission of Bedell Smith's directive gave Roosevelt just enough time to regain the initiative. As he later recalled, Woodhouse

> had faith, or, if one wishes to be cynical, nothing to lose. The British were totally out of Tehran. The AIOC had lost; no more could be taken from them. But Beedle [Bedell Smith] did not want the Americans' hand exposed, particularly in failure. He assumed that no word from me was bad word, and he felt that I should get out. Under the circumstances I can hardly blame him. Had the message arrived earlier – when, in fact, he first sent it – I should have had a real problem.[12]

Instead, chaos reigned until 19 August, when it was Mussadeq's turn to take fright. The CIA's agents stormed

Tehran Radio and broadcast a news bulletin naming General Zahedi as the new Prime Minister. The announcer also claimed, equally falsely, that the Shah was on his way back to Iran. The royalists quickly took to the streets, aided by the police who had been ordered, somewhat rashly, to crack down hard on the Tudeh protesters. The result was a violently pro-Shah demonstration that united the Tudeh activists against Mussadeq. As the Tehran mob approached his house, Mussadeq climbed over the garden wall and fled, leaving General Zahedi to emerge from hiding and take control. A few days later, on 22 August, he was at the airport in his new capacity as Prime Minister to welcome the Shah home.

The coup had been completed with hardly a shot fired, but some 300 civilians died, trampled underfoot, when the mob took over Tehran. Mussadeq was placed under house arrest and later sentenced to three years' solitary confinement. Colonel Nassiry was released and promoted. In December 1953, diplomatic relations were re-established with Britain, allowing Dickie Franks to reopen the SIS station.

Early in the New Year, negotiations commenced so that the oil dispute could be settled. A compromise was reached: the AIOC changed its name to British Petroleum and Zahedi's Government signed an agreement with a consortium of companies in which BP owned forty per cent of the stock; the remaining sixty per cent was bought by five American companies, with Royal Dutch Shell and the French taking a small minority interest.

Neither Woodhouse nor Roosevelt stayed long to enjoy BOOT's success. Woodhouse had already left Cyprus by the time the Shah had been reinstated in Tehran and had embarked upon a tour of the Far East, visiting the SIS stations in Tokyo and Pusan in Korea, before returning to Broadway. He was actually relaxing at the British Ambassador's residence in Korea when the news of Mussadeq's fall came through. For his part, Roosevelt caught a flight out of Tehran the day after the Shah's safe return, having first been thanked by him for saving his kingdom. On his way back to Washington, he stayed in London for a couple of nights, installed at the Ritz by Norman Darbyshire. The next day, a celebration lunch was held by Clutton at the Connaught Hotel's grill room – 'perhaps the best and most expensive place in London, so I assumed Clutton must have authorized it as a business expense'[13] – after which Roosevelt was escorted to 10 Downing Street, where he perched on Churchill's bed and gave him 'in glamorous detail the story of what happened'.[14] Roosevelt then continued his journey home and was later to become head of the CIA's Middle East Operations Division.

Reflecting upon BOOT afterwards, Woodhouse commented:

> Of course there were some things we did not plan. We did not plan the Shah's flight from the scene of action. We did not plan the violence which cost over three hundred lives. In other respects the course of the revolution was more or less what we were trying to bring about. It is possible that events might have taken just such a course without our intervention.[15]

The entire operation was a triumph of co-operation between SIS and the CIA and depended largely on the close relationship that developed between the two partners. There was none of the mutual suspicions that had so marred previous enterprises, such as the Albanian affair. As Woodhouse remarked in his memoirs, *Something Ventured*, published in 1982, 'So far as I know, Operation BOOT was the first such operation successfully carried out by the Americans, and probably the last by the British. It was also the only one they ever carried out together.'[16] It had, nevertheless, been a close-run thing; if Bedell Smith's fatal signal had not been deliberately held up in Cyprus, the entire episode might easily have misfired. As it turned out, the Shah took a tight grip on the country and established a security and intelligence organization, SAVAK, to prevent further instability.

Roosevelt did not wait as long as Woodhouse to give

his version of events. After years of speculation about who exactly had been behind the *coup d'état*, Roosevelt wrote *Countercoup* and released it in 1979. However, its timing was less than perfect, for its publication coincided with the seizure of the American Embassy in Tehran by Muslim revolutionary fundamentalists. It was also thought to be less than discreet about the exact role played by the AIOC and its relationship with the Friends. Pressure was applied instantly and the 7,000 copies of the first edition were quickly withdrawn from sale. In a revised edition all references to British Petroleum were removed, and the names of Clutton, Woodhouse and Darbyshire changed to 'John Cochran', 'Henry Montague' and 'Gordon Somerset' respectively. Omitted from both editions was the unpalatable truth that Clutton was later to be investigated as a suspected Soviet spy.

Certainly, all the essential ingredients for a coup in Iran were present there when SIS had initiated its plan. The political will in London was firm, although with Eden recuperating on a yacht in the Aegean from a bungled gall bladder operation and Churchill recovering from a stroke, there was little fear of top-level interference. Clutton had given SIS a free hand during the Labour Government and, if anything, the policy had become more robust when the Conservatives came to power midway through the undertaking. Another vital contribution was Woodhouse's infectious enthusiasm for the project, which had won support from both the CIA and President Eisenhower's administration. Although Woodhouse could not claim to have Roosevelt's impressive connections (he was Theodore Roosevelt's grandson), he did have extremely useful friendships with Churchill and Eden. On the ground, too, the conditions were very favourable, with widespread resentment that Mussadeq had failed to live up to his extravagant promises, thus alienating the bazaar, the merchants, the wealthy middle classes and even his erstwhile supporters, the Tudeh. With the street mob open to manipulation from a dollar-rich CIA station, and the army and police divided in their support for Mussadeq's eccentric regime, the coup might have happened anyway, without foreign intervention. The CIA and the Friends simply gave Zahedi critical support at exactly the right moment to ensure success.

One essential element in a country where street politics dominate the scene was the role of the radio station. It was not a lesson lost on SIS, which had long maintained an interest in psychological warfare. Officially British involvement with such matters had ended in 1945 with the closure of the Political Warfare Executive. However, two years later Christopher Mayhew, then Bevin's junior minister in the Foreign Office, had pressed for a reappraisal of Britain's propaganda effort in the Cold War. His own experience had been as Hugh Gaitskell's deputy in the Ministry of Economic Warfare, and he was a skilled operator in the field. He knew the potential value of a smooth system of disseminating sympathetic information, and he pressed for the Political Warfare Executive's reinstatement to combat the Soviet propaganda machine. The result was the creation of the Information Research Department (IRD), a small organization which existed uneasily under the Foreign Office's umbrella, but with separate premises at Riverwalk House, Millbank. Its task was to acquire useful intelligence from the secret agencies, principally SIS, and ensure that it was used to good effect against the Russians and their surrogates. In the jargon of the intelligence community, the IRD became known as 'an instrument of news management', distributing material helpful to British policy on an unattributable basis.

The IRD had no opportunity to play a part in the war of words conducted in New York during the Palestine crisis, but it did prove highly effective in Malaya where Alex Peterson and Hugh Carleton Greene had used radio and pamphlets to undermine the Communist insurgents, and in Kenya where the use of 'voice aircraft' had been pioneered to persuade the Mau-Mau rebels to surrender. A similar exercise had been carried out in Cyprus under

the direction of Bernard Fergusson to counter the pro-
EOKA broadcasts from Athens. Inevitably there were, at
IRD's margins, some grey areas that could be usefully
exploited by SIS, and that is exactly what happened. The
first step was the development of the Arab News Agency
(Cairo) Limited, an SIS front organization and a conduit
for IRD-inspired news and feature stories. Virtually all
the important Arabic newspapers subscribed to the ANA,
which was eventually to boast branch offices in almost
every capital in the Middle East. Among its clients was
another IRD operation, the Sharq al-Adna 'voice of
Britain' radio station at Limassol in Cyprus. Among the
directors of the ANA were two career SIS officers, Alan
Hare and Adelaide Maturin, another veteran of SOE.
But although both the ANA and its two subsidiaries, Near
and Far East News Limited and Near and Far East (Asia)
Limited, prospered and proved an extremely useful covert
arm to British diplomacy by the surreptitious manipulation of public opinion, it was their close relationship with
the Friends that brought them to the brink of disaster and
contributed to SIS's greatest post-war catastrophe: Suez.

9

OPERATION STRAGGLE

'Altogether it was an amateur approach for a country which prided itself on the high standards of its more recondite intelligence agencies.'

Roy Fullick and Geoffrey Powell, *Suez: The Double War*[1]

Although nominally an independent kingdom, Egypt had been firmly within Britain's sphere of influence since the Anglo-Egyptian Treaty had been signed by Eden back in 1936, and even before that. This had allowed for a substantial British military presence in the country for at least twenty years and had designated a Canal zone which was to be under Britain's exclusive military control. This arrangement gave Britain an important strategic base from which its interests in the region could be protected. It also ensured free passage along the Suez Canal, the vital shortcut to the Far East for the West's shipping.

In the immediate post-war era growing Egyptian nationalism, combined with discontent over widespread corruption and other grumbles, served to undermine Britain's local standing. The Egyptian army's poor performance against Israel in the 1948 war was also a strong factor, for perfidious Britain had been blamed by the Arab League for handing Palestine over to the Jews and for keeping the army poorly trained and equipped. Thus, in 1950, the Wafd movement was voted into office on a wave of anti-British feeling. These sentiments were expressed by the new Prime Minister, Nahas Pasha, when he announced that the 1936 treaty would be terminated when it came up for renewal in five years' time. He also began applying pressure on the Canal zone so as to have the number of British troops stationed there reduced to the figure agreed in the treaty. The Labour Government's attitude to these developments was firm. Withdrawal was acceptable, but only when suitable arrangements had been made to guarantee security in the region. However, in October 1951, a decision was taken to end the 1936 treaty unilaterally and to declare Farouk king of both Egypt and the Sudan.

Egypt, of course, had long made claims over the Sudan, but that country was the responsibility of a joint British and Egyptian condominium. As the new Conservative Foreign Secretary, Eden insisted that Britain could only agree to the extension of Farouk's kingdom if it had been ratified first by the Sudanese. He also pointed out that international treaties could not be legally ended unilaterally. It was against this political background of rising tension that the CIA intervened.

The US State Department saw no justification for supporting the almost colonial position of the British in Egypt and feared that a British refusal to negotiate might push the country towards the Russians. As the local situation deteriorated, with Nahas Pasha encouraging terrorist attacks on British troops garrisoned in the Canal zone, the Americans began to take an active interest and gave support to the Egyptian claim over the Sudan. As a first step, the CIA Station Chief in Cairo established contact with leaders of a growing number of anti-monarchist Egyptian army officers known as the Society of Free Officers.[2] He reasoned that because they were equally opposed to the Communists and the extremists of the Muslim Brotherhood, the officers might offer a stable and reliable alternative to Farouk's corrupt governments.

By January 1952, the Canal zone was almost completely cut off from the rest of the country. Murderous attacks on individual British soldiers prevented them from visiting local towns, and all the local labour force had been withdrawn. So had the supply of fresh food and water.

One particular guerrilla assault, at the Tel-el-Kebir munitions depot, prompted a fierce counter-attack on Ismailia, where the *fedayeen* had been based. The town was quickly occupied, but the police station refused to surrender. A gun battle followed, in which fifty Egyptians were killed and 100 wounded. Once news of the massacre reached Cairo, a mob took to the streets and went on an anti-European rampage, burning dozens of shops, offices, hotels and cinemas. Eight Britons died in the riot, which also claimed the loss of the exclusive Turf Club and the famous Shepheard's Hotel. The Egyptian army eventually marched in to restore order, but only after the fire-raisers and looters had done their worst, and the threat had been made to send in British troops.

During the following six months Egypt underwent a period of unprecedented instability, with Farouk dismissing Nahas Pasha as Prime Minister and appointing temporary replacements. None survived long and, on 1 July, yet another nominee formed an administration which, like the others before it, was marked only by the scale of corruption it appeared to endorse. Egypt's political structure was in turmoil, ripe for a coup. It happened on 22 July 1952, when General Mohammed Neguib seized power in Cairo. Leading some 3,000 troops and 200 officers, he stormed the army headquarters in Abbasiya, the Radio Cairo building and its relay transmitter at Abu Za'bal, leaving the announcement of the coup to one of his principal lieutenants, Colonel Anwar Sadat. Three days later Neguib entered Alexandria, where Farouk was at his summer residence, the Ras-el-Tin palace, and presented him with an ultimatum: abdicate before noon and go into exile or face execution. Farouk promptly embarked for Naples on the royal yacht *al-Mahrusa* that same evening, accompanied by what was left of the country's gold reserves.

Neguib's bloodless coup had been engineered largely by the CIA in the person of Kermit Roosevelt and, as the CIA's local Station Chief later confirmed, 'official Washington was delighted'.[3] Roosevelt's protégé, and the shadowy leader of the revolutionary Free Officers behind

Neguib, was Colonel Nasser, an inspired nationalist who was to be underestimated by almost every European who met him. He was also the recipient of approximately $3 million of CIA funds via a Swiss bank account. As another senior CIA officer was later wryly to admit, 'We backed the wrong horse there.'[4]

From the British perspective the revolution was not entirely unwelcome. Neguib was half Sudanese and was anxious to settle Egypt's territorial claims. With Farouk gone, the question of his monarchy did not arise, and Neguib accepted Britain's commitment to self-determination for the Sudan. In February 1953, Eden reached a compromise agreement with Neguib, which involved a British withdrawal from the Sudan within three years and a guarantee that the Sudanese could build their own constitution.

The truth about Nasser only began to dawn on the CIA late in February 1954, when Neguib was manoeuvred into resigning, leaving him in control. The only challenge to Nasser came externally from Israel, which made a bungled attempt to destablize his position during the summer with a bombing campaign. The Israelis calculated, wrongly as it turned out, that such lingering CIA support that Nasser enjoyed would evaporate if American premises in Egypt were targeted for attack. The scheme, masterminded and executed by a Mossad network of pro-Zionist Egyptians already well established, involved the placing of incendiary devices in various public buildings, including the US libraries in Cairo and Alexandria. All went well until 23 July, when a Mossad agent, Philip Nathanson, burst into flames in a Cairo cinema. His small incendiary bomb, disguised as a spectacles case, had gone off prematurely. Nathanson was only slightly hurt, but he was in a worse condition by the time the Mukhabarat, Nasser's feared security apparatus, had completed his interrogation. Virtually the entire ring was caught, exposing a well-developed, deep-cover Mossad operation. Two of its key members Max Bennet and an Egyptian Jew named Karmonah, later committed suicide, but six others were eventually tried and sentenced to terms of imprisonment. Two of those convicted, Shmuel Azar and Dr Moshe Marzouk, were hanged.

The affair caused a political storm behind the scenes in Tel Aviv, because the operation had only received prior approval from Benjamin Gibly, Israel's chief of military intelligence. But in Cairo, the incident enhanced Nasser's reputation and made him even more popular. However, the entire episode helped turn the Colonel into a ruthless tyrant, as he was to demonstrate a few months later when, on 26 October, a plumber named Mahmoud Abd el-Latif took a shot at him during a political rally in Alexandria. Nasser responded to the amateurish assassination attempt by the lone religious fanatic as though it was evidence of another huge plot. He ordered a nationwide purge, in which 700 civilians were arrested on charges of high treason and 250 army officers were hauled before military tribunals charged with plotting against him. By the following year, more than 3,000 political prisoners had been detained.

Even though Nasser cracked down hard on dissident elements within Egypt, he still maintained cordial relations with Britain and took every opportunity to repeat that he wished to be on the best of terms with Eden. It was just that he did not want any British soldiers on Egyptian soil. Accordingly, a new Anglo-Egyptian Treaty was negotiated by Eden's Under-Secretary at the Foreign Office, Anthony Nutting, who agreed that all British troops would be withdrawn over a period of twenty months. The small print of the final text actually allowed civilian personnel to remain in the Canal zone for a further seven years.

Nasser's ambitions and his nationalism were not limited to Egypt. He had an Arab vision and used Radio Cairo, now renamed 'Voice of the Arabs', to export his anti-Imperialist message. With the wireless becoming an important medium for propaganda, Nasser had an impact throughout the Middle East; even Britain's most trusted allies, like Iraq and Jordan, were forced by Egyptian-inspired civil disorder to reconsider their links with the West. The main victim of Nasser's fiery anti-colonialism was the Baghdad Pact, Eden's idea for a NATO-style organization in the Middle East. In February 1954, the Turkish Prime Minister signed a mutual co-operation agreement with Iraq's pro-British leader, Nuri es-Said. This was followed by a defence pact with Pakistan, Britain and Zahedi's Iran. It was only when Jordan opened talks about joining too that Nasser flexed his propaganda muscles and directed his attention to Arab nationalist feelings in Amman. Riots broke out and the talks were quickly terminated.

Nasser's extraordinary success during this period took many by surprise, but at least he was determined to capitalize on his achievements and fulfil his most potent ambition: to confront Israel and restore Egypt's lost battle honours. To this end he embarked upon a modernization programme for the army. Since the West was reluctant to supply weapons in breach of an international embargo designed to avoid upsetting the balance of power in the region, Nasser turned to the Soviet Bloc and, in September 1955, made a huge, secret, arms deal with the Czechs. The scale of the purchase was so enormous – involving 300 tanks, 200 MiG-15 fighters, 50 Ilyushin bombers, 100 armoured self-propelled guns, 4 minesweepers and 2 destroyers – that it could not be kept under wraps for long. Almost as soon as the first batch of fifty medium tanks was delivered, reports of the sale started to circulate. According to the Israelis, who viewed this development with considerable alarm, the new equipment would take a year to be brought into active service, but at the end of that period Egypt would represent a formidable threat to regional stability.

From SIS's viewpoint these developments spelt serious trouble, because its role in Egypt had always been limited to gathering intelligence about Soviet Bloc personalities so that the Foreign Office could anticipate Moscow's diplomatic moves. The arms deal, negotiated at a senior level by the Soviet Foreign Minister, Dmitri Shepilov, was worth well over $400 million, ample proof that the Russians intended to increase their influence in the area. The Soviet Embassy in Cairo was also expanding at a prodigious rate. Under normal circumstances these matters would have been the responsibility of SIME, Bill Oughton's regional MI5 office at RAF Fayid, but the withdrawal to Cyprus had left it with only a skeleton staff – which, in reality, consisted of just the local DSO, Gerald Savage, who was based at Moascar, outside Ismailia. But even if it had been within SIME's brief to interfere in Egyptian domestic politics, the organization would have been hard-pressed to find reliable sources within the ranks of Nasser's Free Officers. Several of their number, including Anwar Sadat, had been interned by SIME during the war for their pro-Axis sympathies. Thus, the burden fell on the Friends, who were less than prepared.

Throughout the post-war period, Colonel John Teague had exercised control over SIS's assets in the Middle East. Educated at Portsmouth Grammar School, he had originally intended to become an organist. The First World War intervened and he was commissioned into the Warwickshire Regiment, with whom he won the Military Cross in France; he later transferred to the Indian army and was attached to the Sykes Mission to south Persia. In 1919, he was appointed Vice-Consul in Shiraz and took an active part in the Iraq revolt the following year. Throughout the rest of the 1920s, he served in Iraq, Kurdistan and the North-West Frontier and qualified as a Persian interpreter. The Arab revolt in 1936 found him in Palestine as an intelligence officer, and in 1942 he finally joined SIS as DSO, Iraq. He had an unrivalled knowledge of Arab affairs and occasionally contributed articles to newspapers. He had taken charge of ISLD after Teddy Smith-Ross's departure in 1945 and had later been appointed Controller Middle East, before being replaced by George Young in 1953.

Teague's local station in Cairo was in the hands of Rodney Dennys, a veteran of Section V and ISLD who had been sent to Turkey in 1950 to replace Philby. He had joined SIS shortly before the outbreak of war and had been caught up in the appalling Venlo incident in Holland in November 1940. Thereafter, he had married Graham Greene's sister and run double agents against the Nazis with considerable success. Upon his transfer to Ankara, Dennys's post was taken by Geoffrey Hinton, a graduate of Worcester College, Oxford, who had transferred to SIS from the Ministry of Information at the end of the war.

Although the Cairo Station was powerless to sabotage Nasser's improving relationship with the Soviets, Broadway could monitor the progress of the arms deal with considerable accuracy. Quite apart from GCHQ's technical coverage of the diplomatic traffic passing between Czechoslovakia and Cairo, SIS had recruited a useful agent in the Egyptian Embassy in Prague named Mohammed Hamdi. From his position in the Embassy's commercial section, he supplied detailed reports on each of the shipments. In addition, the ANA in Cairo had built up a large network based on 'freelance correspondents', several of whom happened to be in the Egyptian army and navy. Thanks to the ANA and GCHQ, the Friends were able to keep the Foreign Office well informed about the status of the Egyptian military. However, this position was to change dramatically in 1956, at a most critical moment, just as Nasser announced his intention of nationalizing the Suez Canal.

The Canal concession had been granted originally by the Khedive Ismail in 1866 and was not due to expire until 1969, but Nasser was determined to renegotiate it. In particular, he wanted repatriation of the Canal company's overseas investments, a greater share of the waterway's revenues for Egypt and a controlling interest on the board. Britain's attitude, as articulated by Eden who had succeeded Churchill as Prime Minister in April 1955, was identical to the view previously expressed to Mussadeq: international agreements could not be subject to unilateral change. On 26 July 1956, Nasser simply carried out his threat and took over the Canal. Since the last British troops had left the Canal zone in the middle of June, by the agreed deadline, Britain was powerless to do anything to prevent him.

Britain was not alone in experiencing difficulties with Nasser. Israel was becoming increasingly agitated by the build-up of military hardware in Egypt, and France's overseas intelligence agency, SDECE, blamed Nasser for giving arms to the Arab rebels in Algeria. In addition, Nasser's hand could be detected in other none-too-encouraging developments in the Middle East. In January 1956, an assassination plot against Iraq's Prime Minister was uncovered, implicating the Egyptian Military Attaché; and on 1 March General Sir John Glubb, the British commander of the Arab Legion in Jordan, was suddenly dismissed by the King, supposedly under pressure from Nasser. Even if that assumption was unfounded, it had been Nasser who had actually broken the news of Glubb's sacking to the Foreign Secretary, Selwyn Lloyd, while on a visit to Cairo. Nasser's advance knowledge was clearly indicative of his complicity in the affair, which was certainly in line with his well-known anti-colonialist sentiments.

However, the lynchpin for Operation STRAGGLE, if one was needed, was the Mukhabarat's sudden descent on the ANA on 27 August. The office manager, James Swinburn, a former teacher who had spent twenty-five years in Egypt, was arrested, along with five others, including Charles Pittuck, a local employee of Marconi's who happened to be in Swinburn's flat in Zamalek at the time of the raid, and James Zarb, the Maltese-born owner of a local ceramics factory. Swinburn was the head of SIS's stay-behind network, and Pittuck was to have been his stand-in while he went abroad. Fortunately, Pittuck had only just been introduced to the organization and was later able to plead innocence. The others implicated were not so lucky.

A thorough search of Swinburn's home revealed dozens of compromising documents relating to the Czech arms deal. There were reports from agents on the location of Egyptian army units, the arrival of new Soviet-built tank transporters, details of a new radar station outside Cairo, the delivery of anti-tank equipment to the paramilitary national guard and even an assessment of the competence of the naval defences around Alexandria. Some of the naval papers, which disclosed the movements of a tank landing-ship, the *Akka*, identified the name of Swinburn's principal informant, Sayed Amin Mahmoud, the headmaster of a preparatory school. He had given an account of recent naval manoeuvres in which his son, Captain Ahmed Amin Mahmoud, had taken part, and had speculated that the *Akka* was about to be used as a blockship in the Canal. Another ship, the *Sudan*, was said to have been filled with explosives in order to block the entrance to Alexandria's harbour. Captain Mahmoud had been a particularly well-placed source, as he had previously been General Neguib's naval aide. Another, equally well-informed agent, Youssef Megali Hanna, described how a team of twelve East German rocket scientists had recently been recruited to aid an Egyptian missile programme, and how the Syrians had requested the construction of an aviation college and aircraft repair complex outside Damascus.

One batch of compromising documents revealed the monthly production figures for Egypt's tiny armaments industry and disclosed their origin, an army mechanic named Salah Hassan Bedeir. An Egyptian detective, Massif Morkos Mikhail, had apparently written lengthy reports on Communist activities for the ANA, as had several others working under journalistic cover, including Mohammed Ebeid, an architect; Youssef Bedeir, who was one of Zarb's local employees; Anton Yakoub Abdel-malik, a genuine journalist; Samnel Attiya, formerly a Sudanese civil servant; and Ahmed el-Sayed Rewish, a parliamentary clerk.

The day after the raid two diplomats at the British Embassy, J. G. Gove, the head of the Visa Section, and John Flux the Commercial First Secretary who had worked in Cairo since 1919, were expelled for espionage. Consular access to the prisoners was refused, and over the next few days more than thirty of Swinburn's contacts, both professional and social, were rounded up. Four Britons managed to escape arrest (only to be tried *in absentia* the following year), but SIS's greatest loss was that of Colonel Milovan Gregorivitch, a well-connected, long-serving agent who had been recruited during the war by ISLD and had operated against Eastern Bloc embassies ever since. (He was the nephew of Slobodan Yovanovitch, the wartime Yugoslavian Prime Minister in exile.) Also taken into custody at the same time was one of his sub-agents, Hussein Ali el-Kashef, a guard at the Yugoslav Embassy.

Lengthy confessions were extracted from Zarb and Swinburn, and both were eventually sentenced to terms of imprisonment. However, before they could be put on trial, Operation STRAGGLE was executed.

The military component of STRAGGLE was code-named HAMILCAR, and the details of the Anglo-French invasion of Egypt are well documented. What is not quite so well known is the contribution made by the British intelligence community. At that time, in the summer of 1956, Broadway was recovering from the triple blows of the loss of the Berlin tunnel, the Crabb fiasco and the exposure of the ANA front. Each, in their own way, had been utterly disastrous. The first incident had been written off as an expensive but occupational setback; the next had caused a profound loss of confidence in SIS and had led to the replacement of Sir John Sinclair as CSS by Sir Dick White.

News of White's appointment received a mixed reception at Broadway. It is not so much that Sinclair had been especially popular, but members of SIS were anxious about its future, which had been dropped into the hands of a relative stranger. Worse still, he was a career product of MI5, SIS's long-time rival in Whitehall. Some old-timers talked of 'gamekeepers turned poachers', but White was an exceptional officer in every way. Indeed, his first assignment for MI5 had been a spell abroad as an undercover agent.

Unlike his contemporaries, White had not been educated at a well-known public school. He had, nevertheless, read history at Oxford, where he had won an exhibition to Christ Church, and had spent two years in America at the universities of Michigan and Berkeley, California. When he was approached to join the Security Service in 1936, he had been an assistant teacher at a school in Croydon. He had jumped at the offer and had spent the following nine months based in Munich, travelling around the country making useful contacts. Upon his return he had been indoctrinated into one of MI5's best cases: Wolfgang zu Putlitz, then a diplomat at the German Embassy in London. Zu Putlitz was a confirmed homosexual and Marxist, and was easily one MI5's best sources of intelligence. His information was so valuable that he had been run by a small group of senior British officials which had included Sir Robert Vansittart, the Chief Diplomatic Adviser at the Foreign Office, and David Footman from SIS. MI5's two representatives on this informal committee had been 'Klop' Ustinov, the legendary agent-runner and one-time Press Attaché at the German Embassy, and the youthful White. Zu Putlitz had continued to supply MI5 and SIS until November 1940, when he had been operating from the German Legation in The Hague. Eventually, he had been forced to escape to London when a leak threatened to compromise him, thus ending a highly productive period as one of Britain's key German sources.

When war broke out, MI5's B Division had undergone a sudden expansion to cope with the new demands on its counter-espionage branch; White had been selected to become Assistant Director under his mentor, Guy Liddell. In that post he had supervised many of the most successful wartime operations and had acquired a detailed knowledge of MI5's greatest wartime successes, on which its post-war reputation rested: the 'double-cross' agents used to deceive the enemy and the cryptographic breakthroughs which had betrayed so many of the Abwehr's

The Olympic Stadium Building in West Berlin where the local SIS station operated under cover of the Political Division of the British Control Commission for Germany.

All that remains today of the American radar station in Rudow, West Berlin, where SIS sank the shaft of Operation PRINCE's tunnel.

(Above left) Colonel Grigori Tokaev, SIS's first important Soviet defector who surrendered to the Head of Station in Berlin late in October 1948. *(Above right)* Colonel Harold Perkins, the ruthless sabotage expert recruited into SIS from the wartime Special Operations Executive who planted limpet mines on illegal Jewish refugee ships destined for Palestine.

The bodies of Clifford Martin and Mervyn Paice, the two Security Intelligence Middle East NCOs murdered by the Irgun during the ruthless undercover conflict in Palestine. Moments after this picture was taken a booby-trapped landmine exploded close by.

(*Above*) Sir Stewart Menzies, Chief of the Secret Intelligence Service from 1939 until his retirement in 1952, following his dismissal of Kim Philby.

Kim Philby pictured in 1955 after he had been publicly cleared by the Government of any involvement with the defections of Burgess and Maclean. He was later taken back on to SIS's books as a part-time informant and posted to Beirut under journalistic cover.

(Above left) Monty Woodhouse, SIS's Head of Station in Tehran until 1955 and one of the principal architects of Operation BOOT, the successful coup mounted against Dr Mussadeq, the Iranian Prime Minister.

(Above right) Sir John Sinclair, the SIS Chief who took early retirement following the death of Buster Crabb, even though he had been on leave when the operation had been originally approved.

Buster Crabb, an accomplished diver whose participation in an authorized SIS operation led to his mysterious death under a Soviet cruiser in Portsmouth Harbour in April 1956.

The entrance to 5/6 Pushkin Street, Moscow, where Oleg Penkovsky used a radiator in the hallway as a dead-letter drop to keep his CIA and SIS contacts supplied with secrets.

(Below left) The lamp-post on Kutuzovsky Prospekt used by Penkovsky to signal his Western case officers who lived nearby. A black mark on the plate indicated that he wished to make contact.

(Below right) The entrance to the Peking Restaurant inside the Peking Hotel, Moscow. It was here that Penkovsky kept a rendezvous with Greville Wynne and first spotted a KGB surveillance team.

(Above) Greville Wynne (left) and Oleg Penkovsky at their trial in Moscow. Wynne was swapped for Konon Molody after serving less than a year of his sentence, but Penkovsky was shot.

Greville Wynne, one of several British businessmen recruited by SIS to help maintain contact with agents behind the Iron Cutain. The photo shows him on arrival at Northolt airstrip after being swapped for Konon Molody, April 1964.

(Above left) George Blake, formerly SIS's Head of Station in Seoul. After his release by North Koreans in 1953 he made contact with the KGB and offered his services to them two years later, when he was posted to Berlin. *(Above right)* Maurice Oldfield, the counter-intelligence expert and former SIS Chief who was brought out of retirement in 1979 to co-ordinate security in Northern Ireland.

The old KGB headquarters in Moscow, with its new rarely photographed annexe on the left.

(Right) Oleg Gordievsky (left), once the KGB's *Rezident* in London, who successfully exfiltrated from Moscow in August 1985 after twelve years of spying for SIS.

(Below) The British Embassy in Moscow with one of SIS's two converted Commer vans visible under the portico. It was used in July 1985 to smuggle Oleg Gordievsky across the frontier to Finland.

plans. He had, in short, enjoyed a 'good war' and had ended it as MI5's nominee heading SHAEF's intelligence organization on the Continent after the D-Day landings. He had also conducted the Allied investigation into Hitler's fate. When SHAEF eventually had been wound up, White had been lent to the Control Commission's Intelligence Division and had then undertaken a tour of duty with SIME.

On his return to London White had been appointed Director of MI5's B Division, and it was at that point, in 1949, that his career had threatened to nosedive. A German physicist, Klaus Fuchs, had been identified by GCHQ as a Soviet spy. Fuchs had then been working on top-secret projects at the Atomic Energy Research Establishment at Harwell and had recently been cleared for access to classified material. When MI5's enquiry into Fuchs's background was initiated, it was realized that another B Division officer, Michael Serpell, had already reviewed his personal file and had suggested an immediate investigation. For reasons that never became clear, the recommendation had been filed routinely without any action being taken. When the Director-General, Sir Percy Sillitoe, had been informed of the slip-up, he had disciplined White publicly in the presence of all his staff, a humiliation that nearly had prompted White's resignation. He had only been persuaded to remain in the Service by his friends Guy Liddell and Roger Hollis, who both had persuaded Sillitoe to conceal MI5's gaffe from the Prime Minister. They insisted that the public disclosure of the blunder would undermine confidence in the Security Service and destroy morale. Reluctantly, the Director-General had given Attlee a sanitized version of events, which omitted to mention how Serpell's endorsement of the Fuchs file had been overlooked.

White recovered from this experience, and the errors that enabled Burgess and Maclean to escape abroad undetected, because the essential secrecy of the organization had prevented outsiders from ever learning the truth. However, when Sillitoe retired in 1953, Liddell's well-known friendship with Burgess had precluded him from the succession which, in the opinion of many, was rightly his. Instead, he had gone to the Atomic Energy Authority as its Chief Security Officer and White had moved up to become the new D-G at the age of just forty-seven. His tenure during the following three years is marked by his complete reorganization of the office's six divisions and the establishment, for the first time, of a personnel branch. Many saw White's changes as a sure sign that the traditional amateur status of MI5's officers had gone for ever and had been replaced by a more professional structure which offered a proper career to new entrants. His promotion also marked the end of the flawed elitism which had given Burgess, Maclean and Philby their opportunities to penetrate Whitehall.

Eden's decision to switch White from the Security Service to the Friends, as recommended by Sir Norman Brook, was quite extraordinary, but also quite brilliant. He was an experienced operator, acknowledged in the corridors of power as one of the architects of MI5's acclaimed wartime strategy and widely known as having participated in the running of zu Putlitz, an operation then still regarded as something of a coup. It only became known much later that zu Putlitz had returned to East Germany in 1952 and had been heavily involved with Burgess, Blunt and maybe even the NKVD.

White's task upon his arrival at Broadway was to prevent the Friends from embarrassing the Prime Minister again and to restructure the organization so as to minimize the damage caused by Philby. White, of course, had been intimately involved in the Philby case since his dismissal from SIS in 1951, and had known him as a colleague when they had routinely met to discuss counter-intelligence matters during the war years. He had even interrogated Philby twice immediately upon his recall to London. Although he was later to be called 'ineffective' by Philby,[5] White had been convinced of Philby's duplicity and his subsequent report ensured that Menzies had sacked him. White had also reviewed the case again in 1955 and had arranged for Philby to undergo yet another inquisition, because the Government had commissioned a special report on the Burgess and Maclean defections. Thus, when a few months later White moved into Sinclair's flat 'over the shop' at 21 Queen Anne's Gate, at the rear of Broadway Buildings, he was fully aware of SIS's closely guarded secret: that in contradiction to the Foreign Secretary's supposedly categoric statement the previous year in the House of Commons, there was every reason to beleve that 'Mr H. A. R. Philby . . . had betrayed the interests of this country or [to] identify him with the so-called "third-man", if indeed there was one.'[6]

The irony of White's appointment must be in MI5's belated attempt to help cover up the Crabb fiasco for SIS, and the fact that its hands had never been quite as clean in the affair as the Prime Minister had been led to believe.

White, the newcomer, found that he had to operate without a full-time Foreign Office Adviser as the Crabb affair had cost Michael Williams his job, although officially he was not to go until the end of October 1956; he began finding his feet by reading up all the current cases. Easton, of course, was preoccupied with his anti-Soviet activities, which meant that, because of a set of extraordinarily unusual circumstances, SIS was virtually rudderless and in the hands of a single shadowy, but influential, Whitehall figure, the Chairman of the JIC, Sir Patrick Dean.

Dean had been educated at Rugby and read Classics at Cambridge before switching to law. He had practised as a barrister before joining the Foreign Office in 1939 as a legal adviser. At the end of the war he had moved to the German Political Department, which he headed until 1950 when he served briefly in Rome, his only overseas post. He then returned to take up his appointment as a civilian instructor at the Imperial Defence College and moved to chair the JIC in 1953. As his deputy, Geoffrey McDermott, explained:

Dean . . . was responsible for all relations with the fighting and intelligence services. He was Chairman of the Joint Intelligence Committee which contained representatives, at major-general level, of the three services, MI5, MI6, the Joint Intelligence Bureau, and the Commonwealth Relations and Colonial Offices. The CIA representative attended some meetings. It reported to the Chiefs of Staff and to ministers, through the Permanent Under-Secretary, the late Sir Ivone Kirkpatrick.[7]

Dean was to play a key role in Operation STRAGGLE, but it should be remembered that he was merely the instrument of Eden's determination to 'knock Nasser off his perch'.[8] The Prime Minister was in poor helath, still not fully recovered from a complicated, second operation he had endured in Boston to restore his severed bile duct. Eden saw Nasser as a threat to world peace, with 'his thumb on our windpipe',[9] and was determined to be rid of him once and for all. He made no bones about how he wanted the job done. Anthony Nutting later recalled how, after the House of Commons debate on General Glubb's dismissal, Eden had angrily abandoned the usual Foreign Office euphemisms and demanded immediate action: 'What's all this nonsense about isolating Nasser or "neutralizing" him as you call it? I want him destroyed, can't you understand?'[10] From that moment onwards, SIS commenced work on a series of options to remove Nasser permanently from the scene. Inside SIS, responsibility for producing a plan of campaign fell to the CME, George Young, Cyril Rolo and Nigel Clive.

Young was a big, florid Scotsman from Dumfriesshire with strong right-wing political convictions encouraged by his Dutch East Indies wife Geryke, whom he had met while at university. In fact, he had studied languages at Giessen, Dijon, St Andrews and Yale. Before the war he had worked as a jouranlist on the *Glasgow Herald* and had joined SIS in 1943. At the end of hostilities, he had been appointed Head of Station in Vienna before returning two years later to take charge of R6, SIS's economic section. In 1951, he handed over R6 to Maurice Firth and became Middle East Controller where he took a firm grasp of the crisis in Iran. His solution for Suez was to be equally robust, helped in large measure by Rolo, a veteran of the campaign in the Western Desert whose first assignment for SIS had been in Austria immediately after the war. He had then been posted to Rome before taking over the Berlin Station in 1950. Two years later he was back at Broadway, on the Middle East desk, alongside Clive, a former SOE officer who had fought with the partisans in Greece before joining the Friends in 1945. After two years in Greece with Monty Woodhouse, he had made the brave but doomed attempt to establish an SIS office in Jerusalem. Afterwards he had been recalled to Broadway and then posted in 1950 to the Baghdad Station, where he stayed for the following three years. While Young ran the Cyprus end of CME, Clive and Rolo handled the London desk.

Geoffrey McDermott recalled the remarkable conditions of secrecy in which Operation HAMILCAR was planned:

> Our instructions, passed down by word of mouth from Eden, were both clear and unusual. First, only we three [Dean, Kirkpatrick and McDermott] were to be in on all the intelligence and planning. The three were to be reduced to two at a later stage. Other under-secretaries, for instance the experts on economic matters, Middle Eastern problems, or Anglo-American relations, were to be kept in the dark as far as possible. The task was to be given top priority as well as top secrecy. And the object of our plan was to topple Nasser, by force of course as this could not be done otherwise.[11]

While Eden was urging SIS to come up with firm proposals, the Israelis had persuaded the French to break the Tripartite Declaration of May 1950, which in effect had placed a ban on arms sales to the belligerents in the region. On 22 June 1956, Moshe Dayan, the Israeli Chief of Staff, and Shimon Peres, Director-General of the

Defence Ministry, flew to Paris for a clandestine meeting with senior members of the French administration, including the deputy Chief of Staff of the French air force, General Maurice Challe. The negotiations lasted three days, at the end of which Dayan's party had spent $80 million and obtained a promise of seventy-two Mystère 4 fighters, 200 AMX tanks and enough ammunition to arm the lot. The first shipment was delivered a month later to Haifa, where it was unloaded at night, with the entire dock area cordoned off, but word of it quickly reached the SIS Station in Tel Aviv and was passed on to London.

The first political moves that enabled STRAGGLE, SIS's plot to topple Nasser, to take place happened on Sunday 14 October, when the French acting Prime Minister, Albert Gazier, and General Challe flew into RAF Northolt and were driven straight to Chequers for an afternoon meeting with Eden and Nutting. Gazier was there because Prime Minister Christian Pineau was in New York attending the UN Security Council meeting which was trying to thrash out a compromise agreement for the continued Canal concession with Selwyn Lloyd and Dr Fawzi, Nasser's Foreign Minister.

No account of what took place at Chequers that afternoon has ever been published, but Nutting has been quoted as being 'appalled'[12] by what he witnessed. Since General Challe had participated in the Israeli arms deal and the Chequers meeting, and Eden had learned at least part of its terms, it is very likely that the Prime Minister suggested a combined move against Nasser, involving the Israelis too. In any event, Eden summoned Lloyd back to London on Monday 15 March and the next day, Tuesday, both men flew to Paris for talks with Pineau and his Foreign Minister, Guy Mollet. Once again, no record was made of the meeting, but from subsequent events it is clear that a scheme had been agreed, at least in outline, for recovering control of the Canal. The details, and the involvement of the Israelis in the plan, were left to a further secret conference held on 22 October at a private house near Sèvres, to the south-west of Paris, and organized by Pierre Boursicot, SDECE's Chief. On that afternoon, Lloyd and his private secretary, (Sir) Donald Logan, drove to RAF Hendon and returned to France with Patrick Dean to meet Peres, David Ben-Gurion and Dayan. The British party arrived at the French military airfield at Villacoublay around 7 p.m. and, during the course of the following five hours, negotiated with Pineau and Mollet over exactly how they would complete their 'uncomfortable task'.[13]

On the following day, Lloyd went to Downing Street to report the outcome of his visit and then despatched Logan to the Quai d'Orsay for further consultations with Gazier. However, no sooner had Logan arrived than Pineau decided to see Eden and Lloyd in London. Accordingly, a French plane flew the pair back to Hendon, and Pineau had a short meeting at Downing Street before dining with Lloyd at his official residence at 2 Carlton Gardens. Once again, no record was made of the exchanges, but it may well be that Pineau was urging action. With 250,000 French troops engaged in counter-insurgency operations in Tunisia and Algeria, he had good reason to be anxious. He may also have disclosed that SDECE had intercepted an Egyptian ship, the *Athos*, that very day, loaded with weapons and bound for the FLN rebels in Algeria. Once a Royal Navy minesweeper, the *Athos* had been chartered in Milan to carry a consignment of arms to Pakistan, but thanks to a tip from the Italian Secret Service, SIFAR (the *Servizio Informazioni Forzi Armate Republicane*), SDECE had intervened soon after the ship had called at Alexandria. The cargo of seventy tons of weapons, enough to equip 3,000 men, had been captured, providing incontrovertible proof of Nasser's support for the FLN.

Early on the morning of Wednesday 24 October, Eden briefed Dean on his meeting with Pineau and explained that a joint plan of action had been arrived at. Britain and France would invade Egypt if there was a major threat to the Canal. Dean was instructed to go to Paris and complete the deal. This he did, briefing Logan on the aircraft. The result was an astonishing, typewritten document which set out the role of each of the main participants in HAMILCAR, step by step: Israel was to launch an attack on Egypt and press ahead to reach the Suez Canal within twenty-four hours; Britain and France would issue an ultimatum requiring Egypt to accept temporary occupation of the Canal's key points; and a full-scale Anglo-French invasion would be launched 'within twelve hours' if no reply had been received. In an addendum to the main schedule, it was confirmed that Israel could take possession of the west shore of the Gulf of Aqaba and the strategically important islands in the Tiran Straits. In return, Israel promised not to attack Jordan, and Britain undertook to dissuade Jordan from joining the conflict. The final paragraph imposed secrecy on the agreement for ever. With Logan's consent Dean put his signature to the agreement, and champagne was passed around.

This document, typewritten in French and bearing three signatures, has never been seen because it disappeared soon after Dean delivered it to Eden. Instead of being congratulated for having finalized HAMILCAR, Dean was reprimanded for having put the details down on paper. Eden snatched Dean's copy from him and then insisted that the remaining carbon copies of what he termed 'the protocol' be burned immediately. Thus, the very next morning Dean and Logan made their way back to the Quai d'Orsay and asked Pineau to surrender his copy. Pineau dissembled, and then locked Dean and Logan in a reception-room for most of the rest of the day while he consulted with his advisers. When eventually they were escorted back to Pineau's office, there was bad news. The French Government had decided to keep its copy, and the third carbon was already on its way to Tel Aviv. Nor, indeed, was the French Government prepared to put pressure on the Israelis to destroy their version. Suddenly, Eden had been entrapped by his own scheme. Even if he wanted to pull out, he would be unable to do so. Both the Israelies and the French had absolute proof of his 'collusion'.

In fact, Eden was not to be deterred by the unspoken threat of exposure and lost none of his enthusiasm for the huge military undertaking, which had now acquired the operational codename of MUSKETEER and had been modified to take in the Canal. On 29 October, the Israelis attacked and swiftly took 6,000 Egyptian and Palestinian prisoners of war in the Gaza Strip for the loss of just four Israeli pilots. Almost the entire Egyptian air force was caught on the ground, with only thirty Ilyushins managing to escape to Luxor. Even those were pursued and, eventually, just a dozen survivors took refuge in Saudi Arabia. After the prescribed two days of fighting, the British and French Governments issued their pre-agreed ultimatum, but the Israelis were still more than seventy-five miles from the Canal. This meant that the Anglo-French demand required the beleaguered Egyptian forces to withdraw more than 125 miles! Not surpisingly, Nasser declined to co-operate. Therefore, at dusk on 31 November, Canberra and Valiant bombers attacked nine Egyptian airfields. Two days later, they returned to silence Radio Cairo's transmitters and, on 6 November, a combined force of 100,000 men, supported by 130 warships (including six aircraft carriers), 100 freighters and 20,000 vehicles, began disembarking around Alexandria.

Having played a major role in the planning of MUSKETEER through STRAGGLE, SIS's activites in the field were somewhat limited. A special Counter-Intelligence Unit, along the lines of those deployed on the Continent after the D-Day landings, was formed in Akrotiri, and Gerald Savage, SIME's former DSO in the Canal zone, was appointed to lead it. Its purpose was to prevent any Egyptian stay-behind network from reporting on Allied troop movements or sabotaging the invasion forces. It was also assigned the task of keeping an eye on the Soviet Consul in Port Said, Anatoli Tchikov, and taking possession of the Egyptian Governor of Port Said's office safe. An experienced safe-cracker had been recruited by SIS to blow it open, in the hope that it would contain valuable intelligence, but it proved to be empty.

The military were later to complain bitterly about the quality of intelligence available to them in the two staging points of Malta and Cyprus, but this was not due to any shortcomings on SIS's part. Indeed, the Friends had actually persuaded the CIA to show them aerial reconnaissance photographs of Egyptian airfields and other strategic targets, which had been taken by high-altitude U-2 spy planes on routine overflights. Although several CIA officers suspected what lay behind the requests, no advance warning of MUSKETEER leaked to the US State Department or the White House. The U-2 information was to be of critical importance, especially after 1 November when one of the RAF's photo-reconnaissance Canberras was attacked and crippled by MiGs at 45,000 feet over Syria.

One of the more well-known complaints about the inadequacy of the preparations for the Suez operation concerned the maps provided to the frontline troops by the intelligence staff. They contained a town called Talata, opposite the city of Ismailia, which, in fact, was non-existent. This crucial mistake had arisen because the signal stations along the banks of the Canal had been designated 1–2–3, which translated as *Wahad, Etnein* and *Talata*. Thus the third station, a single building, somehow achieved the status of a town on the maps. And, in spite of the U-2s' clandestine overflights, no one had noticed that the key Gamil Bridge outside Port Said, the only road link to the delta apart from the Canal's twin roads and railway, had been completed. As one eyewitness observed, 'It was startling that plans based on such a failure of intelligence could have been made by officers of an army that had so recently quit the Canal zone.'[14] There were also complaints about the grossly inflated assessments of Egyptian strength on the ground. 'This copybook plan was based on an intelligence picture which exaggerated Egyptian strength in about the same degree as it misread the terrain,' recalled a participant. In reality, it was a classic case of placing too much reliance on the value and accuracy of the U-2 photographs. Although the pictures taken were of excellent quality, and correctly identified the exact number of new Soviet-made planes dispersed on various runways, there was insufficient analysis to determine their readiness. It later turned out that there were not enough trained Egyptian crews to fly them.

MUSKETEER began well enough and the Anglo-French invasion force quelled what resistance it met in Port Said, causing heavy civilian casualties (with the loss of only twenty-six Allied troops). As the invasion force moved south towards Ismailia, more than 1,000 Egyptians were killed and complete success looked imminent. Then, suddenly, the picture changed and, after rather less than a day on Egyptian territory and within sight of its objectives, the army was ordered to stop its advance and give way to a UN peace-keeping force.

The conventional explanation for the swift cancellation of MUSKETEER was the sudden drain on Britain's gold reserves caused by the closure of the Canal by forty-seven Egyptian blockships. This meant buying oil from alternative sources, chiefly America and Venezuela, with catastrophic consequences for the economy. A dollar loan was required as an interim measure, which was refused by the United States unless there was an immediate ceasefire. The sterling collapse precipitated by the Chancellor's heavy purchase on the world financial markets in support of the pound is generally supposed to have forced Eden to abandon his Suez adventure. In reality, the decision to withdraw from Suez was prompted by a Soviet threat to intervene – with nuclear weapons if necessary. The warning from Moscow might have been ignored, except that GCHQ analysts reported a massive mobilization, apparently in conjunction with a Russian invasion of Hungary. According to further information given by GCHQ to the JIC, the Soviet Foreign Minister had promised the Egyptian Ambassador that Khrushchev would authorize a massive operation to repel the Anglo-French invaders. A full-scale war seemed imminent, and Dean was obliged to advise Eden that MUSKETEER should be terminated with immediate effect.

The entire episode proved an embarrassing diplomatic and military defeat for Eden, who was to resign as Prime Minister early in the New Year. He was always to claim that 'there was not foreknowledge that Israel would attack Egypt',[15] and he was loyally supported by Selwyn Lloyd, who confirmed that 'there was no prior agreement between us'[16] when challenged on the collusion. But neither statement was true, and both the French and the Israelis actually possessed the written proof bearing Dean's signature. Eden did not need to be told the implications of the document's existence and he could hardly dissociate himself from Dean if the latter's true position as Chairman of the JIC was ever disclosed. Of course the French and Israeli administrations had their own reasons for concealing the truth about STRAGGLE, but what Prime Minister would wish to continue in office as a hostage of SDECE or even of Mossad? Eden could rely on Dean and Bridges to keep silent and destroy the incriminating evidence of his deception, and he could depend on others, like Sir Anthony Nutting, to remain loyal, but he knew that he could not take the risk with the other participants in the plan.

While Eden could escape the political fallout by pleading ill-health and retreating to Ian Fleming's Jamaican home for a rest, SIS had to suffer further humiliation. Swinburn, Zarb and the rest of the ANA's network, who had languished in Cairo's Barage Prison throughout the military activity, were finally put on trial in May the following year. Eight Britons were charged with espionage including Swinburn, Zarb, Charles Pittuck and John Stanley (the local representative of the Prudential Insurance Company, who had been arrested a week later); the other four – Alexander Reynolds, George Sweet, John MacGlashan and George Roe – were tried *in absentia*. In addition, there were eleven Egyptian defendants and the Yugoslav *émigré*, Colonel Gregorivitch.

The trial was unusual in that as soon as it opened the defence made an application to the judge for the evidence to be heard *in camera*. The request was refused, and lengthy confessions from Swinburn and Zarb were read to the court. The prosecution also produced all the documents seized in Swinburn's apartment, which were more than enough to convict him and his sources. Thanks to the wealth of compromising material recovered, the Mukhabarat really got to the bottom of ANA's organization. This became clear when one of the Egyptian investigators correctly identified 'the British Embassy's intelligence officer, Oliver St John',[17] as having been SIS's mastermind behind the network. In fact, St John had been a colonial civil servant before joining the Friends in 1948 and, thereafter, had been exactly what the Egyptians claimed him to be: SIS's Head of Station in Cairo.

Because Britain still had no diplomatic links with Egypt there were no diplomatic representatives at the trial, but there were two unofficial observers present to monitor the proceedings: Colonel Cyril Banks, the Independent MP for Pudsey, and (Lord) Edmund Davies, then the Recorder of Cardiff. The defence lawyers put forward a whole range of arguments for their clients. Pittuck insisted that, although he had been recruited by Gove and introduced to Swinburn, he had not been given an opportunity to engage in espionage; Zarb claimed he had merely passed on information from Youssef Megali Hanna; Sayed Amin Mahmoud said that the ten sub-agents referred to in his reports were completely fictitious, having been invented to justify his fraudulent expenses; and Abdelmalik protested that his economic assessments were nothing more than legitimate news agency articles. At the end of the trial in July 1957, Swinburn was sentenced to five years' hard labour and Zarb to ten years.

Of the Egyptians, Sayed Amin Mahmoud was sentenced to death, with his son, the naval officer, receiving twenty-five years, along with Salah Hassan Bedeir and Youssef Megali Hanna. The detective, Massif Morkos Mikhail, got fifteen years and a fine of $2,000. Youssef Bedeir was given ten years, as was Alexander Reynolds, although he had already returned to England. Abdelmalik, Ebeid, Attiya and Rewish were also sentenced to shorter terms of imprisonment. Pittuck, Stanley, Mac-Glashan, Roe and el-Kashef were all acquitted. Colonel Gregorivitch was also freed, only to be expelled as soon as the verdicts were announced.

The trial proved to be a profound embarrassment to SIS, although some of the claims made by the prosecution – for example, the suggestion that Swinburn's spy-ring had been operating for more than fourteen years – were obviously fanciful in the extreme. No doubt Mahmoud's defence that he had invented ten notional agents and had constructed their reports, 'webs of falsehood and imagination'[18] from newspaper stories, in order to defraud Swinburn and Gove must have given someone at Broadway cause for thought, but it did not impress the judge. Mahmoud was sentenced to hang anyway.

Undeterred by these events, SIS was still determined to get rid of Nasser and replace him with a more sympathetic regime. Its intended instrument was Squadron-Leader Assam el-Din Kahmoud Khalil, Chief of Intelligence for the Egyptian air force. Khalil had been recruited by an SIS contact, Hussein Khayri, who had himself been Farouk's Deputy Director of Military Intelligence until Neguib's coup. Based in Rome, and related to Farouk, Khayri had cultivated Khalil for SIS and introduced him to two case officers, Major John Farmer MC and David Crichton. Farmer had been in Rome since October 1952 and occasionally flew to Beirut for meetings with Khalil. Officially Crichton, who had previously served in Belgrade and Singapore, was still the accredited British Consul in Alexandria, a cover post he had held since June 1955. Operating from Munich, Crichton's scheme was to assassinate Nasser and replace him with a royalist government led by Mortada el-Maraji Pasha, Farouk's former Minister of the Interior. Khalil had apparently been an enthusiastic participant in the plot and had himself recruited his brother-in-law, Farid Sharif Shaker, as a courier. However, the affair came to an abrupt end on 23 December 1957, when Nasser denounced what he termed the 'restoration' plot in a speech and revealed enough inside information to suggest that Khalil had betrayed the entire enterprise at a very early stage. This was confirmed when Khalil was decorated by Nasser. A military tribunal tried the plotters in their absence in April 1958 and sentenced el-Maraji Pasha and Khayri to life imprisonment. Three others implicated received fifteen years' hard labour.

The entire exercise cost SIS some £162,500 in expenses and bribes paid to Khalil in Rome and Beirut for his nonexistent network. Once again, Nasser had survived an SIS-inspired coup and, contrary to all expectations, was destined to die a natural death.

The collapse of the ANA front, Operation MUSKETEER and the so-called restoration plot, combined with the Buster Crabb incident, left 1956 as one of the least memorable years in SIS's post-war history. The Friends's operations in the Middle East were severely compromised, and the organization itself handicapped by changes at the top. The loss of the ANA was also a setback, forcing the Middle East Controller to rethink his strategy without an Egyptian base of operations. In fact, the Cairo Station was not to be reopened until 1961, when diplomatic relations were resumed.

The SIS officers directly involved in MUSKETEER had mixed fortunes. Jack Easton took a regular diplomatic post in 1958, having accepted reluctantly that being only fourteen months younger than Dick White he would never succeed him as CSS. George Young took over as Vice-Chief, but only stayed until 1961 when, following a clash of personalities with his new Chief, he joined the merchant bankers Kleinwort Benson in the City of London. Norman Darbyshire accepted a two-year tour of duty at the Geneva Station before returning to the Middle East as Head of Station in Bahrain. Cyril Rolo went to Vienna as Head of Station in 1957 and Nigel Clive went to Tunis in the same capacity the following year. The new Controller was Dickie Franks, recently returned from the Tehran Station, and his deputy, Edward de Haan, moved from

Iran to Berne. And what of SIS's team in Egypt immediately before the evacuation? The Head of Station in Cairo was switched to Berlin; Craig Smellie, who had run the sub-station in Alexandria under Vice-Consular cover, was transferred temporarily to Iraq to relieve Stephen de Mowbray before being recalled to London; while Alexis Forter, SIS's ace agent-runner in Port Said, was withdrawn to Broadway and then posted to Baghdad. In 1957, de Mowbray was removed from the scene by a posting to Montevideo, one of SIS's diminishing South American stations. John Farmer went to Vienna in November 1959 and David Crichton was sent to the United States.

The end of the Suez crisis marked a turning-point for SIS. The incoming Prime Minister, Harold Macmillan, had already expressed his distaste for espionage, preferring in contrast to Eden not to know about SIS's illicit activities. However, as a result of the new, supposedly foolproof, system of official clearances for all covert operations, as recommended by Lord Bridges in his second review of the Buster Crabb affair, he had to be informed in advance of any risky undertakings. These also had to be approved formally by the new Foreign Office Adviser, Geoffrey McDermott. Paradoxically, the rules had not prevented MUSKETEER from being launched because the guidelines took no account of a Prime Minister and a Chairman of the JIC conspiring together to prevent the rest of the Foreign Office from learning exactly what they were contemplating. Neither Sir Patrick Dean nor the Permanent Under-Secretary, Sir Ivone Kirkpatrick, had allowed Michael Williams to know what they had in mind and he had been sent on an extended holiday in August just as the tension was rising. His place had been taken, nominally, by Sir Patrick Reilly, who was also not let into the secret. Kirkpatrick retired from the Foreign Office early in the New Year of 1957, and Dean eventually went to the United Nations and then to Washington as British Ambassador. His involvement in the Suez affair effectively prevented him from ever achieving his ambition of becoming Permanent

Under-Secretary. The Labour Party never discovered the full story of Eden's extraordinary behaviour, but it was realized that Dean must have played a key role in the affair and so his career was deliberately blocked. The scale of the deception practised upon the Foreign Office and other Whitehall insiders is breathtaking, even some thirty years after the event. Only a handful have been in a position to learn the complete story, and none have given their version of events. Sir Evelyn Shuckburgh, for example, recalls hearing from another senior diplomat 'that he, too, thought something was going on which the FO did not know much about, but we were not prepared for what occurred'.[19]

Quite why Eden should have behaved as he did has never been explained. Nutting thought his medical condition might have affected him, but another possibility is the confidence Eden had developed for secret intelligence. During the war years he had built up a marvellous relationship with Menzies, who had almost been his contemporary at Eton. They had much in common: both had been decorated with the Military Cross during the First World War in France, where both had served on the General Staff. They mixed in the same social circles and were both inveterate womanizers. It may well be that Eden, having been beguiled by SIS's remarkable achievements during the war, assumed that Menzies's successors would be capable of performing the same feats. If so, the Crabb affair must have been a disheartening experience. Certainly, Churchill had never endured the embarrassing experience of defending an SIS blunder on the floor of the House of Commons. Maybe, knowing from memory what the Friends had achieved in the past, he thought that Dean could get them to rid the world of Nasser. Certainly he was mistaken and, having brought the Allies to the brink of war, he paid the penalty. The excuse for his resignation was his medical condition, and his biographer, Robert Rhodes James, was to state that Eden 'had lost his health and the premiership as a direct result of a medical mistake'.[20] In fact, Eden was to live for a further twenty years, until January 1977.

Dick White's first two years at Broadway were marked by a succession of crises. Virtually his last task as Director-General of MI5 had been to handle the public controversy over Philby, and to advise the Government that there was not sufficient evidence to show that he had been disloyal. Then, in his new job, he had coped with the Crabb fall-out and the aftermath of Suez. His immediate task was to restore the damaged credibility of the Friends and rebuild the special relationship with Washington. He was also to supervise an extraordinary purge of the organization, in a vain attempt to cleanse it of Soviet moles, and was reluctantly to come to the conclusion that SIS had been deeply penetrated at a very high level.

10

THE PENKOVSKY DEFECTION

'There is serious, unresolved evidence that Colonel
Penkovsky was planted on Western intelligence by the
KGB.'

Anatoli Golitsyn, *New Lies for Old*[1]

'Nobody knows exactly when or exactly why the KGB first
became supicious of Colonel Oleg Penkovsky. . . .'

Greville Wynne, *The Man from Odessa*[2]

'It is a misuse of words to say that SIS ran Penkovsky. It did
so but, in a very special sense, he ran himself.'

Anthony Verrier, *Through the Looking Glass*[3]

Sir Dick White initiated numerous changes into the
Friends during his twelve years as CSS; in particular, he
was to usher into the organization 'line management', or
a more obvious chain of responsibility and command.
There was little overt criticism, for he possessed a full
mandate from Eden to make whatever changes were
necessary and was given a free rein by his successor at 10
Downing Street, Macmillan. In any event, most of
White's reforms were recognized as long overdue. Whatever opposition there may have been to him, it was
certainly very muted, perhaps because of the absence of
any exceptionally influential old-timers at Broadway, figures like David Footman (who had left SIS to take up an
academic post at St Antony's College, Oxford, in 1953);

Dick Ellis (who had retired to Australia in the same year); Valentine Vivian (who had retired in 1951); Maurice Jeffes (who died in November 1954); Cuthbert Bowlby (who retired in 1955); Frank Slocum (who went to Oslo in 1954); and Harry Carr (who was appointed to Copenhagen in 1955). The necessity to fill senior posts overseas, away from headquarters, ensured that there was never a chance for cabals to form, as had been so common in MI5, and gave the Chief useful opportunities to move potential troublemakers a satisfactory distance away from the centre. This was not entirely a matter of expediency, or office politics, but a genuine operational necessity to give everyone field experience at a station and then to move them on after the regular two-year stint so as to avoid blowing their cover. Thus, there were sound reasons for exploiting the system to the full.

Many of the old-timers with wartime SIS experience had gone, as had some of the SOE high-flyers like Robin Brook, who had been drafted in immediately after the war. The senior management was in the hands of Jack Easton, who was soon to leave, along with John Teague; George Young, who had only a short time to serve; and the new generation of field operators like James Fulton, Dickie Franks, Nigel Clive and John Bruce Lockhart. Liaison with the CIA, which for the past three years had been in the hands of Leslie Mitchell, a veteran of the 'Shetland bus'[4] ferry service across the North Sea to Nazi-occupied Norway, went to Machlachlan Silverwood-Cope in January 1956 when Mitchell was switched to Berne. In fact, Silverwood-Cope had already spent five months in Washington fulfilling the same role in August 1951, when he had been sent as a replacement for Philby who had been recalled in the aftermath of the Burgess and Maclean defections. Up until that time Silverwood-Cope had run the Stockholm Station; in January 1952, he had been transferred back to London, leaving his post to John Bruce Lockhart. Silverwood-Cope had then been sent to Tokyo in November, a station he was to head for the next three years.

The departure of the old-timers ensured that Broadway shed its time-honoured image of cosmopolitan gentlemen amateurs, many with service backgrounds, stabilized by boffins brought in from the academic world. The previous generation had had few concerns about career prospects, because of family money to fall back on, and could almost automatically draw on a fund of wartime goodwill to ease a difficult situation or open the right door. But the new guard were in the mould of White, not Menzies. None had known the pre-war conditions of financial austerity imposed by a doubting Treasury; few had any experience of anti-Bolshevik intrigues. The new intake were university graduates recommended to intelligence because they had demonstrated an aptitude for the work while doing their compulsory military service. Virtually all had completed their apprenticeship in the BCCG. A tiny handful of legendary relics of an age past, like Edward Boxshall, the pre-war Head of Station in Bucharest, remained to be seen shuffling down corridors because of some obscure knowledge that made them indispensable. For the greater part though, they had given way to their rivals from SOE and had accepted SIS as an adjunct of the civil service, complete with career prospects, two-year tours of station duty overseas and a pension scheme. Foreign accents were out and the technocrats were in.

On the world scene, under Menzies and Sinclair, SIS had become embroiled in a series of what might be termed rearguard actions to defend what was left of the empire. Palestine, Malaya, Cyprus and Suez had all been attempts, with varying degrees of success, to stave off the inevitable and, as far as the Soviet Union was concerned, had been mere side-shows. Covert operations such as those launched in Albania and the Baltic had floundered, and very little had been achieved in the technical field following the enforced termination of the telephone-tapping operations in Vienna and Berlin. Indeed, if the Hungarian uprising and the unrest in East Germany were anything to go by, SIS had missed some important opportunities by being distracted elsewhere. Broadway's pre-occupation with Operation STRAGGLE had effectively prevented any profitable manipulation of the growing anti-Soviet resentment felt in the satellite countries of the Eastern Bloc. Clearly it was time for SIS to go on to the offensive. However, apart from the occasional technical projects against individual Soviet diplomatic missions, there had not been any real prospect of a breakthrough. That depressing status quo altered late in 1960.

Certainly, SIS's performance when fielded against the Soviets in the post-war era had been less than promising. Of the two significant, high-grade Soviet defectors received, Colonels Tasoev and Tokaev, the former had changed his mind within hours of his arrival in London. There had been a couple of low-level turncoats from the Soviet occupation forces in Vienna and Berlin, but they had only been able to supply relatively unimportant material with a short 'shelf-life', such as the identities of intelligence personnel operating undercover locally. Since Tokaev's memorable escape from Berlin in 1948, SIS had failed to attract a single worthwhile defector. On at least three occasions when it looked rather as though a recruitment had gone according to plan, the schemes had misfired. Philby's subsequent behaviour provided an eloquent explanation for at least the first; the second was to remain unexplained for some years to come.

The abortive defection of Konstantin Volkov had taken place back in September 1945, when the NKVD major had made contact with the British Consulate in Istanbul. Volkov had offered to switch sides and betray several Soviet moles in Britain in return for a financially secure future. The proposal had ended up on Philby's desk at Broadway, and by the time he had made his way to Turkey to complete the arrangements Volkov had disappeared, apparently having been forcibly returned to Russia. Philby's report on the incident blamed poor security in the local station and suggested that an indiscretion on an open telephone line may have tipped off the other side. In reality, of course, Philby must have alerted his own London-based case officer to the danger long before he had set out to meet Volkov.

There was a similar episode the following year, when a Soviet lieutenant named Vladimir Skripkin had approached a British naval attaché in the Far East with a view to defecting. The Soviet intended to return to Moscow to collect his wife and then make his escape with her on his next overseas assignment. The Naval Intelligence Division had routinely passed the matter on to the Friends, but Skripkin never turned up in the West. The reason was later disclosed by yet another defector, a KGB lieutenant-colonel named Yuri Rastvorov, who had made contact with another British naval attaché, Commander Michael Tufnell RN DSC, in Tokyo, late in 1953, but who had eventually opted to go to the CIA. During his subsequent debriefing, Rastvorov alleged that Skripkin had been trapped in Moscow by the KGB, which had sent two counter-intelligence experts around to his apartment masquerading as SIS officers from the Moscow Station. Skripkin had accepted them as genuine, and, in so doing, had inadvertently incriminated himself. He had promptly been arrested and liquidated. The affair, however, had received wide circulation in Soviet intelligence circles and had proved a powerful deterrent to those contemplating defection. According to Rastvorov, it was common knowledge that both the British services, MI5 and SIS, were thoroughly compromised. Judging by the experience of Volkov and Skripkin, there was good reason to suspect hostile penetration of the Friends. Indeed, Rastvorov's motive for changing his mind about defecting to the British in January 1954 was his declared fear of betrayal. The deal he had negotiated had stipulated resettlement and debriefing in Australia, and emphatically not in a British colony; it was only when he realized that his RAF transport had filed a flight plan from Tokyo to Singapore that he had fled to the US Embassy. He later told the CIA that he had anticipated being kidnapped in Singapore.

In spite of Rastvorov's testimony, which was entirely hearsay, SIS did not immediately launch a molehunt to investigate his claims. After all, there was only his word for it that the KGB had played the charade on Skripkin in Moscow; there was every chance that Skripkin had somehow betrayed himself. As for Volkov, the incident was not recognized for what it was, a manifestation of Philby's treachery, until January 1963 when he was persuaded to write a confession. Thus, in 1960, when the Moscow Station got the offer of a defector-in-place, it responded with enthusiasm. It was both an opportunity to make up for lost ground and a real chance to prove that the organization was free from hostile penetration. After all, a successful case was the best possible proof of the integrity of an intelligence service's security.

The offer came from Lieutenant-Colonel Oleg Penkovsky, a senior GRU officer who had already made two unsuccessful approaches to the CIA and the Canadians. His first attempt, to the US Embassy in Moscow, had been rejected on the advice of the CIA's counter-intelligence branch as a blatant provocation. Penkovsky had been flagged as a GRU officer some years earlier when he had served in Turkey as a military attaché after the war, but had not taken the opportunity then to make any moves. However, apparently undeterred, he then made a bid to supply information to the Royal Canadian Mounted Police through a Canadian named Oliver Van Vleit, who had close connections with the Department of External Affairs. This, too, had been turned down; in desperation he turned to the SIS Station at the British Embassy, which at that time was headed by Roderick (Ruari) Chisholm, a Russian-speaking graduate of St Catherine's College, Cambridge, who had taken over the Moscow Station in May 1960, following four years in Berlin and two in Singapore. While serving in the army after the war, Chisholm had spent nearly two years in Berlin as a liaison officer with the Soviet forces.

The decision to post Chisholm into the lion's den was an interesting change in policy because previous Heads of Station had been 'blown' almost as soon as they had arrived. One of his predecessors, for example, had run the Czech desk at Broadway while Philby had still been active, so his cover had been almost completely superfluous. As for running or recruiting agents in Moscow, SIS had long since given up trying because of the impossibly hostile environment. KGB surveillance was so comprehensive that even the most casual social contacts with local residents automatically precipitated unwelcome activity. Routine fieldcraft, such as conducting surveys for dead-letter drops and suitable clandestine meeting-places, was a complete waste of time. There was a KGB informer on virtually every street corner and foreigners were far too conspicuous ever to lose their watchers by taking the kind of counter-surveillance measures that invariably worked in Western cities. No sooner was one watcher team shaken off, than another appeared in its place. In addition, the movements of all diplomats were restricted, so that there were few opportunities to engage in large-scale decoy tactics to confound the opposition. Blanket technical coverage of all the telephones, diplomatic premises, hotels and apartment blocks also made life difficult for the intelligence officer used to emptying and replenishing dead-letter drops or even holding the occasional rendezvous with an agent. In truth, the KGB was never short of resources on its own territory and used its advantage to the full. Instead of engaging in the usual liaison and reporting duties normally undertaken by an SIS station, the Friends in Moscow were obliged to confine themselves to giving aid and comfort to the steady stream of English businessmen compromised in honey-traps, and processing the visa applications made by Soviet citizens. After several false starts, the CIA Station in Moscow had also concluded that running agents in the Soviet capital was an unprofitable business: Its last good case, a GRU major named Piotr Popov, had been arrested in October 1959 while in the act of passing a surreptitious message to his case officer. The American had claimed his right to diplomatic immunity and had been released, but his agent had not been so lucky: he had been thrown live into a furnace in front of an audience of his GRU colleagues.

Penkovsky's fortuitous appearance in 1960 was particularly welcome because, as well as being highly placed, he held out the promise of relatively safe personal contact with an SIS case officer. The logistics of arranging a secret rendezvous in Moscow were impossibly dangerous, but Penkovsky's job on the State Committee for Scientific Co-ordination took him abroad quite regularly. Thus, it was reckoned that if direct contact with Penkovsky was limited to meetings held on his overseas trips, there was a good chance that he might be run for some time. Accordingly, one of SIS's stable of businessmen, the 'honourable correspondents' who had volunteered to undertake occasional missions for the Friends, was assigned the task of acting as a cut-out between Penkovsky and SIS until a visit to London could be set up. These individuals were held in deep contempt by Philby. He was later to recall:

> There are, of course, British residents abroad, businessmen, journalists and so on, who are prepared to stick their necks out. There was a Swinburne [*sic*] and a Wynne. But these are usually the lesser fry and their potentialities are limited. The big men, with their big potentialities, are usually unhelpful. They have too much to lose; they have duties to themselves, to their families; they even have duties to their damned shareholders. They would usually agree to pass on anything that 'came their way' – invariably valueless gossip. But patriotism was not enough to induce them to take the risks involved in the systematic search for intelligence.[5]

The agent chosen to link up with Penkovsky was Greville Wynne, an engineer who ran his own small export agency from his home in Chelsea. He had a useful portfolio of client companies whom he represented at trade exhibitions abroad, including one or two firms who had agreed to appoint Wynne to work on their behalf after a discreet approach to the chairman from Wynne's case officer, Dickie Franks. Wynne's business was ideal cover and also enabled SIS to monitor the activities of other British salesmen working regularly behind the Iron Curtain. It was during one of Wynne's visits to Moscow, in December 1960, that he introduced himself to Penkovsky on the pretext of finalizing the details of an official Soviet trade delegation tour of England scheduled for the following year.

The Russian group was to be led by Penkovsky, and elaborate preparations were made to debrief him without arousing the suspicion of the ubiquitous KGB security officer who invariably accompanied all such groups. When the Russian party checked into the Mount Royal Hotel at Marble Arch on 20 April 1961, SIS had already taken over a large suite on the floor above and installed all the necessary recording equipment. On five separate occasions Penkovsky slipped away from his colleagues and made his way upstairs to be debriefed by George Kisevalter, the CIA officer assigned to the case, who was himself Russian in origin, and Harold Shergold, his contact in the Friends. Shergold had been educated at St Edmund Hall, Oxford, and Corpus Christi, Cambridge, and, like Dick White, had become a schoolmaster. In 1940, after three years' teaching at Cheltenham Grammar School, he had joined up with the Hampshire Regiment and had switched to the Intelligence Corps within a year. After a tour of duty with SIME, Shergold had followed many of his colleagues into the Friends and had spent seven years running agents in Germany. Now he was to organize one of SIS's most important agent operations ever.

Penkovsky made a second visit to London in July 1961 and was taken to two safe-houses: a flat in Coleherne Court, in west London, and a borrowed country house. There he was introduced briefly to Dick White, and they chatted for about ten minutes. Although Penkovsky never knew his name, he was later to recall that 'I guessed he was the chief by the behaviour of the others in the room'.[6] He also met Janet Chisholm, Ruari's wife, who was to act as his cut-out in Moscow. The arrangements made for exchanging messages were complicated, but demonstrated the care needed to prevent attracting the KGB's attention in Moscow. Whenever Penkovsky had something to report, he was to telephone a local number on a Monday morning and hang up after an agreed number of rings. The signal would be received by Lieutenant-Commander John Varley RN, the British Assistant Naval Attaché, who would relay Penkovsky's wish for a meeting to the Head of Station, or his secretary, Felicity Stuart. Janet Chisholm would then go to a prearranged, innocuous rendezvous, where Penkovsky would give one of the Chisholm children a box of sweets containing a batch of exposed Minox microfilms. This sophisticated system avoided the kind of direct contact between Ruari Chisholm and Penkovsky that might have jeopardized them. The box of sweets and an envelope containing a picture of Janet Chisholm with her son and two daughters had been handed over to Wynne by Chisholm in Moscow; Wynne had then given them to Penkovsky in the cloakroom of the Bolshoi Theatre's restaurant while apparently attending a French trade fair in the Soviet capital.

Later in 1961, after his two trips to London, Penkovsky went on an official visit to Paris and was met at the airport by Wynne, to whom he handed fifteen rolls of film. He then attended a debriefing session at two safe-houses arranged by the CIA Station Chief, Al Ulmer. He also took in all the usual tourist sights with Wynne, including Versailles and the shows at the Moulin Rouge and the Lido.

In spite of initial scepticism on the part of the CIA, Penkovsky was quickly recognized as a truly extraordinary source. His unique value was two fold: his willingness to continue working as an agent, instead of opting to become a defector, escaping abroad; and his access to vital, top-level Soviet secrets. Penkovsky's determination to remain in place was probably influenced by family considerations: his daughter was at school in Moscow and his wife was pregnant, making it impossible for her to accompany him abroad.

Penkovsky's fortuitous appearance was extremely significant in political terms because the operation was being conducted during a period of unprecedented international tension, with the Berlin Wall suddenly being erected virtually overnight on 12 August 1961. Penkovsky was able to provide an insider's view of the Politburo's decision-making processes and offer his own opinions on particular events. He was also exceptionally well informed about Soviet strategic forces through a close family friend, Marshal Varentsov, who happened to command all the Soviet missile troops and artillery. Thanks to Varentsov's apparent indiscretion, Penkovsky supplied authentic intelligence about rocket strengths and other crucial matters – information that had been denied to the West since May 1960, when President Eisenhower had been forced to curtail all future U-2 overflights following the loss of the American pilot Gary Powers. Without aerial reconnaissance photographs and poor satellite imagery, the West had been left virtually blind in terms of assessing the deployment of Soviet ballistic missiles. Penkovsky's information, codenamed ARNIKA, appeared to be both genuine and timely.

When Penkovsky returned to Moscow after his third trip overseas in 1961, his management was shared between Chisholm and Hugh Montgomery, an American case officer assigned by the local CIA Station Chief. Much the same routine was followed. When arranging to fill an agreed dead-letter drop, Penkovsky would telephone Captain Alexis Davison, the US Assistant Air Attaché, who would empty the cache left in the prearranged hiding-place.

These precautions worked well into the summer of 1962, when Penkovsky began to show the strain of his double life. At his last rendezvous with Wynne, held at the Peking Restaurant in July, he insisted that he had detected KGB surveillance and was increasingly nervous about the new case officers scheduled to take over from Chisholm and Montgomery. In August the Chisholms were to be replaced by Gervase Cowell, and Montgomery was due a stint at headquarters before moving to Rome. Chisholm returned to Broadway for two years before going back into the field, returning to Singapore in 1964. His replacement, Gervase Cowell, had joined SIS in 1951 (and had, therefore, never come into contact with Philby), followed by three years in Germany under BCCG cover. In 1958, he had gone to Amman for a two-year tour. His new task in Moscow was to keep Penkovsky out of the clutches of the KGB, but by the time he took over that was a forlorn hope.

Penkovsky's new CIA case officer was Rodney W. Carlson, listed at the US Embassy as an assistant agricultural attaché. He managed to arrange three meetings with his agent, all at diplomatic receptions, but both men were uneasy. Penkovsky's claim to have spotted KGB surveillance had caused considerable disquiet and, as an added security measure, it had been agreed that Penkovsky should leave a mark on a particular lamppost on Kutuzovsky Prospekt if he had filled his dead-letter drop at 5 Pushkin Street. This would avoid fruitless visits to the spot, which was actually a small box suspended on a wire behind a radiator in a doorway just off an alley. Meanwhile, Peter Deriabin, a KGB officer who had defected in Vienna in 1954, was invited to review the case files at the CIA's headquarters and assess whether Penkovsky's fears seemed justified.[7] He was still considering the matter when, on 22 October, Carlson received his agent's telephone signal. He promptly sent Captain Davison round to Kutuzovsky Prospekt to check the lamppost and, having had that confirmation, assigned a young secretarial assistant, Richard C. Jacob, to empty the dead-letter drop in Pushkin Street. No sooner had Jacob reached behind the radiator than he was arrested by KGB officials. Jacob was expelled and Carlson left the country before he could be declared *persona non grata*.

Evidently Penkovsky was in serious trouble, but contingency plans had been made to allow him to escape to the West. Carlson had given him a forged Soviet identity card, and there was an outside chance that he might be able to make his way to Budapest, where Wynne was taking his new mobile exhibition, essentially a caravan custom-built to demonstrate British engineering equipment. Wynne travelled to Romania from Vienna and then drove into Hungary on 31 October. However, instead of finding Penkovsky, he was arrested by the Hungarian security police on 2 November and shipped straight to the Lubyanka Prison in Moscow. The announcement of his arrest was made four days later, which was followed on 11 December by a statement describing Penkovsky's arrest. An article in *Pravda* on 16 December, entitled 'Caught Red-Handed', confirmed the KBG's intervention and even carried a photograph of the hapless Captain Davison checking the lamppost in Kutuzovsky Prospekt for Penkovsky's signal. It was later disclosed that a secret compartment had been found hidden inside Penkovsky's desk at home and that a Sanyo shortwave radio, three Minox cameras and other espionage paraphernalia had been recovered.

The end of the operation was a devastatingly bitter blow for both SIS and the CIA. The two organizations had achieved an unprecedented level of co-operation, with Maurice Oldfield, as Head of Station in Washington since 1960, managing to rebuild much of the mutual trust that had been so effectively undermined by one of his predecessors, Philby. Penkovsky had become a symbol of the CIA and SIS's joint approach to the Soviet challenge. Now the whole undertaking was suddenly placed in jeopardy, but it could hardly be said that the development was unexpected. Penkovsky had been under appalling strain and, towards the end, had been close to reckless in his attempts to communicate with his case officers at diplomatic receptions. He had made contact with Carlson three times in such circumstances and had used an ingeniously-converted container of Harpic lavatory cleanser at the British Embassy to keep in touch with Gervase and Pamela Cowell. When invited to functions at the Embassy, he would slip into the toilet and place his exposed Minox microfilms into the tin tube of disinfectant, ready for one of the Cowells to collect it later. Penkovsky had certainly acknowledged KGB surveillance, but none of his handlers had been able to ascertain whether this was understandable paranoia, or if he really had good reason to believe that he had come under suspicion. From SIS's viewpoint, the only remaining matter was to determine exactly when Penkovsky had been compromised and establish whether any of his last messages had been written under the KGB's control. This damage limitation exercise was to prove extremely controversial, with Harold Shergold for one remaining insistent that Penkovsky had never been operated as a conduit for disinformation, even at the close.

Apart from expelling those case officers who had not already left Moscow, the KGB made little response to the affair, except for a rather heavy-handed attempt in March 1963 to honeytrap Ivor Rowsell, a transport clerk at the British Embassy who had moved into John Varley's flat after the latter's departure the previous June. Rowsell reported the incident immediately and was withdrawn without delay.

The four-day trial of Penkovsky and Wynne opened in Moscow early in May the following year, with both men pleading guilty to various charges of treason and espionage. Evidently Penkovsky, who resembled something of a zombie in the dock, had given an extremely detailed confession to the KGB; in his testimony on the first day he said that over a period he had passed more than a hundred rolls of film, each with fifty exposures, to his Western contacts. He described having met Janet Chisholm nine times and said that fifteen of the films had been handed directly to Wynne. Throughout this evidence the prosecutor turned constantly to Wynne for his confirmation, which he gave. On a couple of occasions there were some odd exchanges between the two defendants, each accusing the other of misleading the court. For example, Penkovsky insisted that Wynne had asked him to write a biographical account of himself 'for British intelligence', but this was denied by Wynne, who asserted that 'Penkovsky's testimony is not correct'.[8] This was obviously part of Wynne's determined effort to present himself as an unwitting accomplice in Penkovsky's treachery rather than as a willing instrument of British intelligence.

On the following day, 8 May, Wynne took over as the principal witness and gave his version of events. He described himself as an ordinary businessman who had visited Moscow five times between December 1960 and July 1962, and told of his encounters with Chisholm at the Embassy. According to Wynne, he had been approached by Penkovsky in April 1961 (and not the previous December) with a request to be put in touch with the authorities in London. He claimed that a security officer named Hartley, who had worked for one of his client engineering companies, had introduced him to 'Ackroyd of the Foreign Office. I have since heard that he was a member of the British Intelligence'. After lunch at a restaurant, Ackroyd had introduced a certain Roger King to Wynne, and later a third person, their chief, who had completed the recruitment. 'I thought they were from the Foreign Office and very trustworthy gentlemen,' said Wynne. He had received 'assurances from King's and Ackroyd's chief, a very powerful figure, that this was nothing to do with espionage'. Wynne claimed to have been threatened by King:

> He said that my business would suffer if I did not help and they would make things very difficult for me in England. . . . I was very concerned because, knowing official people, it is quite possible that they would pick up the telephone and speak to the directors of my companies, and just one little word might give a bad impression of me. . . . I did not want to risk that. I have spent my life building up my own business.

Asked whether he had been deceived by his fellow countrymen, Wynne replied, 'Yes, indeed they did. That is why I am here. A thousand miles from here there are my own people – responsible people – who have landed me in this dock.'⁹

Wynne's claim to have worked in this 'dirty business' under duress, having been 'deceived, threatened and blackmailed', earned him an eight-year prison term, five to be spent in a labour camp, while Penkovsky received a death sentence, confiscation of his property and deprivation of his military rank. The announcement of Penkovsky's execution by firing squad was made on 16 May, but this was far from the end of the Penkovsky affair. The Cowells were declared *personae non gratae*, as were the remaining CIA personnel named during the trial. In April 1964, eleven months after Penkovsky's death, Wynne was swopped at Checkpoint Heerstrasse in Berlin for Konon Molody, the KGB 'illegal' known as 'Gordon Lonsdale' who had been arrested in London in January 1961 along with the rest of the Portland spy ring: Harry Houghton, Ethel Gee and the Krogers.

Once Wynne had been returned to Britain, to RAF Northolt from Gatow in Berlin, and had made a recovery from the mental breakdown he experienced upon his release, he became a thorough pest to SIS. As soon as he learned that a book called *The Penkovsky Papers* was being prepared, he demanded his right to add a foreword. Reluctantly he was given permission to do so, on condition that he did not compromise his public standing as an innocent businessman. The result was a brief, bland contribution to a book which, having been edited heavily by Peter Deriabin and Frank Gibney, the *Newsweek* and *Time* journalist, was predictably denounced as a poor reconstruction of Penkovsky's real autobiography. *The Penkovsky Papers*, combined with the publication in the same year of *Spy* by Gordon Lonsdale, led Wynne to write his own account, entitled *The Man from Moscow*, in December 1967. The prospect was greeted with horror by the Friends, but the book proved to be less embarrassing than had been anticipated, with Franks's true identity concealed after a little discreet pressure had been applied.

He was simply referred to as 'James' and described as one 'of my friends in Intelligence, the men whose Christian names were false and whose surnames I never knew'.[10]

Shergold's colleague 'Roger King', who had been named in the trial in Moscow, was also protected. Far from being the domineering thug who had coerced him into co-operating, Wynne revealed that 'the villain is a British agent whom I will call Robbins. He was a charming man who never bullied me at all.'[11] This belated attempt to avoid identifying King was not entirely successful because, apart from an initial introduction to 'Robbins', the text also mentioned a certain 'Roger' whose exact role was unexplained. Sharp-eyed readers must have wondered why Wynne had been persuaded to change Roger's surname from King to Robbins, unless the first was indeed his true name. 'Robbins' and 'Roger King', of course, was actually Roger Andrew Ivan King, an experienced agent-runner who had been born in Zurich and had operated in southern Germany after the war. Occasionally confused with C. Andrew B. King, one time Head of Station in Vienna, Controller of the German Stations, joint head of Operation PRINCE and, up until 1961, Head of Station in Hong Kong, both Kings had links with the Communist Party of Great Britain. In 1940 Roger King had reportedly been in contact with a senior GRU agent in England.

Andrew King had originally joined SIS before the war and had operated under commercial cover in Austria before being taken on to the British consular staff in Switzerland upon the French collapse in 1940. Educated at Wellington and Magdalene College, Cambridge, and a lifelong bachelor, he had been acquainted with Philby at university and had joined the Communist Party of Great Britain. Although he never went to any lengths to conceal his inclinations or his political past, he was to become the victim of an MI5-inspired purge when he eventually came to retire in 1967 at the relatively early age of fifty-seven.

The Penkovsky operation effectively compromised the Chisholms and, in 1964, Ruari returned briefly to Singapore. In 1970, he was posted to South Africa for four years as Head of Station and later served a second term at Pretoria in 1977. While there he wrote *Ladysmith*, an acclaimed account of the Boer War siege, but at the end of his tour, *en route* to London, he caught a particularly malignant form of malaria in Dar-es-Salaam. He later died in Scotland, his second, promising career as a military historian unfulfilled. The Cowells, who were also named at the trial, were posted to Bonn the following year; they later went on to serve at the Paris and Tel Aviv Stations. Franks was destined to become Chief in 1978.

Wynne himself never recovered from his experience in Russia and became obsessed with the Penkovsky case. His first marriage ended in divorce, the second in separation and he retired to the Spanish island resort of Mallorca. In 1981 he published a second version of his original book, *The Man from Odessa*, in which he claimed to have played a vital role in the defection of a GRU major named Sergei Kuznov in 1959. The official comment on Wynne's first book was simply that 'certain passages . . . would almost certainly have been objectionable on security grounds, had they been true'.[12]

Penkovsky's own veracity was also to be challenged during the course of the post mortem, which was held routinely in order to see if any lessons could be learned from the operation. The first part of the inquest consisted of a joint CIA-SIS counter-intelligence review to establish exactly when and how the Soviets had tumbled to Penkovsky. This never reached a satisfactory conclusion because the evidence was so conflicting. There were, of course, the initial fears as expressed by Penkovsky himself, which had prompted Deriabin's abortive study of the problem. Then there was the occasionally obvious manifestation of hostile surveillance spotted by Wynne and Penkovsky. The difficulty was to decide whether the deployment of watchers in Moscow was normal coverage, or something more unusual which might have indicated the KGB's sudden interest.

During Wynne's debriefing, he revealed that the KGB had taped fragments of conversations he had held with

Penkovsky in the Ukraine Hotel, months before their arrest. If Penkovsky had come under suspicion at such an early stage, had he ever been run, willingly or unconsciously, as a double agent? As the experts pondered these conundrums, more evidence accumulated to undermine Shergold's star agent. According to Yuri Nosenko, a KGB defector to the CIA, Penkovsky's original approaches to the US Embassy and the Canadians in 1961 must have been monitored and could not have been overlooked. He insisted that the room in which an American diplomat had first rebuffed Penkovsky's offer to work as a spy contained a hidden microphone. He also suggested that the KGB had the technical means to filter the sound of voices from a background of running water, the standard counter-measure used by Wynne and Penkovsky when they met in hotel bathrooms. So why had Penkovsky been allowed to continue contact with the West until his eventual recruitment? Questions were also raised about the intelligence product itself. It was undoubtedly of the highest quality and conveniently timely, but it did cause the military strategists to rethink their assessments of Soviet strength and, in particular, end the then-popular concept of the 'missile gap', Russian numerical superiority in ballistic weaponry. According to Penkovsky, the Soviets were lagging behind the West in nuclear technology, did not pose a real threat and had 'no existing means of combating enemy missiles'.[13] Such information might have been a trifle academic if events had turned out differently, and Khrushchev had not been planning to site Soviet missiles in Cuba during Penkovsky's most active period. There was certainly a plausible case to be made for portraying Penkovsky as a conduit for disinformation, a kind of clandestine, direct contact between the Kremlin and the West's most influential military analysts.

Neither George Kisevalter nor Harold Shergold would entertain such a proposition, but the fact that the matter had been raised at all was enough to ensure that Penkovsky's case was to some extent tainted. When the CIA's counter-intelligence specialists conducted their own examination, they found more apparent inconsistencies. For example, the intelligence product code-named RUPEE, which identified Penkovsky's GRU colleagues operating under diplomatic cover around the globe, failed to expose a single GRU 'illegal'. Although RUPEE seemed to present a fascinating insight into the GRU's activities, it was quite worthless in operational terms. There were also reservations expressed about Penkovsky's *modus operandi*. He had purloined original rocket training manuals, instead of photographing the contents and replacing the documents so that they would not be missed. In the view of some officers, such behaviour could not go undetected for long. There was also Penkovsky's remarkable agility with a miniature camera, and his extraordinary access to classified material outside his limited sphere of responsibility. Were the Soviets guilty of appalling recklessness when it came to physical security, or was there a more sinister explanation? One body of opinion reckoned that the breach was on such a scale as to be uncharacteristic; the other insisted that bureaucratic, departmental rivalries, together with Penkovsky's rank and his useful family connections, delayed the KGB's intervention until very late in the affair.

None of these matters have been fully resolved although the more extreme ideas, like the suggestion that Penkovsky had always been a sophisticated provocation or instrument of disinformation, have been rejected by those who have obtained confirmation from secret sources that he was indeed executed when the announcement was made in Moscow. Nevertheless, the suspicion of a well-orchestrated plot proved durable. The West lost many strategic advantages during the relevant period. The Berlin Wall had been constructed and Khrushchev had demanded the removal of the American Jupiter missiles from Turkey in return for the Soviet withdrawal from Cuba. President Kennedy had also been forced into giving a humiliating guarantee of Castro's regime in the aftermath of the disastrous Bay of Pigs invasion. In human terms, Wynne, SIS's civilian cut-out, had been swopped for a well-trained, long-term Soviet 'illegal', Konon Molody. It had hardly been a fair trade. Whichever way you looked at the critical months of 1961 to the end of 1962, the Kremlin seemed to come out on top. Yet SIS insisted on sticking to the belief that Penkovsky represented a major breakthrough.

Re-examining the Penkovsky affair later, it was noted that two items tended to stand out. One was the remarkable achievement of sustaining the operation for so long, given the necessarily very wide distribution of ARNIKA and RUPEE. Penkovsky's continued freedom from KGB interference could be interpreted by some as an indication, or even proof, of the integrity of all the Western intelligence agencies involved. After all, it would not have required enormous powers of deduction for even a middle-ranking mole to have realized from the sheer volume of high-grade Russian material that the CIA and/or SIS had acquired an extremely useful Soviet source. The corollary was that both organizations must have been free of penetration. It was also noticed that Penkovsky had expressed a view of the Berlin tunnel, which he had described as 'a very serious failure on the part of Soviet counter-intelligence'.[14] How could such an opinion be justified in the face of overwhelming evidence pointing to the existence of an as yet unsuspected Soviet mole, active deep inside the Friends; someone who had actually supervised the technical aspects of Operation PRINCE? If a proven spy had been indoctrinated into the secrets of the tunnel right at the start of the project, how could Penkovsky say that 'many important secrets and much valuable information had fallen into enemy hands'?

11

THE BLAKE CATASTROPHE

'Born in Holland, the son of an Egyptian Jew, Blake was the "odd man out" in the cliquish world of British intelligence.'

David C. Martin, *Wilderness of Mirrors*[1]

Word that SIS had been penetrated at a high level by yet another Soviet spy was first given by the CIA's Soviet Bloc Division in 1959. An anonymous source, codenamed SNIPER, had already proved his bona fides by supplying enough information to indirectly incriminate Harry Houghton, the KGB's agent inside the Admiralty sensitive Underwater Weapons Research Establishment at Portland. MI5 had handled that investigation, which eventually resulted in the convictions of Houghton, his girlfriend Ethel Gee, and their illegal contact, Konon Molody. Lengthy surveillance on Molody had led to Morris and Lona Cohen, who had adopted the identities of Peter and Helen Kroger and had run a wireless station in west London to communicate Houghton's secrets to Moscow. All five had been arrested on 7 January 1961.

SNIPER wrote a total of fourteen letters, in rather poor German, to the CIA. The first was addressed to the American Ambassador in Switzerland and, once contact had been established, the rest were picked up from prearranged dead-letter drops in Warsaw. In one message, dated November 1959, he claimed that up until recently the KGB had been in receipt of material from someone in the Friends known by the cryptonym DIA-MOND. He later mentioned that he had actually examined three SIS papers. At first there had been some scepticism about the story, until it was realized that SNIPER's description of the three documents was sufficiently precise to identify them. He had accurately recalled particular internal documents which had not circulated outside SIS. For example, SNIPER gave an authentic account of SIS's annual R Sections Report of 1959. This key list itemized the needs of each of the R Sections for the coming year and could easily be analysed to reveal SIS's relative strengths and weaknesses. The second document was a Warsaw Station list of likely Polish prospects for recruitment by a specialist unit. The third was an extract from the annual brief from R6's Polish Section. Where had they all come from? The problem was made all the more difficult because the CIA had no idea who their anonymous correspondent really was. They guessed that he was in the Polish Intelligence Bureau, the *Urzad Bezpieczenstwa* or UB, but they could not be completely sure.

SIS's immediate priority was to establish how SNIPER had acquired three of its documents, and a molehunt was launched to track down DIAMOND. There were only a few clues to narrow the field: much of SNIPER's authentic knowledge seemed to be either Polish or German in origin, which suggested a leak from either Warsaw or one of the German field stations. In addition, some significance was attached to the fact that it had been derived from the 1959 R Sections Report, rather than the one for the current year. There were about ten possible candidates who fitted DIAMOND's profile, and each was investigated by MI5 and cleared. After further enquiries, the molehunt concluded that the most likely source for the leak had been a burglary at Guy Bratt's station in Brussels some three years earlier in 1957. Certain routine security precautions had revealed that the Head of Station's office safe had been tampered with, and it had been assumed at the time that the contents had been compromised. No definite record had been kept of all the papers lost in the burglary, so there was no proof that all of SNIPER's information had come from this incident. However, MI5 concurred that the break-in at Brussels was the most likely source for SNIPER's information.

This assessment was changed early in 1961 when SNIPER was suddenly made available to SIS in America. He had turned up in Berlin on Christmas Day and had requested political asylum for himself and his German girlfriend, Irmgard Kampf. They had been flown on a military aircraft from Frankfurt to Andrews Air Force Base outside Washington on 11 January 1961 accompanied by SNIPER's CIA case officer, Howard Roman. Once in America, SNIPER had been driven to a secluded country estate in Maryland for intensive debriefing. It was there, on 16 January, that he answered the detailed questions put to him by Maurice Oldfield and Harold Shergold. SNIPER was revealed to be Michal Goleniewski, a lieutenant-colonel in the UB who had also acted as an informant for the KGB. Instead of simply liaising with the KGB, as he was required to do as head of the UB's industrial and scientific branch, he had actually worked for them as an active agent. During his frequent contacts with his KGB handlers information had passed in both directions, so Goleniewski was well qualified to disclose knowledge of both UB and KGB operations. Before his defection, he had even stashed several hundred documents in a hollow tree in Warsaw. Once these had been retrieved by the CIA, they disclosed even more data and served to establish his credentials. From SIS's viewpoint, the conclusion was inescapable: the Friends had sustained an appalling haemorrhage of highly classified secrets. It seemed likely that SNIPER's position had necessarily restricted his indoctrination to material directly relevant to Polish affairs, in which case it was possible that the KGB had actually acquired a better source with much wider access. In all probability, SIS had been penetrated at a senior level and the burglary in Brussels was no longer a valid explanation for the loss of the documents. Shergold returned to London determined to identify the traitor, and a new molehunt was launched.

In February 1961, immediately following the start of the second molehunt for DIAMOND, further incriminating evidence was provided by the West German BfV. One of the ten original candidates suspected of having leaked SNIPER's three reports had been a successful young SIS officer named George Blake. He had been investigated, but had been given a clean bill of health by the molehunters. However, according to the BfV, one of Blake's star agents in Berlin had turned out to be a double agent controlled by the KGB, who, after his arrest, had identified Blake as having collaborated with him. Horst Eitner had been working for both sides in the *agentensumpf* since 1955, but had evaded capture until October 1960 when the BfV finally amassed enough evidence to charge him with his duplicity. After several months in custody, Eitner saw the weight of the prosecution's case against him and offered a deal. He declared himself willing to incriminate his KGB contact, whom he had known as Max de Vries, in return for lenient treatment from the authorities. 'Max de Vries' had been Blake's cover name during his tenure at the Berlin Station and, as soon as Eitner's allegation reached Broadway, Blake was reinvestigated.

Blake's record was unusual, for under SIS's regulations all officers were required not only to have British citizenship, but to have been born in England. This rule had been waived on the authority of the Chief Production Officer, Kenneth Cohen, when Blake had been offered a permanent post in SIS at the end of the war.

Blake's file showed him to have been an ideal member of SIS's wartime Dutch country section and a skilled linguist, fluent in French, German and Dutch. In April 1945, he had been seconded to Naval Intelligence in Hamburg to assist in the interrogation of U-boat crews. In October 1947, he had enrolled in a Russian-language sandwich course at Downing College, Cambridge, and, on 1 September 1948, had been sent to Seoul under consular cover to open SIS's first station in Korea.

Blake had run the Seoul Station from the British Legation's compound at Chongdong until late June 1950, when he and the rest of the diplomatic mission had been taken into custody by the North Korean invaders. He had remained a prisoner of the Communists until April 1953, when he had been taken by train to Moscow and released. On 21 April, the RAF had flown him to Gatow and, the following day, his ordeal ended when he arrived at Abingdon. After a period of rest, Blake had been trained as a technical operations officer and assigned to the London end of Operation PRINCE. Soon after his arrival, the quality of the 'take' began to deteriorate. Eighteen months later, he married Gillian Allan, the youngest of Colonel Arthur Allan's two daughters, who both worked as secretaries in Broadway, where their father had been one of SIS's veteran Russian translators. In April 1955, Blake began a four-year tour at Peter Lunn's Berlin Station, which ended in April 1959. Since September 1960, he had been studying Arabic at the Middle East College for Arabic Studies, the Foreign Office's language centre located in the old monastery of Shemlan, outside Beirut.

At the end of March 1961, the Head of Station in Beirut, Nicholas Elliott, who had recently taken over from Frank Steele, asked Blake to return to London for consultations regarding a possible promotion. Apparently unconcerned, Blake accepted Elliott's spurious reason for the recall and flew home on 3 April. He reported to Dick White at Broadway the following morning, but instead of being offered a new job, he was ushered into a room where he was challenged with being the KGB spy known as DIAMOND. His interrogators were Shergold (who was about to take on the handling of Penkovsky) and Terence Lecky, another counter-intelligence expert who had joined the Friends in 1946 and had spent four years in Germany, followed by two in Zurich. During his first session with Shergold and Lecky, Blake gave reasonable answers to many of the points raised by his interrogators, and it was agreed that the interview would be continued after lunch. Blake promptly left the building, apparently not suspecting that he was under constant MI5 surveillance. In fact, he had been kept under observation from the moment he arrived at London airport.

During the lunchtime break he was seen to approach a public telephone kiosk and his behaviour was that of someone tormented by indecision. He walked up to it as though about to make a call, but then seemed to think better of it. He eventually returned to SIS headquarters to continue answering Lecky's questions, but in the meantime MI5's watchers had reported Blake's evident distress. As soon as Blake walked into the room, Lecky demanded to know who he had considered telephoning. His wife was still in Beirut, and Blake was caught off-guard. Suddenly he broke down and made a full statement. Two Special Branch detectives, Louis Gale and Ferguson Smith, were called in, and the spy repeated his confession while under a formal caution. In it he admitted that, earlier in the day, he had panicked and had seriously considered contacting the Soviet Embassy in London to demand an emergency escape. At the last moment he had decided against it, hoping to bluff his way through the rest of the interview, but he had lost his nerve. His confession was read out at the Old Bailey on 3 May 1961, *in camera*, and he was sentenced to a record term of forty-two years' imprisonment by the Lord Chief Justice. Blake was completely unprepared for the length of the sentence and promptly collapsed. He had been led to believe that his co-operation with Shergold and Lecky had ensured that he would receive some leniency; instead, he had to be treated in the Wormwood Scrubs' infirmary wing for shock.

Blake's background was a matter of considerable embarrassment to SIS and the organization made a variety of attempts to conceal his long-term employment. Indeed, the Prime Minister was even persuaded to state in the House of Commons on 4 May 1961, somewhat disingenuously, that 'Blake was never an established member of the Foreign Service'. A D Notice was also issued to restrict newspaper comment on Blake's trial, but it was ignored when leaks disclosed that Blake had been a regular SIS officer. While Fleet Street editors were often prepared to co-operate with the Ministry of Defence on matters of genuine national security, they were not willing to save the Friends from embarrassing publicity over what amounted to a first-rate blunder. The attempt to gag the press was seen as just that, and proved thoroughly counter-productive. Nevertheless, SIS continued its efforts to distance itself from Blake and tried to portray him as having had only a brief, post-war involvement with the Friends. A former SIS agent named Edward Spiro, who wrote books under the pseudonym E. H. Cookridge, perpetuated the legend in his account of Blake's case entitled *Shadow of a Spy*.

The reality was somewhat different and, because Blake was such a significant source for the KGB, it is worth tracing his career in some detail. He was born in Rotterdam on 11 November 1922 to Catherine Beijderwellen and Captain Albert Behar, an Egyptian Jew who had served with the British army in France during the First World War. He had been educated at the English School in Cairo, where he had stayed with his uncle, a rich banker. In 1938, he returned to Holland and attended high school in Rotterdam. Soon after the Nazi invasion, he was interned at Schoorl, near Alkmaar, north of Amsterdam, but late in October he escaped and lived underground with the resistance. His cover name, Max de Vries, was the one he had adopted upon joining the *Orde Dienst*, one of the principal Dutch resistance movements.

In July 1942, Behar contacted an MI9 escape line and made his way to Spain, where he was interned briefly at both the Modello Prison in Barcelona and the notorious Miranda de Ebro camp. Upon his release, he reported to the British Embassy in Madrid, where arrangements were made for him to travel to England via Gibraltar. In London he underwent the routine refugee screening process at the Royal Victoria Patriotic School in Wandsworth and, after he had been cleared and his British citizenship confirmed, he volunteered to join the Royal Navy.

In November 1943, Behar changed his name by deed poll to Blake (as his mother and two younger sisters, Adele and Elizabeth, had done already) and was accepted to join an induction course at Portsmouth. For a short time he served on coastal minesweepers and then was recommended for an Officers Training Course at HMS *King Alfred*, the shore base at Hove. There he was commissioned as a sub-lieutenant RNVR and opted to join a submariner's programme at Fort Blockhouse, Portsmouth. This he never completed, because it was discovered that he suffered from impaired hearing which would be damaged further if he worked in a pressurized atmosphere, such as underwater in a submerged submarine. The Royal Navy had no further use for him, so his name and impressive language qualifications were passed on routinely to the Naval Intelligence Division. NID, in turn, gave his details to John Cordeaux, the DNI's Deputy Director in SIS, and Blake was duly interviewed at Broadway by Charles Seymour, then the Head of A2, SIS's Dutch Section (before the post-war reorganization).

Seymour was not much older than Blake and had transferred to SIS in 1941, having originally been recruited into SOE from the Royal Tank Corps. His father had been the managing director in Holland of British American Tobacco (BAT), so he had spent most of his school holidays there and spoke fluent Dutch. After his arrival at Broadway, he had been appointed assistant to Ewen Rabagliati, then Head of A2. It is a reflection of SIS's pre-war amateur approach to intelligence that Rabagliati, who was responsible for intelligence operations in Holland and Denmark, spoke not a word of Dutch or Danish. Rabagliati eventually clashed with Kenneth Cohen, his colleague in A4, the French Section, and resigned from SIS when the CSS ruled in Cohen's favour. Thus, somewhat unexpectedly, Seymour succeeded him and became SIS's youngest head of a country section.

Another member of A2 was Kenneth Dulling, an army

officer on temporary secondment whose father had worked for Unilever in Holland. Dulling had suffered a nervous breakdown in the Middle East and had been sent home where, as a Dutch speaker, he was considered ideal material for SIS. Seymour's principal agent-runner was a colourful character known as Duggie Childs. A former Merchant mariner, he had operated a seaside boat rental business in Scheveningen and had also supplied the Passport Control Officer in The Hague with the occasional item of intelligence. When the Nazis invaded, he had tried to get his family on a ship to England and, in the attempt, had been badly wounded in an air raid. One of his legs had been amputated and the Germans had repatriated him through the Red Cross. A2 was completed by two junior officers, Captain Makin and Harry Druce, and two secretaries, Diana Legh and Iris Peake.

The Misses Legh and Peake came from prominent English families: Diana's father was Colonel the Hon. Sir Piers Legh, Masters of the King's Household; and Iris's father was the Rt Hon. Osbert Peake, Conservative MP for North Leeds and Parliamentary Under-Secretary of State in the Home Office (later to be ennobled Viscount Ingleby). Her mother was Lady Joan Capell, daughter of the seventh Earl of Essex. There is a purpose for emphasizing Iris's blue-blooded background: soon after Blake's arrival in A2, he became hopelessly infatuated with her.

There has been much speculation about Blake's apparent conversion to the Soviet cause, and the commonly accepted version is that he succumbed to some kind of 'brainwashing' technique while a prisoner of the Koreans between June 1950 and his release in April 1953. However, there are also those who believe that another, earlier incident played some part in his subsequent behaviour. One weekend, Blake had been invited to stay with the Peakes at their country home at Snilesworth, near Northallerton in Yorkshire. After dinner one evening, Iris's father had taken Blake aside and had made it quite clear that there was absolutely no question of him even contemplating marriage to his daughter. Blake had interpreted his remarks as offensively anti-Semitic and had never got over it. It had never occurred to him that he might have been regarded as 'unsuitable' by English Society. The Hon. Iris Peake continued her wartime service in SIS and eventually went on to become a lady-in-waiting to Princess Margaret.

As to the damage sustained by SIS through Blake's switch in loyalties, he himself admitted to having passed to the Soviets every conceivable detail of his work from 1 September 1963, when he resumed his duties at Broadway after five months' leave. A particularly depressing aspect of the case was that Blake was judged to have been one of the new breed of professionals. He had not slipped into the organization under some old pals' act, but had been selected and promoted on merit and his performance had been excellent. He was a brilliant linguist with a natural aptitude for intelligence work. Nobody had detected signs of his disaffection or even his social insecurity. His unprecedented sentence reflected the gravity of his offence. As he subsequently confirmed to Lecky during a series of debriefing sessions conducted at Wormwood Scrubs after his appeal had been rejected, he had effectively nullified all the German stations' anti-Soviet activities throughout his four years in Berlin.

Geoffrey McDermott, formerly SIS's Foreign Office Adviser and the British Minister in Berlin at the time of Blake's arrest, made this observation about the scale of his betrayal:

> Looking back with hindsight it is now clear that our intelligence was not too good. British intelligence which a few years back had greatly flourished in Berlin had taken a hard knock as a result of the activities there of George Blake, the double agent, which had only recently been exposed. No doubt our Allies' intelligence was affected to some extent too by his skilled treachery.[2]

In reality, Blake had compromised everything he could get his hands on in Berlin, regardless of whether the source was from SIS or the CIA. He certainly blew Operation PRINCE at a very early stage, but the KGB appear to have allowed the project to continue for fear of jeopardizing him. It is also the belief of William Hood, the CIA case officer who ran his organization's lone mole in the GRU, Piotr Popov, that his case had been betrayed by Blake. Popov had been arrested in Moscow in October 1959 and executed. A post mortem of the affair showed that inadvertently Blake had been given two opportunities to warn the KGB of the penetration. Once, in an unguarded moment, David Murphy, then in charge of the CIA's local anti-Soviet operations, had mentioned the existence of 'a hot one' while visiting SIS's Berlin Station. On another occasion, Popov had tried to renew contact with the CIA by slipping a message to a British military observer in East Germany. His note had been passed on to the CIA via the office in the Olympic Stadium buildings, just when Blake was routinely rifling through the desks of his colleagues during their lunch-hours.

Blake described his lengthy career as a KGB agent in detail to Lecky and, despite the severity of his sentence, proved an exceptionally useful source. As well as identifying the Soviet intelligence officers who had handled him in London while under diplomatic cover, such as Sergei Kondrashev, Blake also confirmed the kind of information he had supplied. By going back over the material, the Friends were able to assess the scale of Blake's betrayal. The final damage report made shattering reading. Not only had Blake compromised documents and agents, but he had also given the KGB a comprehensive order of battle for the Friends, identifying every currently serving officer and reconstructing the personnel of every SIS station in the world. In short, Blake had blown the Friends sky-high. The implications were appalling, not least for the Penkovsky case, because Blake admitted having identified Ruari Chisholm back in 1960. This was further evidence to undermine what had been hailed as SIS's greatest post-war coup, for it had to be assumed that the KGB must have concentrated its considerable resources on Chisholm almost as soon as he arrived in the Soviet capital. If indeed that had happened, how had Penkovsky kept his liberty for so long and how had Janet Chisholm been able to hold so many meetings with him? As the awful consequences of Blake's treachery sunk in, the Friends found additional reason to suspect that the penetration was even worse than they had feared.

12

THE MOLEHUNT ERA

'The resultant contest between Soviet intelligence and British counter-intelligence resembles – at least until the late 1950s – a football match between Manchester United and the Corinthian Casuals in the years of the decline of amateurism.'

Robert Cecil, *The Missing Dimensions*[1]

The identification and elimination of George Blake as a Soviet mole was not to be the end of SIS's anxiety about Soviet penetration. In fact, it was to herald the start of what might be termed the molehunt era.

In April 1961, Blake's was the only proven incidence of treachery within the organization although, of course, Philby's case was still unresolved. And far from having been abandoned after the 'third man' debate in the House of Commons in 1955, Philby had actually been taken back on to SIS's books, albeit unofficially, at the Beirut Station where his old friend Peter Lunn had taken over from Nicholas Elliott as Head of Station in 1962. Apart from peddling the occasional titbit of information and running the odd informant, Philby's overt occupation was that of a 'stringer' for the *Observer* and the *Economist*, cabling routine despatches on political developments in the Middle East back to London. His renewed connection with his old office is supposed to have shocked Dick White, who had apparently assumed that the sacking of his old adversary had been the final chapter in his duplicitous career. Whether true or not, the embargo on contacts with Philby was certainly breached by several officers who had not been indoctrinated into the details of the case against him. In any event, following his public exposure and clearance in 1955, Philby had eked out a living as a jouranlist and, for a short time, had been employed in Ireland to 'ghost' the history of a family firm owned by his friend David Allen.

The event which dramatically changed Philby's cosy relationship with the Friends was the defection, in December 1961, of a KGB major named Anatoli Golitsyn in Helsinki. Golitsyn had been planning his escape, together with his wife and daughter, for months and arrived well prepared with his 'meal-ticket': enough information about the KGB's moles in the West to identify dozens of them. In particular, Golitsyn confirmed that Philby had been a long-term Soviet agent and was still operating as a spy.

Golitsyn's revelation was a useful piece in the jigsaw of evidence that had been accumulated since the original investigation back in 1951, but in legal terms it was merely hearsay and far from conclusive. The clincher was to come later in the year when White was approached by an old wartime MI5 colleague, Lord Rothschild. It was his introduction of Flora Solomon that was to provide the key to extracting a confession from Philby.

Flora Solomon was a senior executive of Marks and Spencer and had known Philby before the war. She had also employed his second wife, Aileen, and had attended their wedding in 1946. According to Mrs Solomon, Philby had not only hinted at his secret work for the Soviets before the war, but had actually attempted to recruit her by inviting her to join him in his 'important work for peace'. Why had Mrs Solomon waited so long before denouncing Philby? On her own admission she had delayed more than twenty years before approaching the authorities. She gave various explanations, but the most convincing was her admitted anger and frustration caused by the anti-Zionist tone of his newspaper articles. Rothschild had reported her remarks to White, who, in turn, arranged for the Security Service to interview her.

Although her statement was less than comprehensive, MI5 was convinced that, combined with Golitsyn's testimony, it might be enough for a skilled interrogator to confront Philby. The only remaining difficulty was the problem posed by Blake's recent conviction. The savage sentence of forty-two years' imprisonment was a powerful disincentive for Philby to co-operate and he was a sufficiently wise counter-intelligence operative to know the practical limits of MI5's jurisdiction. There seemed little chance of persuading him to return to London to face further questioning, and there was even less likelihood of him falling for pretext like the one used to tempt Blake back to London. After all, Philby was no longer an SIS officer and could not simply be recalled to headquarters. Indeed, assuming that he had been alerted to Golitsyn's defection, he would be anticipating just such a move against him.

Even in the unlikely event that he volunteered a confession to MI5, there was no guarantee that he would agree to face the music in England. Why should he? His offences against the Official Secrets Act were not extraditable from a foreign country and, provided he avoided British territory, he could escape arrest for the remainder of his life. The nature of the evidence against him would also look decidedly weak in a court of law, as it rested upon the unsubstantiated allegations of a Soviet defector (assuming, of course, that Golitsyn could be persuaded to go into the witness-box) and the denunciation of an old friend who might easily lose her nerve. All in all, it was far from promising.

Given these unpalatable facts, White conferred with his former deputy, Sir Roger Hollis, now Director-General of the Security Service, and came up with an ingenious solution. On the basis that there was only an intelligence advantage to be gained from Philby's confession and that any thought of a public prosecution was likely to be futile, there was still the option of an official immunity from prosecution sanctioned by the Attorney-General.

Turning Queen's evidence is an established method of

obtaining useful information from individuals who would otherwise not be expected to co-operate. In Philby's case the proposal put to the Attorney-General, then Sir John Hobson, was even more straightforward. The only hope of obtaining his co-operation, a prize highly valued by both MI5 and SIS, was the offer of a formal immunity from prosecution. The Attorney-General gave his consent to the plan, leaving White and Hollis to arrange its delivery.

Initially, it had been MI5's intention to send a D Branch case officer to Lebanon to make the offer to Philby, but at the last minute White took matters into his own hands and decided that, as the affair was strictly an internal one for the Friends, Nicholas Elliott should fly to Beirut and put the proposition to his old friend. Despite resistance from the counter-espionage staff who had been briefed to undertake this assignment, Hollis concurred with White's decision. Accordingly, Elliott arrived in Beirut early in the New Year of 1963, briefed his successor at the Station and rented an apartment, which was then wired for sound.

The exact circumstances of the meeting between Elliott and Philby have never been disclosed. Elliott's own version of it has yet to be published, but two things are known: Philby expressed no surprise at the offer of immunity and accepted it without a moment's hesitation. Furthermore, he typed up a two-page summary of his confession and handed it to Elliott before he flew back to London, to report his mission accomplished to White.

Any jubilation at Elliott's apparent success was short-lived, because Philby disappeared from Beirut on 23 January. It was only then that SIS and MI5 took a closer look at Philby's 'confession' and realized that an off-hand remark made to Elliott about having expected him sooner might have had an added significance. Perhaps Philby had been warned of Elliott's imminent arrival, and the two-page document he had drawn up was not as spontaneous as it purported to be.

The confession acknowledged Philby's dual role since his recruitment to the Soviet cause in 1934 and disclosed his part in the abortive Volkov defection in 1945. On the sensitive matter of the identity of other moles, Philby cleared his old university friend Anthony Blunt of ever having been involved in Soviet espionage, but confirmed that Tim Milne, who had been his protégé in the Friends, had been a fellow conspirator.

Philby's allegation against his lifelong friend was eventually proved to be baseless but only after Milne had been suspended from duty, interrogated and forced to resign. It was a devastating experience for him and an indication of just how low Philby had sunk. Milne's record in the Friends was faultless and his one overseas posting, to Edward de Haan's Station in Berne for two years from 1956, had been a success. Yet he was dispensed with, chiefly to eliminate a risk perceived by the Americans. He was later found a job as a clerk in the House of Commons, a post he kept until 1976.

Philby's disappearance prevented him from being taken to task about the veracity of his confession and left SIS in a state of turmoil. Was any of his statement true? Did his remarks about Blunt's loyalty make him more or less likely to have been an accomplice? Had he really been expecting Elliott to turn up, or had his initial reaction been a revealing slip? There was little way to judge these matters on the basis of the tape-recording made by Elliott, because the window had been left open in the apartment in Beirut throughout the confrontation and the noise of the traffic had drowned the conversation. Nevertheless, it did seem odd that Philby should have been so willing to admit his treachery when, on previous occasions, he had defended himself with vigour. What had made him concede defeat so easily? Was his subsequent disappearance a further clue to a well-planned operation? The evidence seemed to point that way when the Lebanese security authorities reported that, shortly before Elliott had arrived in Beirut, a Soviet diplomat named Yuri Modin had paid a fleeting visit to Lebanon. Modin had already served in London twice – from 1950 to 1953 as Second (then First) Secretary, and from 1957 to 1959 as Press

Attaché – and had been flagged by MI5 as being a senior KGB officer. Was his unexplained appearance in Beirut at such a critical moment a coincidence, or an indication that he had delivered a vital message to his star agent, perhaps alerting him to the build-up of evidence against him in England? If the two did hold a rendezvous, it was unlikely to have been a routine affair, but rather a lengthy meeting at which the experienced case officer had given Philby an up-to-date assessment of recent developments, altogether too secret and complicated to be entrusted to an enciphered radio signal.

Whatever the truth of the situation, there was no mistaking Philby's absence. Yet another damage assessment was prepared on the basis that he had been a Soviet spy continuously since 1934 and, like Blake, had betrayed everything that had passed his way. Once again, like Blake, it did nothing to enhance SIS's special relationship with the CIA.

It could be argued that Philby's most effective periods as a Soviet mole were during the time he headed R5, shortly before his departure to Turkey, and throughout the eighteen months he served in Washington, where he was in a powerful position to influence SIS policy and obtain almost unrestricted access to many of the CIA's operations. Although he may have been useful during the war, his knowledge was necessarily limited, in the latter part at least, to matters directly affecting the Iberian Peninsula. Of course he must have compromised many of his colleagues in Section V who remained in the service after the war, but the damage sustained by the Friends must have been less than devastating. Similarly, there is some evidence to show that the Volkov episode in 1945 was an experience he had no wish to repeat. Volkov's mysterious removal before Philby could negotiate his defection had all the hallmarks of a betrayal, and Philby must have known that any similar incidents on his file would be bound to attract unwelcome attention. Accordingly, he had exercised great caution when passing current, operational matters to the KGB. This circumspection can be seen in his handling of another defector, Ismail Akhmedov, in 1948.

Akhmedov had been a GRU lieutenant-colonel, who had been working under press attaché cover at the Soviet Consulate in Istanbul during the war. Calling himself Grigori Nikolayev, Akhmedov had fallen foul of the NKVD and, in May 1942, had decided to defect. He had made contact with the brother of a local station officer, Jack Whittall, who had been running the family's merchant business in Turkey, and a message had been passed on to the SIS Head of Station, Harold Gibson. However, when the moment came for Akhmedov to defect, he chose to throw himself upon the mercy of the Turkish Security Inspectorate. This proved to be a wise move, because it subjected him to only the most superficial of debriefings and then set him up with a permanent body-guard and a new identity.

It was not until 1948, when Philby had already been established in Istanbul for eighteen months, that Akhmedov became restless and asked the Security Inspectorate to put him in touch with either the British or the Americans in the hope of obtaining a residency permit elsewhere. The price, of course, was a thorough debriefing, which was undertaken by Philby at an SIS safe-house, a comfortable, fifth-floor apartment in Jihangir, overlooking the Bosphorus. Akhmedov later recalled his introduction to Philby, 'the Head of the British Secret Service in Turkey, the son of the famous St John Philby':

> Philby was all smiles and courtesy: the impeccable English gentleman full of attention. For starters we had a drink and then got down to business, business which was going to last approximately four weeks – each day from nine to five, with short interruptions for lunch, which was served in the same room. Oh, my God. If only I had known that this smiling courteous Englishman named Philby was the man who had tipped the KGB about Soviet Vice-Consul Konstantin and had sent him to certain death! If

only I had known that here in this most luxurious
apartment I was actually sitting in a KGB den and
was being interviewed by a KGB agent![2]

Philby was thoroughly professional in his approach to
Akhmedov, and the defector had no reason to suspect his
interrogator:

> While neglecting my background, Philby showed an
> intense interest in my reasons for defecting, in the
> circumstances surrounding it, in how I was handled
> by the Turks, and finally in the attempts, if any, of
> the KGB to whisk me out of Turkey or to liquidate
> me. He was obsessed with learning the smallest
> details of the Turkish handling of my
> protection. . . .
>
> He was extremely interested to find out how much
> I knew about Soviet espionage activities in England.
> Here he tried his best to grill me. Of course, I did
> my best to tell him everything I knew of all those
> matters, because I wanted to expose the scale of
> Soviet world-wide espionage activities conducted
> through all channels. Also, I was hoping, as a result
> of our long association during these meetings, that
> he might help me settle in England.[3]

Akhmedov's interviews with Philby were recorded by his
secretary in shorthand and backed-up by a hidden tape-
recorder, so there was little opportunity for Philby to
conceal his testimony, but almost everything he said was
more than six years out of date. Akhmedov was passed
over to the Americans and eventually in 1953, he obtained
asylum in the United States.

As the holder of a senior rank in the GRU, Akhmedov
must have been high on the Soviet's assassination list and,
no doubt, Philby reported his meetings with him, but
there was no repetition of the Volkov episode which had
proved so difficult to explain to the molehunters in 1951,
and again in 1955. Philby's final escape prompted White
to order a massive purge of the Friends, in parallel to a

similar exercise then being conducted inside the Security Service. MI5's enquiries were to lead, in April 1964, to Blunt who, like Philby before him, agreed to confess his espionage in return for an immunity from prosecution. Unfortunately, from SIS's viewpoint, he professed ignorance of any Soviet spies at work in SIS, apart from John Cairncross, who had worked briefly in Section V at the end of the war.

SIS's counter-intelligence branch had several good reasons to believe that the organization had been penetrated even further. Firstly, there was the obvious possibility that Blake and Philby might have either recruited one or two of their colleagues, or have recommended them to their KGB controllers, leaving the Russians to make the approach. Certainly, both men had had plenty of time to sound out like-minded colleagues and, given the nature of the work the Friends undertook, must have noticed opportunities to entrap vulnerable personnel. Talent-spotting of this type would have been a matter of routine, and it seemed improbable that no one had succumbed to temptation or blackmail. There was also the chance that they had deliberately acquired tainted sources, which were still supplying material of a dubious value. Then there were the accusations made by previous defectors, all of which had to be re-examined in the light of the exposure of Philby and Blake. And, finally, there were some unexplained incidents, like the suicide of Harold Gibson at his apartment in Rome in August 1960, which could be seen as having some connection with MI5's molehunt.

There were other, vaguer indications which might be interpreted as evidence of Soviet penetration: the inability to recruit worthwhile Soviet moles; the paucity of authentic defectors; the lack of any major breakthrough in spite of the numerous double-agent operations mounted against Moscow; the odd circumstances of the Petrov defection in Australia which so nearly ended in catastrophe (see page 213); the almost uncanny ability of the KGB to deter would-be defectors; the failure of so many technical surveillance operations around the world; the absence of a conclusive counter-espionage case in either GCHQ or MI5, two of the KGB's most obvious targets; the high proportion of SIS personnel with Russian or foreign backgrounds; and the apparent ease with which Cairncross, Blake and Philby had been able to get themselves into positions where they could inflict the greatest damage. And so the list went on. While none of these items in isolation added up to anything other than the flimsiest of circumstantial evidence, when reviewed *in toto* the situation looked depressingly clear. The only antidote was a further dose of hunting through the files for the telltale clues to disloyalty that, in retrospect, were so obvious in the major investigations experienced to date.

The most immediate cases to be reinvestigated were those individuals named by Volkov as having been Soviet assets. He had identified Robert Zaehner as a Soviet source, an allegation later repeated by an MI5 informant of doubtful reliability, Goronwy Rees. At the time of Rees's denunciation, Zaehner had been working for Norman Darbyshire and Monty Woodhouse at the Tehran Station. He had returned to academic life at Oxford shortly before the culmination of Operation BOOT and, therefore, did not pose a threat. Nevertheless, he was interviewed again and made aware of the investigation into his background.

Another on the list of Foreign Office staff fingered by defectors was Sir Anthony Rumbold. Although a regular diplomat, he had originally been named as long ago as 1936 by a GRU defector. When the files were reopened, it was realized that Rumbold had enjoyed a life-long friendship with Donald Maclean, who had been best man at Rumbold's first marriage. There was no new evidence against Rumbold, so the case was passed to MI5 and shelved.

More significance was attached to the case developed against Sir George Clutton, the senior diplomat who had been appointed as SIS's Foreign Office Adviser in 1952 and had played a major role in Operation BOOT. In

1955, he had been succeeded by Michael Williams and had gone to Manila as British Ambassador. Thereafter, he served in the same capacity in Warsaw, where his homosexuality may have made him susceptible to blackmail. In any event, he too came under intensive investigation when a junior, local employee based at the British Embassy in Vienna, and already suspected of peddling low-grade information around town, was put under close surveillance. One weekend he was followed to London where, to the astonishment of the watchers, he visited Clutton at his flat in St James's. A pretext was found to sack the man from the Embassy, and the case against Clutton lapsed when he died soon afterwards.

None of these enquiries really fulfilled the profile of the Soviet spy in SIS as described by Anatoli Golitsyn, who had always insisted that the Friends harboured KGB moles. But when his allegations had been looked at by Geoffrey Hinton, who had been appointed Head of Counter-intelligence in 1960 upon his return from the Bangkok Station, they had been considered too vague to pursue. Hinton had been unable to make any headway with Golistyn's claims.

According to Golitsyn, whose information had proved so valuable on other matters and had helped expose Philby and Blunt, the KGB had been running several agents in London, and both MI5 and SIS had been penetrated. Very little progress had been made by the Friends on this issue because it was widely believed that the most likely candidate had been Blake, who had already been dealt with. However, when Hinton was posted to the Paris Station in 1966, his place was taken by Christopher Phillpotts, who had just completed two years in Washington and was determined to carry on the molehunt where Hinton had left off.

Phillpotts was hugely popular within the intelligence community, a much-respected, larger-than-life figure who had originally come into contact with the Friends by complaining about their illicit cross-Channel activities during the war. The son of an admiral, Phillpotts had been a regular naval officer before the war and, in 1940, had found himself in charge of inshore patrols around the Devonshire coast. He had been in constant conflict with Frank Slocum's private navy, then based in the Helford estuary, which he had regarded as a nuisance and a waste of time. For his trouble he had been given a nominal posting to Naval Intelligence and placed in charge of the entire operation. He had also covered himself in glory as Head of Station in Athens and had been decorated with the CMG in 1957 for sabotaging the efforts of *enosis* gunrunners, who had unwisely attempted to smuggle weapons to Cyprus in the Emergency. In 1966, Phillpotts was fifty-one and was due to retire in four years' time. There had been a chance, just before his departure to Washington in 1964, that he might have been promoted to be White's Vice-Chief, but Maurice Oldfield had got the job instead, by recommending himself, according to rumour. Phillpotts, therefore, had no ambition to succeed White, for the post was effectively promised to Oldfield, so he moved into his new offices in SIS's recently acquired anonymous tower block at 100 Westminster Bridge Road, unimaginatively called Century House, and renewed the molehunt by going back to the allegations made against Rumbold, the very earliest claims of Soviet penetration dating from 1936.

When run together, the claims made by a series of separate defectors over a long period of years followed a similar pattern. Walter Krivitsky, the GRU agent-runner who had been one of the first to defect rather than face a purge in Moscow in the 1930s, had described how one of his best sources in Paris had been closely involved with a British intelligence officer who had sold information about SIS. Krivitsky had been found shot dead in his Washington hotel room in February 1941, so he could give no further help, but another defector, Igor Gouzenko, had talked in 1945 of a spy run by the GRU in 'British Counter-intelligence', with the cryptonym ELLI. Gouzenko had only been a low-level cipher clerk, so his further usefulness as a witness was limited. Nevertheless, he was interviewed in Canada, where he reiterated his belief in a traitor codenamed ELLI. Volkov had also mentioned a total of five Soviet agents in British intelligence and two in the Foreign Office. Skripkin had disappeared before he could elaborate on what he knew and his colleague, Yuri Rastvorov, later confirmed that he had been betrayed by someone inside the Friends. Michal Goleniewski, the Polish defector from the UB, had said much the same and had talked of a 'middle-ranking' agent in SIS. There seemed to be a consistency in these claims, from people who had already established their credentials as reliable sources, which pointed to further Soviet penetration above and beyond Philby and Blake.

The first two victims of the molehunt organized by Phillpotts were almost certainly innocent of any contact with the KGB. Andrew King's offence was to have owned up to his pre-war membership of the CPGB when a student at Magdalene, Cambridge. He had told Kenneth Cohen of this indiscretion when he had first been approached to join SIS, and had brought the matter up again in 1951 when he had been serving as Head of Station in Vienna. On that occasion Menzies had said that there was already enough trouble with MI5 and had advised him to keep quiet. When subjected to a hostile interrogation by the Security Service in 1967, King agreed that he had always known about Philby's membership of the CPGB. Unfortunately, Cohen had been unable to remember King's original declaration about his Communist past and had been unwilling to corroborate King's version of events. When pressed, King admitted that in some ways it was surprising that Philby had not passed his name on to the KGB for possible recruitment, but he insisted that the Soviets had never even come close to making an approach. This was accepted, and King retired.

He was followed into premature retirement by Donald Prater, who was recalled from the Stockholm Station, which he had run since 1965, to face questions about his pre-war connections with the CPGB. Prater had attended the Ealing County School before going up to Corpus

Christi, Oxford. After war service with the Royal Fusiliers in North Africa, he had joined the Friends in May 1946 and completed a two-year tour in Singapore before going to Germany under BCCG cover in August 1949. Thereafter, he had served at the Beirut Station from February 1955 to October 1957 and had then moved to Vienna as Cyril Rolo's deputy, until his return to Broadway in November 1959. Prater's whole career had been in the Friends, yet he too opted to resign soon after his fiftieth birthday. He moved to New Zealand to take up a university post lecturing in German.[4]

Neither King nor Prater were spies, but under the tough regime imposed by Phillpotts their political past had wrecked their careers. Some even believed that mere association with a suspect who had been put through the wringer was enough to blight a promising future; Nicholas Elliott, the man who had extracted Philby's confession, opted to find a new job in the City of London.

The atmosphere of the molehunt inevitably brought morale to a low ebb, and some of the cases pursued by searches through ancient files were impossible to conclude, causing further uncertainty. Much time was devoted to following up Golitsyn's belief that the elusive master spy in British intelligence had something Russian in his background. This vague clue fitted any number of the old-timers who, like the Gibson brothers, had been born in pre-revolutionary Russia and had spent a lifetime fighting Bolshevism. Roman Sulakov, Biffy Dunderdale, Major Steveni and the Gibsons had all worked for SIS and had immersed themselves in anti-Communist, White Russian circles in order to cultivate sources. It was also true that the KGB had proved itself to be a past master at fronting bogus resistance movements so as to manipulate and even control the opposition. All the SIS White Russians, for different reasons, must have been targeted by the KGB at some time. Sulakov had worked closely with Philby at the Istanbul Station; Dunderdale had managed Tokaev's defection in 1948; Steveni had received Boris Bajanov, Stalin's personal assistant back in 1928;

the Gibson brothers had worked for SIS throughout Eastern Europe and the Middle East.

Harold Gibson's suicide had been a particularly puzzling affair. The last three years of his extraordinary career had been spent as Head of Station in Rome, where he retired in 1958 and been succeeded by Craig Smellie. After his first wife, Juliet Kalmanoviecz, died in 1947, he married another Russian, Ekaterina Alfimov. For reasons that were never fully explained, he apparently shot himself in his apartment in Rome on 24 August 1960.

The emergence of the Counter-Intelligence Branch as a powerful, sometimes feared, instrument to invesitgate Soviet penetration was in part a reflection and consequence of the dedication of Phillpott's staff. Two officers in particular proved to have an exceptional talent for trawling through the old files to construct new dossiers: Arthur Martin and Theo Pantcheff.

Martin had been swopped from the counter-espionage, D Branch, of the Security Service, with Terence Lecky, in November 1964 following a series of internal rows among MI5's molehunters. It was a convenient move, for Lecky was still handling Blake, then serving his sentence at Wormwood Scrubs, and Martin, the acknowledged expert on Philby, had been placed in charge of SIS's long-neglected Registry. There he had unrestricted access to the old case histories and a free hand to reopen old enquiries. Pantcheff, who had operated under BCCG cover in Munich in the early 1950s, was assigned to investigate the allegations made by Krivitsky. With White's approval, the occasionally strained relationship between the two organizations had been patched up because of their combined commitment to root out the moles. Stephen de Mowbray, for example, who had returned from the Montevideo Station in 1961, had been seconded to the Security Service to assist in the pursuit of a highly placed suspect and continued to have regular meetings with his opposite numbers from Curzon Street until his posting to Washington as Phillpott's successor in 1966. A specialist working party, codenamed FLUENCY, was set up to direct the activities of the molehunters from both services. Staffed by experienced counter-intelligence officers, the FLUENCY Committee was to supervise a series of investigations and recommend Phillpotts to dispense with several career officers who, for one reason or another, had come under its scrutiny.

One of the most controversial cases dealt with by FLUENCY was that of Dick Ellis, the Australian-born former Controller Far East who had taken early retirement in 1953 to go back to Sydney. There he had worked briefly under contract for the fledgling Australian Secret Intelligence Service (ASIS), before turning up again in London. At the time of the investigation into his past, codenamed EMERTON, he had been re-employed on a temporary basis in the Registry at Century House, 'weeding' redundant files from the records.

Like so many of the investigations inspired by FLUENCY, the basis of the case against Ellis began as a series of coincidences, evidence of the most circumstantial kind which, when linked together, cried out for closer examination. His career in SIS had stretched back to 1924, when he had been sent to the Berlin Station, fresh from the Sorbonne, under consular cover. A talented linguist, with family connections through his first wife, Lilia Zelensky, to the exiled White Russian community on the Continent, Ellis used the cover-name Howard to run agents, one of whom was his brother-in-law, Alexander Zelensky.

Shortly before the war, Ellis had been brought back to London and had been given the task, along with a team of other personnel fluent in German, to translate and transcribe recordings made of telephone conversations intercepted from the German Embassy in Carlton House Terrace. This highly secret monitoring operation, conducted with the clandestine help of the Post Office, had continued almost to the outbreak of war, but appeared to lose its value as a source of high-grade intelligence at a particular moment when new security procedures had been introduced on the Embassy's supposedly secure direct line to Berlin. Ellis had remained at Broadway until June 1940, when he had been posted to SIS's New York Station, then located in the Cunard building on Wall Street, as deputy to the newly appointed British Passport Control Officer, William Stephenson, whose station was later retitled the BSC. Towards the end of 1944, Ellis had returned to Broadway, before being posted to Singapore. At the conclusion of his tour in the Far East Menzies had appointed him Chief of Production in Europe, in succession to Frederick Vanden Heuvel, and this was the post he had passed on to Herbert Setchell in 1953 upon his short-lived premature retirement to Australia, which was alleged to have been recommended by his doctors on medical grounds. Those who knew him had been puzzled by his decision to return to Australia and had not been convinced by his excuse of ill-health. In fact, he was to live for another two decades and remarry twice.

In many ways Ellis's career resembled one long adventure. After a short spell at Melbourne University, where his studies were interrupted by the outbreak of war in 1914, he had joined up as a private soldier in the Royal Fusiliers. He was later commissioned into the Middlesex Regiment and spent two years at the front in France. This had been followed by postings to Egypt and India, and then his attachment to General Malleson's military mission in Tashkent. In 1963, Ellis wrote an account of his part in the Allied intervention on the side of the White Russians, entitled *The Transcaspian Episode*. When he eventually returned to civilian life in 1920, he began a course at St Edumund's Hall, Oxford, but then moved to Paris without completing it. There he studied languages at the Sorbonne and started to contribute articles to the London *Morning Post* and other newspapers on a free-lance basis. Thanks to an introduction to Major Langton, then the SIS Head of Station in Paris, Ellis had also begun an undercover life as a British agent. His marriage to Lilia had not lasted long and he had married again in 1934, to Barbara Burgess-Smith, whom he divorced in 1947. Oddly, Ellis later made a clumsy attempt to conceal his marriage to Lilia by omitting it entirely from reference books like *Who's Who*; instead, he listed Barbara as his first wife.

By sifting through the files, the molehunters managed to construct an interesting parallel of coincidences which neatly fitted Ellis's career: an Abwehr officer undergoing a debriefing session immediately after the war had identified Alexander Zelensky as the source of some extremely accurate intelligence about SIS's pre-war internal structure; there was an old file which raised the possibility of a leak having been responsible for the unexpected imposition of security measures on Ribbentrop's telephone line at the German Embassy; according to Soviet wireless decrypts and information from the Americans, BSC had accommodated several Soviet sympathizers during the war years; and one of the R5 dossiers detailing allegations against a certain 'Captain Ellis' had been dismissed and shelved, on Philby's authority.

According to testimony from Blunt, who had been co-operating with MI5 since April 1964, there might have been a direct link between Ellis and Philby. Blunt recalled having been alerted by Philby, shortly before the defection from Canberra of Vladimir and Evdokia Petrov in April 1954, that just such an event was about to take place and that he should take extreme caution for a while. Blunt had heeded the warning, and the Petrovs, who both held senior ranks in the KGB, had indeed volunteered some useful information about Soviet espionage in Britain to the Security Service, which, at the time, had only seemed of passing relevance to Burgess and Maclean. But how had Philby been tipped off to the impending defection and why had the Soviets failed to prevent what must have been a catastrophe for them? It turned out that the Russians had made an abortive attempt to stop Petrov from defecting, but the two thugs assigned the task had arrived too late. Instead, they had had to settle for Mrs Petrov, whom they tried to manhandle on to a plane. She had been rescued by the Australian authorities, but only after the aircraft had broken its journey to refuel.

The molehunters speculated about Ellis's role in the Petrov affair and concluded that he had been handily placed in ASIS to learn in advance of Petrov's cultivation and his decision to defect. While it was certain that Ellis had returned to London early, in breach of his employment contract with ASIS, and had then arranged to meet Philby for lunch, there was no proof that he had been the source of the tip-off which Philby had swiftly relayed to Blunt.

The substance of the case against Ellis fell into two categories: illicit pre-war connections with the Abwehr and post-war contact with the KGB. When invited to explain the coincidences, Ellis vigorously protested his innocence of both charges and indignantly showed his anti-communist credentials, including the fact that he was at that time working on an anti-Soviet book entitled *The Expansion of Russia*. Painstaking cross-examination of Ellis by Pantcheff and Phillpotts revealed a few flaws in his denials, and gradually Ellis's defensive façade began to crumble. At one moment he had insisted on not having taken part in the telephone-tapping operation on the Ribbentrop line, but had then been forced to agree that, in fact, he had after all. As a new interrogation session at Century House was about to begin, and apparently convinced that a former Abwehr officer had consented to fly to London to describe his relationship with him before the war, Ellis suddenly produced a short, typed statement which he had prepared overnight. Somewhat reminiscent of Philby's confession, the Ellis document contained the admission that he had, indeed, been forced through circumstances to supply the Germans with information about SIS's structure and some of its personnel before the war. The conduit used had been his former brother-in-law in Paris. As regards any post-war contacts with the KGB, Ellis continued his vehement denials and could not be persuaded to budge, even with the offer of an immunity from prosecution.

Had the molehunters stumbled on to an as yet undetected Soviet master-spy willing to make small concessions in order to avoid revealing the scale of his duplicity, or was Ellis really what he claimed to be, a pathetic victim of SIS's parsimony which had forced him to trade a few worthless secrets to the Abwehr so as to survive? Opinion was divided. Phillpotts was satisfied that Ellis had made a clean breast of his treachery, but some MI5 officers, principally Peter Wright, remained convinced that Ellis had been let off the hook too easily. They argued that if the Soviets knew that Ellis had dealt with the Abwehr, as seemed likely from their penetration of Russian *émigré* circles in Paris, they would never have missed the chance to exploit the situation and apply pressure on him. Whatever the truth, Ellis was allowed to go back into retirement to Eastbourne, where he died in July 1975. Soon after his confrontation with the molehunters, Ellis, who was to write two further books, *Soviet Imperialism* and *Mission Accomplished*, pleaded financial hardship to the CIA and, in recognition of his war service, which had already been rewarded with the American Legion of Merit, was granted a small pension. At least one CIA officer regarded Ellis's behaviour as little short of blackmail.

This unsatisfactory conclusion to the Ellis affair was not to mark the end of the molehunt era, although the investigations sponsored by the FLUENCY Committee gradually were wound down. On 22 October 1966, much to the embarrassment of both the Friends and the Security Service, George Blake successfully escaped from Wormwood Scrubs and made his way, undetected, to East Berlin and then to Moscow. The Friends were convinced that the entire episode had been carefully stage-managed by the KGB, but MI5 insisted that the known KGB and GRU intelligence officers at the Soviet Embassy in Kensington Palace Gardens appeared to have been equally surprised by Blake's dramatic escape, over the prison's perimeter wall with the aid of an improvised rope-ladder fashioned from knitting needles. A massive police search had ensued, but although Blake's getaway car had been found abandoned after an anonymous tip-off, and the owner traced to an Irishman who had been discharged from the prison the previous June, very little trace of Blake was found. A warrant was issued for the arrest of Sean Bourke, who was known to have been friendly with Blake while in prison with him, but he proved every bit as elusive as the convicted Soviet spy.

The first definite news of how the escape had been accomplished came from SIS's Head of Station in Moscow, when, in September the following year, Bourke unexpectedly called at the British Embassy and requested travel documents to the West. He claimed to have arrived in the Soviet Union on a forged British passport and to have been sharing a flat in Moscow with Blake. However, as an Irish citizen, the Embassy officials could not issue him with a passport and he was advised to return in a week, so that the authorities in Dublin could be contacted. In fact, he never went back to the Embassy. In 1968, his brother flew out with a travel document good for a trip back to Dublin, where Bourke was arrested by the Garda on an extradition warrant alleging that he had conspired to help Blake escape from prison in London. The application was refused by the High Court, which judged Bourke's offence to have been political, and he was released. He subsequently wrote his own candid account of these events, *The Springing of George Blake*, in which he stated that the KGB had played no part in Blake's escape, and that most of the financial and other assistance given had been provided by two leading members of CND, whom he discreetly referred to only as 'Michael Reynolds' and 'Pat Porter'. Their true names, Michael Randle and Pat Pottle, were not disclosed until 1987, when H. Montgomery Hyde's biography *George Blake: Superspy*, was published. In July 1989 both men were formally charged with aiding Blake's escape. Blake had apparently realized that he stood no chance of being swopped for a British spy, as he had nothing left to offer the KGB, and had decided that he would have to arrange his own escape. Bourke's motive for agreeing to help him seems to have been a combination of adventurism and innate anti-British Republican sentiments.

Blake's successful escape served to nullify much of the intelligence advantage achieved by Lecky who, after hours of interrogation, had been able to build a comprehensive damage assessment report of Blake's work for the Soviets. Of course, Blake's co-opeation in this exercise had been kept a closely guarded secret, but this was no doubt revealed to the KGB once Blake arrived behind the Iron Curtain. Even as late as 1987, when the amateurish nature of the whole escape plot was confirmed for the first time, some retired members of the Friends seemed unwilling to accept that Blake's escape had been masterminded not by the KGB's *Rezident* in London, but by a group consisting of nobody more sinister than an Irish petty criminal and a few rather naive left-wing political activists.

13

THE DEFECTOR SYNDROME

'Penetration is the technique *par excellence* of counter-espionage operations.'

James McCargar, *The Spy and his Masters*[1]

Although it had generally been widely anticipated that Maurice Oldfield would succeed White upon the latter's retirement in 1968, the appointment was not made. Nor, for that matter, did White actually retire. Instead, he moved into the Cabinet Office with the new title of Intelligence Co-ordinator to the Cabinet. In his place Labour's Foreign Secretary George Brown chose Sir John Rennie, a regular diplomat whose only experience of the secret world had been one posting behind the Iron Curtain, in Warsaw, and five years running the Information Research Department during the turbulent mid-1950s when propaganda seemed one of the few effective weapons left in Britain's depleted arsenal. Rennie's promotion must have been a cruel blow for Oldfield who, despite his donnish, relaxed appearance, was intensely ambitious. Perhaps worse was the verdict expressed in Rennie's eventual obituary in *The Times* in November 1981 which claimed that Rennie had been made CSS because 'No suitable candidate was at that time available from within the Service.' There may well have been a struggle for power in the top echelons of Whitehall as White's departure approached, after twelve years as CSS, but in operational terms the change was not to make much difference until the civil rights campaign in Northern Ireland exploded into Republican-sponsored violence and the Friends were asked to intervene. Craig Smellie, the Arabist who had served in Alexandria before the Suez crisis, and had subsequently headed the stations in Baghdad, Rome, Khartoum and Tripoli, was posted to Belfast to reinforce the very limited intelligence apparatus already in existence. At the end of a stormy, two-year tour, Smellie moved on to Athens, leaving MI5, the Special Branch and numerous military intelligence units, all with overlapping briefs, to continue the rivalry and muddle.

Because of SIS's continuing presence in Belfast, and the nature of its activities, little can usefully be said about intelligence operations in the province. They are quite obviously at the 'sharp end' of the clandestine effort to suppress terrorism, a role that cannot be undertaken with any hope of success if its methods are to be disclosed. Nevertheless, there have been a couple of rare occasions when outsiders have been given an opportunity to glimpse SIS in action. One was the imaginative project launched by an untraceable travel firm called Casuro, based in an accommodation address in central London and equipped only with a telephone answering machine. Letters from Casuro addressed to various people informed them that they had won a competition and awarded prizes. The individuals selected by Causro happened to be leading members of extremist Republican parties and, having accepted an invitation to enjoy an all-expenses-paid holiday in Torremolinos, they were approached by other 'contestants' who were really SIS personnel making a bid to recruit them as informers. The scheme was eventually wound up after a couple from Dublin, both founder members of the Irish Republican Socialist Party, the political wing of the Irish National Liberation Army, went on a free trip to Spain sponsored by Causro but then rejected SIS's offer and denounced Casuro in the press. SIS's hidden involvement in the affair was revealed when it was learned that Casuro's single telephone line terminated inside the building occupied by SIS's London Station.

In another incident which was reported publicly, in December 1972, a Garda Special Branch detective was arrested in a Dublin hotel on a charge of supplying a Briton named John Wyman with classified reports about the IRA from the Garda's files. Much secrecy surrounded the subsequent prosecution which was concluded with the conviction, *in camera*, of both defendants and their immediate release. Observers suspected that the case had the familiar ring of 'unofficial assistance' that had somehow come unstuck. Both these examples demonstrate the high-risk character of intelligence-gathering in Ireland, but the fact that they ended in failure does not imply ineptitude. Certainly, the Casuro was an ingenious contrivance to lure potential informers with proven access to neutral ground where, surrounded by a friendly but alien environment, congenial case officers, could undermine the resistance of Republican activists with minimal danger. Given the fluid composition and methodology of the terrorist movements deployed in Northern Ireland, and the strict limitations imposed on the security forces, the authorities have only a narrow range of resources to fall back on. Signal interception, covert surveillance, aerial photography, prisoner interrogation and other standard techniques can offer tactical advantages, but are unlikely to provide the key, strategic information that can be supplied by a well-placed informant. The recruitment of agents and the infiltration of moles into the various target groups represents the most effective, and the most hazardous, means of acquiring the kind of useful data that, when skilfully exploited, could lead to the complete elimination of a modern terrorist organization.

Since containment, let alone elimination, is an objective that still eludes the authorities in Northern Ireland, continued discretion should be exercised and we should turn to SIS's main preoccupation during the remainder of Rennie's tenure: the threat posed by the Soviets.

By the time Christopher Phillpotts retired in 1970, he was entirely satisfied that his task of cleansing the Friends of hostile penetration had been completed and that the Service was free of any moles. How could he have been so certain?

There are several ways of judging the relative integrity of a security or intelligence agency, but the best is a demonstrable ability to keep secrets and run good cases. The definition of the latter is not the kind of operation like Operation PRINCE or the Penkovsky affair, which seemed to go well while they lasted, but rather the more concrete achievement of running an agent, protecting him as a source, and ensuring his safe arrival when eventually he decides to complete his defection by escaping. When Phillpotts left Century House two such projects had been initiated and were to go smoothly to reach a successful conclusion.

One of the results of the molehunts had been the division of the Security Service's counter-espionage branch, D Branch, into two K Branches, designated 'KX' and 'KY' respectively, to separate investigations from counter-intelligence operations. It was one way to mark the end of an era and start afresh. Now SIS was to embark upon a new period of co-operation with the Security Service, targeting the numerous Soviet 'legal' facilities in London for joint attention.

Of course SIS had long enjoyed its own London Station which, under Nicholas Elliott back in 1956, had run Buster Crabb's ill-fated mission. In more recent years it had operated independently of the Security Service, almost like any other overseas station, as though the host territory was in a foreign captial. From its local station in the Vauxhall Bridge Road, SIS mounted routine operations in support of the Belfast Station, exercised clandestine technical surveillance of target diplomatic missions and liaised more closely with MI5.

One of the first such operations had started out as a possible honeytrap, organized by MI5's K Branch, involving a member of the Soviet Trade Delegation named Oleg

Lyalin who, through routine surveillance, was discovered to be conducting an illicit affair with his Russian secretary, Irina Teplyakova. The approach made to Lyalin proved entirely welcome, and he offered to defect with his girlfriend there and then. The two case officers in charge of the operation persuaded him to remain in place, at least for the time being, and gather information. Lyalin turned out to be an undercover KGB officer, so he was able to supply invaluable data concerning the Soviet order of battle at the trade mission's headquarters and the Embassy. The case went extremely well but was eventually terminated, at the end of August 1971, when Lyalin was arrested by the police in London for drunken driving. As a trade official and not a regular diplomat, Lyalin could not claim immunity and was taken to a police station for the night before appearing in a magistrates court the following morning. Another KGB officer, Aleksandr Abramov, turned up in court to pay Lyalin's bail, but the charges against him had been dropped, on the Home Secretary's sanction, and he had already been reunited with Irina in preparation for months of debriefing. The most immediate consequence of Lyalin's defection was the rounding up of his network, which had included two Greek Cypriots and a Malayan, who worked in the vehicle registration department of the local authority. He had been providing the KGB with details of cars used for surveillance by MI5 and SIS. All three agents were convicted and sentenced to terms of imprisonment.

Partly due to testimony from Lyalin, ninety Soviet diplomats were expelled from Berlin and a further fifteen who were already abroad were excluded from returning. Overnight, London had been transformed into a hostile enviornment for the KGB. Over the following fifteen years, as a result of greater liaison and co-operation, the KGB was forced on to the defensive all over the world and more than 700 Soviets were to be thrown out of countries for 'activity not compatible with diplomacy', the polite international euphemism for spying.

The second crucial case, already in the development

stage when Phillpotts retired, was that of Oleg Gordievsky, then Third Secretary at the Soviet Embassy in Copenhagen, a city that Phillpotts knew well, having been Head of Station there in the early 1950s. Gordievsky had arrived in Denmark in January 1966, his first posting abroad, and was to remain there until the end of February 1970. He was later to return in October 1972 with the rank of Second Secretary and after a promotion in November 1976, fulfilled the role of Press Attaché until July 1978.

Although Copenhagen may seen an unlikely centre of espionage, the key high-flyers chosen by the Friends to run the local station are an indication of its standing in the league tables of international intrigue. The station had been opened after the war by Leslie Mitchell, and among his successors were Harry Carr, formerly the Controller Northern Area, Charles de Salis and Machlachlan Silverwood-Cope who, like Mitchell, was to run the Washington Station in the late 1950s.

Gordievsky's recruitment by SIS, perhaps with the assistance of the Danish intelligence service, was revealed on 12 September 1985 when the British Foreign Office announced his defection. The official statement disclosed that Gordievsky, aged forty-six, had made his move 'several weeks' earlier and was 'in a position to know the full details of Soviet intelligence activities and personnel in this country'. A brief biography of him suggested that he had graduated from a KGB training school in 1963 and had 'spent much of the next ten years dealing, both in Moscow and abroad, with Soviet "illegals"'. He had come to Britain in June 1982 with the rank of Counsellor and 'had recently become the head of the KGB residency in London'. A further statement announced the immediate expulsion of twenty-five Soviet officials who had been named by Gordievsky as intelligence officers. The Danish authorities were quick to leak their involvement in the operation, prompting Michael Lyngbo, deputy head of Denmark's tiny intelligence service, to fly to London for hasty consultations with the Friends. By the time he had returned to Copenhagen, the gossip had been stopped but the damage had already been done. Far from being a spontaneous defector, as the KGB might have suspected, or a recently recruited source. Gordievsky was revealed in his true colours as an agent of remarkably long-standing.

During Gordievsky's period in Copenhagen, one Dane had been discovered spying for the Russians and seven diplomats had been declared *personae non gratae*, but evidently the Soviets had not suspected that their own *Rezidentura* might have been penetrated. A similar incident took place in London within months of his arrival to act as deputy to Arkadi Gouk, the local KGB *Rezident*. Early on Easter Sunday, Gouk had received an anonymous letter purporting to come from someone with access to secret information. To establish his bona fides the correspondent had enclosed a genuine document, prepared by MI5's K Branch, describing the circumstances of the recent expulsion of three Soviet diplomats. Surprised by this windfall, Gouk had consulted with his deputy and concluded that it was nothing more than a clumsy provocation. In reality, it was a genuine attempt by Michael Bettaney, a thirty-three-year-old misfit, to betray his colleagues in the Security Service.

Bettaney made two further offers to Gouk using routine tradecraft to avoid detection, but meanwhile Gordievsky had alerted the Friends, who had organized their own surveillance operation to catch the anonymous traitor in MI5's K Branch. Bettaney was spotted when he made a third, late-night visit to Gouk's London home on 10 July 1983, leaving a final set of instructions on how he should be contacted. Having identified Bettaney as the spy, he was placed under skilled observation until sufficient evidence could be found to justify his arrest. One additional problem that had to be taken into consideration was Gordievsky's security. The reason for Bettaney's arrest had to be plausible enough to convince Gouk that there had not been a leak from within his own organization. Bettaney was eventually arrested on 16 September while planning an approach to the Soviet Embassy in Vienna. When the evidence of Bettaney's duplicity was later presented at his trial, it was alleged that Bettaney's own eccentric behaviour and some of his indiscreet questions had been enough to compromise him and initiate a molehunt. In reality, of course, Gordievsky must have experienced some anxious moments pondering whether the unknown mole in K Branch was aware of his own secret role, or whether Bettaney could be identified and eliminated before Gouk decided to take him up on his offer and establish contact with him.

Gordievsky's position proved resilient enough to cope with the pressures of Bettaney's arrest and trial, and he was later promoted to *Rezident* when Gouk was expelled for receiving Bettaney's messages. Thus, ironically, the incident which at one moment threatened to jeopardize Gordievsky actually helped improve his standing within the KGB. However, he was recalled unexpectedly to Moscow for consultation in July the following year and seized the opportunity to vanish there, leaving his wife and two children behind. The circumstances of his passage back to England were quite extraordinary. It took place while Moscow's local security apparatus was at full stretch coping with some 30,000 students attending the 12th World Festival of Youth. Coincidentally, a cocktail party was held at the British Embassy by the Ambassador, Sir Bryan Cartledge, and Gordievsky was smuggled past the Soviet militiamen guarding the Embassy gates in the back of a guest's diplomatic car.

After spending the night in the Embassy, Gordievsky climbed into one of the two specially adapted Commer vans that periodically carry non-urgent diplomatic freight north by road to Helsinki via Leningrad. Once across the frontier at Vybourg-Vaalimaa where, by convention, diplomatic vehicles and their passengers are exempted from checks, Gordievsky's arrival in the Finnish capital was concealed by the unusually large retinue accompanying the British Foreign Secretary to attend a European Security Conference. Once his journey to England had been completed, the lengthy debriefing sessions began.

Throughout the tense months of Gordievsky's double life in London, the Friends kept in constant contact with him and his acquaintances so that his behaviour could be monitored. One of those in touch with both Gordievsky and Colin Figures, who supervised the case personally, was Neville Beale, a senior member of the Conservative group on the Greater London Council, elected by the Prime Minister's constituency, Finchley, and a former Chairman of the Chelsea Conservative Association. Beale, who had met Figures socially some years earlier, had been introduced to Gordievsky by a Conservative Party official at a reception held by the Embassy and invited him to lunch at the GLC's headquarters. Thereafter, they met occasionally for lunch. After each meeting Beale would prepare a report for one of Figures's case officers and undergo an informal debriefing session, usually conducted discreetly in a restaurant. This arrangement continued until Gordievsky sent a message to Beale cancelling a long-standing luncheon appointment because of his sudden recall to Moscow. That was the signal for SIS to put into operation its contingency plans for an emergency rescue, not entirely dissimilar from those which failed to exfiltrate Penkovsky. Whilst there had always been a residual danger that Gordievsky's role in the exposure of Bettaney might be compromised, SIS went to considerable lengths to avoid jeopardizing him. When, for example, the Security Commission made its own investigation of the Bettaney case, a conflict arose. It was recognized that the preservation of Gordievsky as a source was absolutely vital and, accordingly, the Commission's final report, part of which was made public in May 1985 while Gordievsky was still in place in London, was not entirely frank on the issue of exactly how Bettaney had originally been identified as a traitor. The report claimed that Bettaney had drawn attention to himself 'by his asking questions about sensitive matters, completely unrelated to his work'. It was hoped that this misleading explanation would satisfy the Soviets and allow Gordievsky to continue his covert work for SIS. If the ruse achieved the desired effect, the London *Rezidentura* would escape suspicion and Gordievsky would be free to carry on with his career. The rather more fundemental issue of who took the decision to mislead the Commission, or whether the Commission willingly collaborated in order to protect Gordievsky, has not been revealed, or publicly debated, in spite of the obvious implications. After all, if the Commission had complied with an understandable request to participate in a deliberate deception, as can be seen to have been practised, how would it answer the charge that it had abandoned its integrity and maybe discredited itself for the future? The alternative scenario, demanding full candour from both MI5 and SIS, whatever the consequences for 'blown' sources, could hardly be expected to find favour either. Thus Gordievsky's hair-raising experience of fending off Bettaney did not end with his arrest. Indeed, it was that very act which proved to be the catalyst for some hard decision-making.

Gordievsky's defection and his successful escape from the Soviet Union were both extraordinary coups, but they were far from unique. At about the time Gordievsky was preparing himself for his new post in London in 1982, one of his KGB colleagues, Major Vladimir Kuzichkin, was making contact with the SIS Station in Iran and negotiating his defection. He had been attached to the Soviet Consulate in Tehran since 1977, with special responsibility for running 'illegals'. Once again, with his defection, the KGB sustained appalling damage to its organization in the Middle East, and SIS received a powerful boost to its morale. On that occasion selected journalists were invited, one at a time, to the Carlton Tower Hotel in Knightsbridge to meet him and hear, first-hand about Soviet objectives in the region. This useful defection was also turned into a neat propaganda exercise.

In recent years the pressure on the KGB from defections has escalated dramatically. In March 1985, Igor Gezha, a Third Secretary at the Soviet Embassy in Delhi, switched sides; he was followed in May by Sergei Bokhan, the ranking GRU officer in Athens who turned himself over to the CIA. Then, in the last week of July 1985, Vitali Yurchenko, a senior KGB officer who had once been in charge of security at the Washington Embassy, defected to the CIA in Rome. This particular episode only lasted until 2 November when Yurchenko, depressed by three months of intensive debriefing and a rejection from his former lover, the wife of a Soviet diplomat in Montreal, sought sanctuary at his old Embassy. Whatever the cause of his change of heart, his 'meal-ticket' had been worthwhile to the CIA.

Such defections are important to intelligence agencies, not just for the value of the data received, but the implicit assurance that all is well within the organization itself. The Friends agonized for years over the probability that they had been penetrated at a high level, and went through the trauma of tracking down and isolating Philby and Blake. Steps were then taken, judged ruthless by some, to eliminate the possibility that other ideologically motivated traitors had followed in their path. Various officers, who had fallen under suspicion, had had their careers terminated. The successful resettlement of Oleg Lyalin, Oleg Gordievsky and Vladimir Kuzichkin is eloquent testimony to the eventual success of the counter-measures taken to ensure the integrity of what Monty Woodhouse termed that 'department in the Foreign Office known politely, but not very sincerely, as the Friends'. The price, however, was often painfully high, as Maurice Oldfield, who succeeded Sir John Rennie as CSS in February 1973, could testify.

The circumstaqnces of Oldfield's succession were inauspicious. John Rennie's son and daughter-in-law had been charged with illegal possession of heroin and the publicity that followed made his position untenable. Accordingly, his Vice-Chief took over and, instead of taking up another intelligence post in the Cabinet Office as Dick White had done on his retirement when he had been made Intelligence Co-ordinator, Rennie moved down to the country permanently.

Oldfield had little in common with his six predecessors.

He was an academic at heart, who might have pursued a useful career as a medievalist at some university. He came from a humble background, being the eldest of eleven children born to a tenant farmer in the tiny Derbyshire village of Over Haddon. He had been educated at local state schools and had never married. His commission in the Intelligence Corps had been gained after lengthy service as an NCO in a Field Security Section in the Middle East during the war, and his recruitment into the Friends had been fortuitous, owing to the appointment of his direct superior in SIME, Douglas Roberts, to R5 in 1946. If this was not enough to distinguish him from the other men who had held the post of CSS, he was the first to attend a redbrick university (he went to Manchester, while his two predecessors, Rennie and White, were both Oxford men) and the first to rise through the organization, having served at SIS stations abroad. He had completed two tours in Singapore and had followed John Briance to Washington in 1960, where he had been based for four years before returning to understudy White. He was also the first to have been commissioned from the ranks, having ended the war as a lieutenant-colonel.

Perhaps because of his academic inclinations, Oldfield made a good professional intelligence officer who fitted well into SIS's post-war regime. He had many supporters among those who had served with him in SIME and had made the same switch to SIS, some of whom were also to rise to senior positions in the organization. Oldfield's role was first identified to the public when Philby paid him the compliment in his autobiography of describing him as 'formidable' and 'an officer of high quality'. Evidently this accolade did not cut much ice somewhere in Whitehall, for its publication coincided with the decision to appoint Rennie, an outsider, to take over SIS upon White's retirement in 1968.

Although Oldfield was well liked by his colleagues in Cairo, Singapore and Broadway, his greatest contribution to the intelligence community probably took place during his tenure of the Washington Station, a post that just nine years earlier had been occupied by Philby. The four Heads of Station who had served in the intervening period had all been made perfectly aware of the acute sensitivity of their position, which demanded a high degree of goodwill and mutual trust if the liaison was to be fruitful. Many of the old guard, on both sides of the Atlantic, had been willing to give the personable Philby the benefit of the doubt when he was still ensconced in Lebanon, in frequent contact with both the CIA and SIS Stations in Beirut; for as long as his case was unresolved, the Americans were willing to be cautious, even sceptical, but never hostile. That situation was to alter in January 1963 when Philby unexpectedly fled to Moscow, leaving Oldfield to break the news to John McCone, the CIA's Director. Suspicion is one thing, but absolute confirmation of treachery is quite another, and it fell to Oldfield to heal the wounds.

Oldfield's success, in spite of being a bachelor, was in part due to his commitment to Penkovsky at a time when the world seemed on the brink of atomic war. Penkovsky's data gave the West a unique insight into the Kremlin's strategy and reassured those analysts who had succumbed to the missile gap theory. Although there were to be recriminations and an enduring debate much later over the authenticity of Penkovsky's information, it was regarded at the time as an invaluable motherlode and a rare opportunity to restore the special relationship between SIS and the CIA. To a large extent the donnish Oldfield fulfilled his mission and smoothed the way for Phillpotts, who was to take over the station in 1964.

Oldfield's return to London coincided with the election of a Labour administration and an intention, fuelled by political and economic arguments, to reduce Britain's role as a world power. The most immediate impact of the change in government for the Friends was a new era of strict financial control, and the first of a series of station amalgamations which served to eliminate certain stations judged to be relatively unproductive. Even though the Friends were to take over responsibility for some of the former colonies like Nigeria (and South Africa, which had left the Commonwealth in 1961), where previously MI5's E Branch had, by convention, posted Security Liaison Officers, their brief was on the decline. This process was eventually to leave SIS with just one station in South America, increasing the burden on the Buenos Aires Head of Station and diminishing the quality and flow of useful information from the continent. The gradual but deliberate run-down of SIS's overseas representation may have been a factor in the lack of advance warning for the conflict with Argentina more than a decade later, but it also changed the nature of the new relationship with the CIA and emphasized the trend towards acceptance of GCHQ's product which, thanks to technical break-throughs in the data-processing field, was proving both reliable and cost-effective. SIS was to be trimmed to reflect Britain's status as a small debtor nation, with a scaled-down army, manoeuvring to join the EEC. In November 1967, the remaining troops fighting a rearguard action in Aden were evacuated, leaving Britain with few overseas assets left to defend. Even Rhodesia, which had declared independence unilaterally in 1965 and was a high political priority for the Government, needed few intelli-gence-gathering resources devoted to the problem given the long relationship the Friends had enjoyed with the Rhodesian Central Intelligence Organization. Indeed, the CIO's Director, Ken Flower, 'contrived to visit relatives in the UK several times a year from 1968–80' and met the Friends every time.

The concern that SIS's leaner profile would inhibit Britain's ability to conduct military operations abroad was tested in Oman in 1971, when the Government authorized a covert intervention by a Special Air Service squadron to suppress a rebellion against the Sultan. The campaign was eventually concluded five years later when the insurrec-tion was quelled, with only peripheral political help from the Friends.

There were numerous consequences of the financial squeeze on SIS during the late 1960s. The reduced demand for personnel enabled the Friends to pick only the best of those opting for a career in the Foreign Service. It was occasionally said that the best way to identify a Head of Station in a British diplomatic mission was by judging the secretarial staff: SIS secretaries were often smarter and brighter than the Foreign Office regulars. In some places the overseas stations were cut to just two people, forcing them to concentrate on liaison rather than acquisition. In strategic terms the lower volume of assessments from key stations altered the balance of the intelligence input to the JIC in favour of GCHQ, with the result that rather more weight was given to SIGINT analysis. Perhaps not surprisingly one factor accounting for the absence of any sensible advance notice of the Argentine invasion of the Falklands in 1982 was the assurance given by the signal interpreters that certain troop movements, such as those by crack Argentine commando units moving away from their usual positions on the Chilean frontier, would betray an intention to prepare for an amphibious assault. The junta would certainly deploy its best-trained troops for a complex operation, and the wireless traffic of the units concerned was monitored constantly. The slightest hint of a change in procedure, or anything that might indicate a transfer to a new location, would be noted instantly. Withdrawal, assembly and embarkation, it was confidently stated, would be accompanied by a perceptible increase in Argentine signal patterns which, in turn, would be scrutinized. In the event, and contrary to all the appreciations made at the time, untried marine conscripts spearheaded the landings, and the regular commandos who had attracted the close surveillance were never deployed beyond the Andes. In those circumstances the SIGINT analysts were caught by surprise and never delivered the promised alert.

The tighter budget also bore some internal security implications for the Friends: a smaller order of battle makes for greater vulnerability to hostile penetration and an easier target for the opposition. As has already been seen, the most damaging and divisive molehunts were conducted during this period, and Oldfield was in the thick of them upon his return to London.

During the latter period of his career Oldfield was necessarily preoccupied with the menace of an expanding KGB presence in the West and the messy conflict in Northern Ireland. On one memorable occasion he gathered his staff into the canteen in Century House to assure them that SIS's activities in the province, which had commenced early in 1971 in spite of Oldfield's initial objections, did not include authorizing bank raids, as had been claimed by a freelancing part-time informant and armed robber named Kenneth Littlejohn.

Oldfield ended his career with the Friends in April 1978, having recommended his Vice-Chief, Dickie Franks, to succeed him. Franks was the last of the wartime intake from SOE and his career had taken him to stations in Cairo, Tehran and Bonn.

When Oldfield retired, he moved into digs in Iffley so as to undertake a year of historical research at All Souls, apparently in order to see whether he wanted to return to academic scholarship. However, in September the following year he was offered a job by the new Prime Minister, Margaret Thatcher, as Co-ordinator of Security and Intelligence in Northern Ireland. This post was an innovation, but was founded on the work done by Dick White after his official retirement from the Friends back in 1968. As Intelligence Co-ordinator to the Cabinet, a special niche had been created for him to bridge the CSS, the Director-General of MI5 and the Chairman of the JIC. White had stayed until 1972 when Sir Leonard Hooper, the retiring Director of GCHQ, had taken up the role; he had been succeeded in 1978 by Sir Brooks Richards, a regular diplomat and former SOE hand.

Richard's task had been to oversee the work of the two organizations, but his brief had not extended to Ulster where, until 1971, domestic intelligence had been handled exclusively by the Royal Ulster Constabulary's Special Branch. However, with the establishment of SIS's Station in Lisburn, and MI5's local office in downtown Belfast, there was plenty of opportunity to exacerbate the scene which had already been complicated by differing objectives of the army's military intelligence units and the Special Branch. A disastrous conflict had arisen between the detectives, who were anxious to play a lengthy game of careful surveillance and infiltration, and the soldiers, who were under pressure to produce quick results. The incompatability of their motives had led to some awkward incidents and seemed likely to bring their operations to a state of paralysis. Inter-service communications had almost broken down and several of those directly involved were openly distrustful of each other. The assassination of Airey Neave just before the general election in 1979 demonstrated to the incoming Prime Minister the urgency and magnitude of the threat posed by the terrorists, who evidently could not be contained in the province by the existing security arrangements. The neat solution to the overlapping intelligence briefs was the appointment of a co-ordinator of sufficient stature as to command the respect of all the interested parties in Belfast's recondite intelligence apparatus. Oldfield's mission was to move into Stormont Castle, sort out the personality clashes and restore co-operation.

Oldfield stayed at his post in Ulster less than six months. His departure, at the end of March 1980, followed his volunteered admission to the Cabinet Secretary that he had not been entirely candid when he had been routinely interviewed for his Positive Vetting security clearance. Like all his subordinates, the CSS was required to undergo the PV procedure every five years. The first stage of the system is a detailed questionnaire which has to be completed by the PV candidate. Once completed, the form is followed up with an interview conducted by a field investigator, usually a retired SIS officer, who will seek answers to highly pertinent questions about homosexuality, drug and alcohol abuse, indebtedness and membership of political parties. Although Oldfield had consistently denied ever having been a homosexual since the introduction of the measure in 1952, the truth was that he had indeed had such experience, albeit not very recently. The statement meant his access to secret material was suspended automatically and he never went back to Ireland. In fact, he was already in failing health and early in March the following year he died of cancer of the stomach.

Oldfield's post at Stormont was quickly filled by Brooks Richards, with a trouble-shooting diplomat, Sir Antony Duff, taking over as Cabinet Intelligence Co-ordinator. Following the publication of the Franks Report into the background of the Falklands crisis, and the criticism it contained of the management of the JIC's assessment staff, Duff supplanted (Sir) Patrick Wright as Chairman of the JIC; in 1985, he was to move yet again, to replace Sir John Jones as Director-General of the Security Service in the wake of the Bettaney case.

The Joint Intelligence mechanism in Whitehall proved itself to be unable to collate all the different strands of data, and consequently certain key items of information were overlooked. Too much emphasis was placed on the SIGINT component and too little attention given to the reports from people on the spot in Argentina: the captain of HMS *Endurance*, the Royal Navy's single vessel in the area; the hopelessly overburdened Defence Attaché; and SIS's last Head of Station in South America. All sent timely warnings to their respective organizations in London about what they saw as dangerous developments, but the JIC drew quite the wrong conclusions. Thus, for all the sophistication of satellite surveillance systems, and GCHQ's many interception sites dotted across the globe, it fell to one of the Friends to cable his misgivings, only to have his message pigeon-holed . . . as nothing more than advice from friendly circles.

NOTES

Introduction

1 These files, in the FO 369–72 series at the Public Records Office, provided much of the documentary basis of *MI6: British Secret Intelligence Service Operations 1909–45*.

2 J. C. Masterman, *On the Chariot Wheel* (OUP, Oxford, 1975); Sir Percy Sillitoe, *Cloak without Dagger* (Cassell, London, 1955); Derek Tangye, *Moonlight on a Lake in Bond Street* (Norton, New York 1961) and *The Way to Minack* (Michael Joseph, London, 1978); Lord Rothschild, *Random Variables* (Collins, London, 1984); Peter Wright, *Spycatcher* (Heinemann, Sydney, 1987).

3 Gerald Glover, *115 Park Street* (privately published).

4 F. H. Hinsley, E. E. Thomas, C. F. G. Ransom, R. C. Knight, *British Intelligence in the Second World War* (HMSO, London, 1979, 1983, 1984, 1988).

5 Sir Harry Hinsley and C. A. G. Simkins, *Security and Counter-Intelligence* (to be published by HMSO).

6 A censored version of *Greek Memories* was released by Cassell in 1939. A new edition, with all the original 1932 text restored, was published in 1987 by the University Press of America, edited by Tom Troy.

7 Bill Graham, *Break-In* (Bodley Head, London, 1987). Others in this genre include Patrick Seal, *The Hilton Assignment* (Temple Smith, London, 1973); Leslie Aspin, *I, Kovaks* (Everest, London, 1975); Gayle Rivers (pseud.), *The Specialist* (Sidwick & Jackson, London, 1985); Peter Stiff, *See You in November* (Galago, 1985).

8 *Falklands Island Review. Report of a Committee of Privy Counsellors*, Cmnd 8787 (HMSO, London, 1983).

9 Peter Hennessy, *Cabinet*, p. 120.

10 *Ibid.*, p. 113.

1 Transition

1 Geoffrey McDermott, *The Eden Legacy*, p. 144.
2 David Footman wrote four novels – *The Yellow Rock*, *The Mine in the Desert*, *Pig and Pepper* and *Pemberton*; two books of short stories, *Half-Way East* and *Better Forgotten*; and a travelogue, *Balkan Holiday*.
3 David Footman, *The Russian Revolution*, p. 121.
4 Robert Carew-Hunt, *The Theory and Practice of Communism*, p. 263.
5 Kim Philby, *My Silent War*, p. 123.
6 Now the 9th Duke of Portland; see Patrick Howarth's *Intelligence Chief Extraordinary*.
7 Kenneth Strong, *Intelligence at the Top*, p. 223.

2 The British Control Commission for Germany

1 John Bruce Lockhart, *Intelligence: A British View*, p. 37.
2 This individual is still alive but, although confirming his pre-war membership of the Communist Party of Great Britain, he has always denied having spied for the Soviets.
3 James McGovern, *Crossbow and Overcast*, p. 201.
4 *Ibid.*
5 G. A. Tokaev, *Comrade X*, p. 357.
6 Reinhard Gehlen, *The Service*, p. 122.
7 *Ibid.*, p. 123.
8 *Ibid.*, p. 154.
9 Commander Courtney, later Conservative MP for Harrow East 1959–66, was subsequently the victim of a Soviet honeytrap; see *Sailor in a Russian Frame*, p. 55.

3 Palestine 1945–8

1 PRO/CO537/2270.
2 Sir Noel Charles to Foreign Office, 10 January 1946.
3 Bickham Sweet-Escott, *Baker Street Irregular*, p. 27.
4 Menachem Begin, *The Revolt*, p. 99.
5 *Ibid.*, p. 97.

4   Malaya 1948–54

1   Quoted in Harry Miller, *Jungle War in Malaya*, p. 70.
2   Sir Robert Thompson, *Defeating Communist Insurgency*, p. 85.
3   Lord Chandos, *Memoirs of Lord Chandos*, p. 366.

5   Kim Philby and VALUABLE

1   Anatoli Golitsyn, *New Lies for Old*, p. 71.
2   Philby, *op. cit.*, p. 13.
3   *Sunday Times.*, 27 March 1988.
4   Philby, *op. cit.*, p. 72.
5   PRO FO/37171687.
6   Philby, *op. cit.*, p. 116.
7   *Ibid.*, p. 135.
8   *Ibid.*
9   *Ibid.*, p. 142.
10   David Smiley, *Albanian Assignment*, p. 163.
11   Philby, *op. cit.*, p. 162.
12   *Ibid.*, p. 161.
13   Smiley, *op. cit.*, p. 164.
14   Philby, *op. cit.*, p. 165.
15   H. Montgomery Hyde, *The Quiet Canadian*. p. 18.
16   Philby, *op. cit.*, p. 117.

6   Cyrpus 1953–60

1   Lockhart, *op. cit.*, p. 41.

7   Buster Crabb OBE GM RNVR

1   Anthony Eden, *Full Circle*, p. 108.
2   Marshall Pugh, *Frogman*, p. 172.
3   Geoffrey McDermott, *The Eden Legacy*, p. 129.
4   *The Times*, 30 April 1956.

5   *Hansard*, 4 May 1956.
6   *Ibid.*, 14 May 1956.
7   *Ibid.*
8   *Ibid.*
9   *Daily Express*, 11 June 1957.

8   Operation BOOT

1   Miles Copeland, *The Real Spy World*, p. 93.
2   C. M. Woodhouse, *Something Ventured*, p. 111.
3   *Ibid.*
4   *Ibid.*, p. 110.
5   *Ibid.*, p. 116.
6   *Ibid.*, p. 117.
7   *Ibid.*, p. 118.
8   Kermit Roosevelt, *Countercoup*, p. 107.
9   *Ibid.*, p. 123.
10 Woodhouse, *op. cit.*, p. 125.
11 See Sir Shapoor Reporter's entry in *Who's Who*.
12 Roosevelt, *op. cit.*, p. 190.
13 *Ibid.*, p. 205.
14 *Ibid.*
15 Woodhouse, *op. cit.*, p. 230.
16 *Ibid.*, p. 132.

9   Operation STRAGGLE

1   Roy Fullick and Geoffrey Powell, *Suez: The Double War*,
    p. 62.
2   For differing versions of the scale of the CIA's involvement
    with the Free Officers, compare Miles Copeland in *The
    Game of Nations*, p. 62, with Wilbur Crane Eveland in
    Ropes of Sand, p. 97.
3   Copeland, *ibid.*
4   Former CIA Station Chief in Paris, 24 August 1987.
5   Philby, *op. cit.*, p. 192.
6   *Hansard*, 7 November 1955.
7   McDermott, *op. cit.*, P. 133.

8   Field Marshall Montgomery speaking in the House of Lords, 16 March 1962. (*Hansard*, vol. 238, cols 1002–3).

9   McDermott, *op. cit.*, p. 132.

10 See Brian Lapping's *End of Empire* (Granada, London, 1985) for Nutting's confirmation that he had toned down Eden's exact words in his autobiography, *No End of a Lesson*.

11 McDermott, *op. cit.*, p. 133.

12 Anthony Nutting, *No End of a Lesson*, p. 99.

13 Eyewitness account.

14 Fullick and Powell, *op. cit.*, p. 61.

15 *Hansard*, 20 December 1956.

16 *Ibid.*, 31 October 1956.

17 Keesings Contemporary Archive, 1957, Col. 15679.

18 *Ibid.*

19 Evelyn Shuckburgh, *Descent from Suez: Diaries 1951–6*, p. 362.

20 Robert Rhodes James, *Anthony Eden*, p. 369.

10   The Penkovsky Defection

1   Anatoli Golitsyn, *New Lies for Old.*, p. 54.

2   Greville Wynne, *The Man from Odessa*, p. 217.

3   Anthony Verrier, *Through the Looking Glass*, p. 213.

4   See David Howarth's *The Shetland Bus* (Nelson & Sons, London, 1951).

5   Philby, *op. cit.*, p. 147.

6   Kessings Contemporary Archives, Col. 19623.

7   Interview with Peter Deriabin, 22 September 1987.

8   Keesings Contemporary Archives, Col. 19625.

9   *Ibid.*

10 Greville Wynne, *The Man from Moscow*, p. 25.

11 *Ibid.*, p. 130.

12 Wynne, *The Man from Odessa*, p. iii.

13 Frank Gibney and Peter Deriabin, *The Penkovsky Papers*, p. 340.

14 *Ibid.*, p. 370.

11   The Blake Catastrophe

1   David C. Martin, *Wilderness of Mirrors*, p. 99.
2   McDermott, *op. cit.*, p. 182.

12   The Molehunt Era

1   Robert Cecil, *The Missing Dimension*, p. 197.
2   Ismail Akhmedov, *In and Out of Stalin's GRU*, p. 191.
3   *Ibid.*, p. 197.
4 · Donald Prater later wrote *European of Yesterday* (OUP, Oxford, 1972), a biography of Stefan Zweig, and *A Ringing Glass: The Life of Rainer Maria Rilke* (Clarendon Press, Oxford, 1986).

13   The Defector Syndrome

1   James McCargar, *The Spy and his Masters*, p. 131.

BIBLIOGRAPHY

Akhmedov, Ismail, *In and Out of Stalin's GRU* (Arms & Armour Press, London, 1984)

Begin, Menachem, *The Revolt* (W. H. Allen, London, 1979)

Bourke, Sean, *The Springing of George Blake* (Cassell, London, 1970)

Carew-Hunt, Robert, *The Theory and Practice of Communism* (Geoffrey Bles, London, 1950)

Cavendish, Anthony, *Inside Intelligence (privately published, 1987)*

Cecil, Robert, The Missing Dimension (Macmillan, London, 1984)

Chandos, Lord, *The Memoirs of Lord Chandos* (Bodley Head, London, 1962)

Chisholm, Roderick, *Ladysmith* (Osprey, London, 1979)

Cookridge, E. H., *Shadow of a Spy* (Leslie Frewin, London, 1962)

Copeland, Miles, *The Game of Nations* (Weidenfeld & Nicolson, London 1969)

Copeland, Miles, *The Real Spy World* (Weidenfeld & Nicolson, London, 1974)

Courtney, Anthony, *Sailor in a Russian Frame* (Johnson, London, 1968)

Eden, Anthony, *Full Circle* (Cassell, London, 1960)

Eveland, Wilbur Crane, *Ropes of Sand* (W. W. Norton, New York, 1980)

Footman, David, *Red Prelude* (The Cresset Press, London, 1944)

Footman, David, *The Primrose Path* (The Cresset Press, London, 1946)

Footman, David, *The Russian Revolution* (Faber & Faber, London, 1962)

Fullick, Roy, and Powell, Geoffrey, *Suez: The Double War* (Hamish Hamilton, London, 1979)

Gehlen, Reinhard, *The Service* (World Publishing, New York, 1972)

Gibney, Frank, and Deriabin, Peter, *The Penkovsky Papers* (Doubleday, New York, 1965)

Golitsyn, Anatoli, *New Lies for Old* (Bodley Head, London, 1984)

Hennessy, Peter, *Cabinet* (Basil Blackwell, Oxford, 1986)

Howarth, Patrick, *Intelligence Chief Extraordinary* (Bodley Head, London, 1986)

Hutton, J. Bernard, *Frogman Spy* (Neville Spearman, London 1960)

Hutton, J. Bernard, *Commander Crabb is Alive* (Tandem, 1968)

Johns, Philip, *Within Two Cloaks* (William Kimber, London, 1979)

Jones, R. V., *Most Secret War* (Hamish Hamilton, London, 1978)

Landau, Henry, *All's Fair* (Putnam, New York, 1935)

Landau, *Secrets of the White Lady* (Putnam, New York, 1937)

Landau, Henry, *The Enemy Within* (Putnam, New York, 1937)

Lockhart, John Bruce, *Intelligence: A British View* (RUSI, London, 1987)

Lonsdale, Gordon, *Spy* (Neville Spearman, London, 1965)

Mackenzie, Compton, *Greek Memories* (ed. Tom Troy) (University of America, New York, 1987)

Martin, David C., *Wilderness of Mirrors* (Harper & Row, New York, 1980)

Masterman, J. C., *On the Chariot Wheel* (OUP, Oxford, 1975)

McCargar, James, *The Spy and his Masters* (Secker & Warburg, London, 1963)

Bibliography

McDermott, Geoffrey, *The Eden Legacy* (Leslie Frewin, London, 1969)

McGovern, James, *Crossbow and Overcast* (William Morrow, New York, 1964)

Miller, Harry, *Jungle War in Malaya* (Arthur Barker, London, 1972)

Montgomery Hyde, H., *The Quiet Canadian* (Hamish Hamilton, London, 1962)

Montgomery Hyde, H., *George Blake: Superspy* (Constable, London, 1987)

Nutting, Anthony, *No End of a Lesson* (Constable, London, 1967)

Philby, Kim, *My Silent War* (McGibbon & Kee, London, 1968)

Pugh, Marshall, *Frogman* (Charles Scribner, New York, 1956)

Rhodes James, Robert, *Anthony Eden* (Weidenfeld & Nicolson, London, 1986)

Roosevelt, Kermit, *Countercoup* (McGraw Hill, New York, 1979)

Seton-Watson, Hugh, *The East European Revolution* (London 1950)

Seton-Watson, Hugh, *The Pattern of Communist Revolution* (London, 1953)

Seton-Watson, Hugh, *Neither War Nor Peace* (Methuen, London, 1960)

Shuckburgh, Evelyn, *Descent to Suez: Diaries 1951–6* (Weidenfeld & Nicolson, London 1986)

Sillitoe, Percy, *Cloak without Dagger* (Cassell, London, 1955)

Smiley, David, *Albanian Assignment* (Chatto & Windus, London, 1984)

Strong, Kenneth, *Intelligence at the Top* (Cassell, London, 1968)

Sweet-Escott, Bickham, *Baker Street Irregular* (Methuen, London, 1965)

Tangye, Derek, *The Way to Minack* (Michael Joseph, London, 1978)

Thompson, Sir Robert, *Defeating Communist Insurgency* (Chatto & Windus, London, 1967)

Tokaev, G. A., *Betrayal of an Ideal* (trs. Alec Brown) (Indiana University Press, Indiana, 1955)

Tokaev, G. A., *Comrade X* (Harvill Press, London, 1956)

Verrier, Anthony, *Through the Looking Glass* (Jonathan Cape, London, 1983)

West, Nigel, *A Matter of Trust: MI5 1945–72* (Weidenfeld & Nicolson, London, 1982)

West, Nigel, *MI6: British Secret Intelligence Service Operations 1909–45* (Weidenfeld & Nicolson, London, 1983)

West, Nigel, *Molehunt* (Weidenfeld & Nicolson, London, 1987)

Whitwell, John (alias Leslie Nicholson), *British Agent* (William Kimber, London, 1967)

Winterbotham, Fred, *The Ultra Secret* (Weidenfeld & Nicolson, London, 1974)

Woodhouse, C. M., *Something Ventured* (Granada, London, 1982)

Wright, Peter, *Spycatcher* (Heinmann, Sydney, 1987)

Wynne, Greville, *The Man from Moscow* (Hutchinson, London, 1967)

Wynne, Greville, *The Man from Odessa* (Robert Hale, London, 1981)

INDEX